1972

VOLTAIRE
Historian

VOLTAIRE
Historian

BY

J. H. BRUMFITT

OXFORD UNIVERSITY PRESS

Oxford University Press, Ely House, London W.1

GLASGOW   NEW YORK   TORONTO   MELBOURNE   WELLINGTON
CAPE TOWN   SALISBURY   IBADAN   NAIROBI   DAR ES SALAAM   LUSAKA   ADDIS ABABA
BOMBAY   CALCUTTA   MADRAS   KARACHI   LAHORE   DACCA
KUALA LUMPUR   SINGAPORE   HONG KONG   TOKYO

First published in the
Oxford Modern Languages and Literature Monographs
1958

REPRINTED LITHOGRAPHICALLY IN GREAT BRITAIN
(WITH NEW PREFACE)
AT THE UNIVERSITY PRESS, OXFORD
BY VIVIAN RIDLER
PRINTER TO THE UNIVERSITY
1970

PREFACE

THIS book first appeared in 1958, and is here reprinted with a bare minimum of corrections. In form and style it would no doubt have benefited from a more complete revision. However, my views on the significance of Voltaire's historical writings have not changed appreciably in the intervening years, and I take this as an indication that the time for such a revision has not yet arrived. Instead, I shall content myself, in this preface, with a short review of some of the more important works on Voltaire as an historian which have appeared in recent years and which amplify, modify, and in some cases contradict, my own arguments.

In the first place, new editions are now available of many of the historical writings themselves. The most valuable of these are the work of René Pomeau. His Pléiade *Œuvres historiques*, which includes all the historical writings except the *Essai sur les mœurs* and lesser works of controversy, was published in 1957. It was followed, in 1963, by his edition of the *Essai* itself (Classiques Garnier, 2 vols.). Though neither of these is fully 'critical' in the most rigid sense of the term, both give all the more important variants and have extensive introductions and notes. The edition of the *Essai* is particularly rich in illustrative material and in explanatory notes drawn largely from information in Voltaire's library at Leningrad. For the general reader, these volumes are likely to remain, for a long time, the most reliable standard text. For the specialist, however, they may soon be superseded by the relevant volumes of the new *Complete Works of Voltaire*, an edition which is now being prepared by an international team of scholars (M. Pomeau is prominent among them) and published under the aegis of Theodore Besterman and the Institut et Musée Voltaire of Geneva. As I write, only one volume of the historical writings has yet appeared: my own edition of *La Philosophie de l'histoire*. However, there is much to interest the student of Voltairian historiography in the two volumes of Besterman's new, and much augmented, edition of the *Notebooks*, and some of the major histories are likely to be published in the next year or two. They will contain a fully critical text and an extensive commentary.

Two major studies of Voltaire the historian have appeared since my own was published; they are both considerably longer than mine, and treat some questions much more fully. The first, Furio Diaz's *Voltaire storico* (1958), is particularly illuminating in its detailed discussion of Voltaire as an historian of modern times. Diaz demonstrates the link between his political thinking and his historical writing, showing the extent to which the latter is a function of the former. He is a very sympathetic commentator, and his case for regarding Voltaire as a historical thinker of the first magnitude with a flair for appreciating the dialectic of history is powerfully argued, though his enthusiasm, to my mind, can sometimes be excessive.

Diaz writes from an avowedly, though by no means dogmatically, Marxist standpoint. So too does the author of the other major study of Voltaire historian, Charles Rihs, whose *Voltaire: Recherches sur les origines du matérialisme historique* was published in 1962. However, their interpretations differ widely, for whereas Diaz's Voltaire is almost 'pre-Marxist' ·in his insight, Rihs's is the epitome of the 'idealist' historian and represents the antithesis of Marx and the materialists. The two cases are ably argued, though that of Diaz seems to me the more convincing. However, rather than accepting either view, it seems to me better sense (and possibly better 'Marxism') to conclude that Voltaire was simultaneously both 'idealist' and 'materialist'—in short that he reflected all that was most active in the ideological conflicts of his day.

Rihs's book has much else to recommend it; it is particularly thorough in those fields where my own coverage is most superficial, especially in its discussion of aspects of the development of historical thought from Saint Augustine onwards and of the way in which Voltaire absorbs, modifies, and at times rejects this tradition.

Of the many shorter contributions to our understanding of Voltaire the historian, I wish to mention only a few. O. R. Taylor has given us a first class edition of what might be called Voltaire's first historical work, *La Henriade* (*Studies on Voltaire and the Eighteenth Century*, Vols. XXVIII-XL, 1965) and has developed his views on the historiographical significance of the work in an article in *The Age of the Enlightenment* (1967). Enzo Caramaschi has examined the relationship between Voltaire and an important precursor in his 'Du Bos et Voltaire' (*Studies*, Vol. X, 1959). The same relationship also plays its part in an interesting study of Voltaire's attitude to the Renaissance, to be found in Franco Simone's *Il Rinascimento francese* (1965). Basil Guy has studied afresh Voltaire's attitude to one of his utopias in 'The French Image of China before and after Voltaire' (*Studies*, Vol. XXI,

1963). Finally, insight into the nature of Voltaire's historical artistry is to be found in Lionel Gossman's 'Voltaire's *Charles XII*: history into art' (*Studies*, Vol. XXV, 1963).

In short, this book is already out of date in some of its details. In its essentials, however, it still remains, I believe, a valid analysis of Voltaire historian.

J. H. B.

St. Andrews
March 1970

CONTENTS

ABBREVIATIONS

EXCEPT where otherwise stated, references to the works of Voltaire are to the edition by L. Moland (Paris, Garnier, 1877–85, 52 vols.). In such references, volume and page number alone will be given (e.g. xvi. 177).

References to the edition of *Voltaire's Correspondence* by Th. Besterman (Geneva, 1953–) will have the same form except that they will be preceded by the abbreviation: Best.

When works are referred to in the footnotes by their short titles, fuller information will be found in the bibliography.

INTRODUCTION

WHETHER or not Voltaire is, as some of his more enthusiastic admirers have asserted,[1] the father of modern historical writing, he is certainly the most typical and the most universal of the historians of the Enlightenment. Moreover, recent studies have shown how unjustified was the nineteenth-century tendency to dismiss Enlightenment historiography as being fundamentally anti-historical.[2] It is true that its exponents felt little reverence for the past, and that they rarely succeeded in dissociating themselves from the problems of their own times. It is true that their attachment to the mechanistic science and psychology of their age often led them to ignore the variations in human conduct throughout the centuries, and that their belief in the new society which they were attempting to create led to a contemptuous attitude towards earlier forms of society and, in particular, to a systematic disparagement of the Middle Ages. But if they were often lacking in historical imagination, they nevertheless brought about a profound revolution in historical thought. They created a new type of social history, interesting themselves in laws and constitutions, in economic progress, in the arts and sciences. They strove to separate history from legend and to make the past appear as rational as the present. They were unwilling to confine themselves within national traditions, or even within the European Christian tradition, but aimed at being truly universal and at showing how all nations had contributed to the progress of mankind.

If Enlightenment historiography was a natural result of the social and philosophical theories of the *philosophes*, it was also a conscious reaction against the historical writing of the previous century. The majority of seventeenth-century historians continued the humanist tradition of the Renaissance,[3] and sought, above all, to follow the precepts of Cicero and the examples of Livy and Sallust. They aimed at moral instruction and artistic excellence. To achieve the

---

[1] e.g. Lanson, *Voltaire*, p. 132, and Brailsford, *Voltaire*, p. 84.
[2] See Dilthey, 'Das 18te Jahrhundert und die geschichtliche Welt'; Meinecke, *Die Entstehung des Historismus*, and Cassirer, *Die Philosophie der Aufklärung*. One of the most recent defences of Enlightenment historiography is to be found in Luporini's *Voltaire e le 'Lettres Philosophiques'*.
[3] For a general account of this development, see Fueter, *Geschichte der neueren Historiographie*.

INTRODUCTION

first of these, they concentrated their attention on the individual, good or bad, who made the moral decision. To achieve the second, they described the glorious deeds of the battlefield and the colourful activities of the court, embellishing their narrative with traditional rhetorical devices, and excluding any facts, details, or discussions which might spoil the aesthetic effect.[1]

The facts in which the humanist historians were interested were not likely to appeal to the more socially minded writers of the Enlightenment. Moreover, many of the humanists were not particularly interested in the facts at all. For if a moral purpose and an artistic presentation were what mattered most in historical writing, it seemed unreasonable to give too much attention to factual accuracy, especially when a little rearrangement of the incidents of a story could produce a much more moving or exciting narrative. Towards the close of the seventeenth-century, there arose a school of historians, among whom Saint-Réal and Vertot are the best known, who were only interested in psychological and dramatic effect, and who altered historical fact almost as freely as did dramatists like Corneille or Racine.[2] Vertot's famous words, 'J'en suis fâché, mais mon siège est fait',[3] epitomize their attitude.

Such degeneration is not, of course, characteristic of all seventeenth-century historians. Some, like Mézeray or Daniel, tried to maintain the best traditions of humanist historiography. But even they show the same artistic and moral preoccupations, the same concern for court pageantry, military prowess, and diplomatic intrigue. And more often than not, they exhibit a naïve credulity in the face of the myths and miracles of the distant past.[4]

If the seventeenth century saw the degeneration of humanist historical writing, it also witnessed an unprecedented growth of historical scholarship. Men like Duchesne, Baluze, Mabillon, and Montfaucon created the science of history and placed new tools such as palæography, archæology, and diplomatics in the historian's hands.[5] However, the beneficial results of these developments were

[1] See Thierry's *Notes sur quatorze historiens antérieurs à Mézeray* (*Œuvres*, 1859, vol. iii). In 1670 the Jesuit theorist Le Moyne still insists, in his *De l'histoire* (1690), that harangues are a necessary part of history.
[2] See Dulong, *L'Abbé de Saint-Réal.*
[3] See D'Alembert, *Discours sur la meilleure méthode d'écrire l'histoire*, p. 193.
[4] See Evans, *L'Historien Mézeray*, particularly p. 133.
[5] Some account of the development of erudition in seventeenth-century France may be found in Molinier, *Les Sources de l'histoire de France*, Pt. V

not immediately apparent. For if increasing erudition tended to show up the inadequacies of the humanists, it also tended to create almost as many problems as it solved. In particular it resulted frequently in the destruction of traditional certainties, and only rarely in the achievement of new ones. The discoveries of the chronologists tended to make a literal interpretation of the Old Testament impossible and thus cast doubt on the one document for which absolute historical certainty had been claimed. Similar uncertainties were found in Greek and Roman history,[1] and they appeared to be so numerous in the accounts of the religious wars of the sixteenth century, that Bayle asserted that he read the historians of this period not in order to find out what happened (a hopeless undertaking), but merely to discover what each side *said* about what happened.[2]

Masters as they were of 'lower criticism' the scholars lacked any principle by which they could distinguish fact from fable. Nor had they any social or historical theory to tell them what type of fact it was important to establish. The one thing of which they were certain was that history itself was largely uncertain. 'Le Pyrrhonisme de l'histoire' became the watchword of men like Bayle, whose *Dictionnaire* is a vast compendium of all the unconnected facts which could be salvaged from the ruin of history. If the majority were unwilling to accept historical Pyrrhonism, they were far from agreed as to the certainty which might replace it. Hardouin, suspicious of all written records, put his trust in coins and inscriptions; but Bierlingius had already demonstrated that many of these were forgeries too.[3]

The early decades of the eighteenth century saw the culmination of this wave of Pyrrhonism. Evidence of this is to be found not only in the great debate on early Roman history which split the Académie des Inscriptions and ended in the triumph of the sceptics,[4] but also in handbooks of historical method like those of Lenglet du Fresnoy or Juvenel, which are full of exhortations to

(Paris, 1901); in L. Traube, *Vorlesungen und Abhandlungen zur Paläographie und Handschriftenkunde*, Munich, 1909; and in the studies devoted to Mabillon in the *Archives de la France monastique*, vol. v (Paris, 1908).

[1] See Hazard, *La Crise de la conscience européenne*, pp. 30 ff.

[2] *Critique générale de l'histoire du Calvinisme* (*Œuvres diverses*, ii. 10).

[3] See Hazard, loc. cit., and Momigliano, 'Ancient History and the Antiquarian' pp. 301–2.

[4] See Flint, *Historical Philosophy in France*, pp. 255 ff., and Giarrizzo, *Edward Gibbon*, pp. 93 ff.

doubt.[1] But the same period also witnessed various attempts to overcome the crisis. An increasing number of historians who remained within the humanist tradition, such as Daniel, Fleury, or Rapin de Thoyras, tended to adopt something of the methodological exactitude of the *érudits*.[2] Others attempted to approach history in a more scientific spirit. The fables of antiquity were shown up for what they were in works like Fontenelle's *Histoire des oracles*, and both Fontenelle and Banier tried to explain the origin of fables in a manner which showed some understanding of primitive human nature.[3] Most important of all, attempts were made to evolve a new conception of the purpose of the historian and of the sort of material which ought to form the subject-matter of history. Bayle and Fontenelle both urge the historian to study 'l'histoire de l'esprit humain', and Fénelon demands a more thorough study of the development of social institutions and forms of society. After the death of Louis XIV, in a world tired of war and despotism, these demands become more general and are linked with a feeling of hostility towards the history of wars and diplomacy.[4] Greater interest is shown in economic developments, not only as a result of the growth of economic thought originated by men like Vauban and Boisguillebert, but also as an outcome of the financial crisis of the Regency. A growing concern with social and constitutional questions is shared by the aristocracy, interested in restoring their old privileges, and the middle classes, increasingly imbued with the ideas of parliamentary democracy and the concept of the rights of man. Boulainvilliers's *Histoire de l'ancien gouvernement de la France* of 1727 gives a new vitality to history by bringing it back into the field of political controversy.[5] Significantly, Boulainvilliers himself is one of the more outspoken champions of a more social type of history.[6]

With Boulainvilliers, and still more with Montesquieu, whose *Considérations sur les Romains* appears in 1734, Enlightenment historiography becomes a reality. But Boulainvilliers and Montesquieu both deal with restricted subjects. The task of interpreting history as a whole from the point of view of the Enlightenment is reserved for Voltaire.

[1] Lenglet's *Méthode pour étudier l'histoire* appears in 1713, and Juvenel's *Principes de l'histoire* in 1733.　　　　　　　　　[2] See pp. 27 ff.
[3] For Fontenelle's attitude, see the edition of *De l'origine des fables* by J.-R. Carré, and for that of Banier, Giarrizzo, *Edward Gibbon*, pp. 70–73.
[4] See pp. 32 ff.　　　　　　　[5] See p. 64.　　　　　　　[6] See p. 38.

I

APPRENTICESHIP

THE age of historical Pyrrhonism and of attempts to solve the problems which it presented was also the age in which Voltaire grew to manhood and achieved fame as poet and dramatist. But the young Voltaire was, for the most part, unaware of the problems which beset the historians. He could never have said, as Gibbon did of his childhood, that:

> The dynasties of Assyria and Egypt were my top and cricket ball, and my sleep has been disturbed by the difficulty of reconciling the Septuagint with the Hebrew computation.[1]

References to historical questions in his early works and his early correspondence are extremely few. It was not until 1731 that he produced his first historical work of real significance, and it was not until the later thirties and the forties that he began to elaborate his own theory of history and to write the major works which appeared in the following decade.[2]

Indirectly, however, the attitude of the future historian was already being formed in his early years. For if he was not concerned with the interpretation of the past, the young Voltaire took considerable interest in the political events of the world around him. At the Collège Louis-le-Grand he came into contact with fellow pupils, such as the brothers D'Argenson, who were later to hold important office in the state. One of his teachers, P. Porée, remarks of him that 'il aimait à peser dans ses petites balances les grands intérêts de l'Europe',[3] and he himself, in later years, confirms this.[4] That something of his later republican spirit had also developed at a relatively early age is revealed by his letters from Holland with their comments on Dutch democracy and commercial prosperity.[5] The future social historian was already interested in society, if not yet in its origins and development.

[1] Gibbon, *The Autobiographies* (ed. J. Murray, London, 1896), p. 59.
[2] *Le Siècle de Louis XIV*, 1751; *Essai sur les mœurs*, 1756.
[3] See Desnoiresterres, *Voltaire et la société au 18ᵉ siècle*, i. 28.
[4] In a letter to D'Olivet, xxxv. 19.
[5] e.g. xxxiii. 73.

Again, if the young Voltaire knew nothing of the Pyrrhonism of history as such, he probably became acquainted at an early age with one of its principal manifestations—scepticism regarding the miraculous. If it is an exaggeration to say that Voltaire was born a Deist, he nevertheless absorbed the scepticism of the Société du Temple at an early age.[1] His godfather, the abbé de Chateauneuf, who introduced him to this society, himself elaborated a criticism of miracles,[2] and though this was only published in 1725, it is more than likely that Chateauneuf communicated his ideas to his young protégé.

But Voltaire's interest in history proper appears to have been first aroused in 1715 when, after the scandal of Le Bourbier,[3] he spent a period of exile at Saint-Ange, the home of the aged Caumartin, a former Conseiller d'État and 'très savant dans l'histoire'.[4] Caumartin related many anecdotes about the previous century and succeeded in interesting Voltaire particularly in the career and personality of Henri IV.[5] As a result, the young poet embarked upon the epic which was finally to be known as La Henriade.

La Henriade is a work of poetry rather than of history, and contains all the improbabilities which might be expected in a pastiche of Virgil. Yet it is not devoid of certain pretensions to historical accuracy. Even the 1723 version, published under the title of La Ligue, contained a considerable number of footnotes in which the author cited his historical authorities, and in subsequent editions these notes became more numerous.[6] Work on La Henriade probably introduced Voltaire not only to seventeenth-century humanist historians such as Mézeray[7] and earlier annalists such as De Thou,[8] but also to Bayle, whose Réponse aux questions d'un Provincial is quoted,[9] and whose Dictionnaire may well be the source of much information.[10] It is very possibly through Bayle that Voltaire first makes contact with the problems of history.

[1] See Ascoli, 'Voltaire historien', p. 504.
[2] See Pomeau, La Religion de Voltaire, pp. 32–33.
[3] See Desnoiresterres, i. 8.
[4] Commentaire historique (i. 4).   [5] See p. 10.
[6] See viii. 82, 83, 122, 124, and 125.
[7] Mézeray is frequently quoted (e.g. viii. 75, 83, 100, 177), and appears to be Voltaire's principal source.
[8] viii. 67, n. 2.   [9] viii. 75, n. 3.
[10] See Haxo, 'Pierre Bayle et Voltaire avant les Lettres Philosophiques'. He also discusses other sources of La Henriade.

His interest may well have been further stimulated by his visit in 1722 to the exiled Bolingbroke at the latter's residence at La Source. In the enthusiastic account of his stay which he sends to Thiériot, he mentions particularly the extent to which he has been impressed by the English statesman's knowledge of both ancient and modern history.[1] Two years later he writes to Thiériot urging him to become 'bien savant dans l'histoire,' and adding 'vous me donnerez de l'émulation et je vous suivrai dans cette carrière'.[2] Thiériot is then at La Rivière-Bourdet near Rouen, and the Rouen circle grouped around Cideville and including Voltaire, Thiériot, and Mme de Bernières, appears to have been interested in history.[3] A letter of Voltaire's in the following year suggests that Thiériot was engaged in writing a life of Mahomet, though, like most of Thiériot's projects, this work was never completed.[4]

Thus, even before his exile in England, Voltaire shows signs of an interest in social history, of a sceptical attitude towards the fabulous, and of a certain concern for historical accuracy. Yet history is still for him primarily a means to an end: the raw material of drama or epic poetry. He has not yet begun to think deeply about its problems. The seeds of Enlightenment historiography, though sown in his mind, have not yet begun to ripen.

In England, Voltaire publishes not only the new version of *La Henriade*,[5] but also his first historical work, the *Essay upon the Civil Wars of France* of 1727. This short essay (it occupies less than 20 pages in the Moland edition) is, however, little more than a brief account of the principal events of the civil war together with a number of anecdotes. It shows greater partiality for the Protestant cause than Voltaire is later to exhibit,[6] but this may be due to its association with a poem praising Henri IV or with the fact that it was written for English readers. Otherwise it has no particular originality, except that it reveals something of Voltaire's gift for rapid, forceful, if somewhat superficial analysis as in a passage like the following:

The Superstition, the dull ignorant Knavery of the Monks, the over-grown Power of Rome, Men's Passion for Novelty, the Ambition of

---

[1] xxxiii. 84.
[2] xxxiii. 122.
[3] See Pomeau, *La Religion de Voltaire*, pp. 90–91.
[4] Best, i. 325.
[5] 1728.
[6] e.g. viii. 270. Cf. p. 58.

Luther and Calvin, the Policy of many Princes; all these had given rise
and countenance to this Sect, free indeed from Superstition, but running
as headlong towards Anarchy as the Church of Rome towards Tyranny.[1]

Voltaire's sojourn in England, however, was the occasion of a
much more important work. His interest in the life of Charles XII
of Sweden was probably of long standing, for as far back as 1717
he had met the then Swedish Foreign Minister, Baron Goertz, at
the house of the banker Hogguers, and he claims to have been one
of the first witnesses of the intrigues in which Goertz was engaged
at this time.[2] However, in 1727, Baron Fabrice, friend of George I,
and former Holstein envoy to Charles XII during the latter's
captivity in Turkey, arrived in England. He stayed at Lord Chester-
field's and moved in the same society as Voltaire.[3] It was their
meeting which led to the writing of the *Histoire de Charles XII*,[4]
and Fabrice was one of Voltaire's most important sources of
information.[5]

In all probability, he consulted other authorities at the same
time; among them Bolingbroke, the Duchess of Marlborough, and
the former English ambassador Jeffries.[6] But we have no precise
evidence as to when these consultations took place, for Voltaire's
correspondence contains no mention of the *Histoire de Charles XII*
until after his return to France. He then writes to Thiériot about
the 'Swedish manuscript'[7] in terms which suggest that the work is
almost complete. The suggestion is supported by the appearance,
in the *Mercure* of May 1729, of an announcement of the forth-
coming publication. However, if a version of the work was complete by this time, it probably differed considerably from that
finally published in 1731; for Voltaire continues to bombard
Thiériot with requests for information,[8] and the memoirs of some
of his important informants, such as Villelongue, do not reach him
till later.[9] He probably continued to revise the work until its
publication.

The first volume of the *Histoire de Charles XII* should have
appeared earlier, for Voltaire had arranged, with official approval,

[1] *Essay upon the Civil Wars of France* (London, 1728), pp. 6–7.
[2] xvi. 564.
[3] See Chase, *The Young Voltaire*, pp. 137–8.   [4] See p. 10.
[5] i. 87–88.   [6] See xvi. 226 and 294–5.
[7] *Correspondance* (ed. Foulet), p. 194.
[8] e.g. ibid., pp. 197–200 and 298.   [9] See p. 18.

for its publication in Paris. But while the edition was being printed, the Garde des Sceaux changed his mind and ordered its seizure.[1] The reason was doubtless Voltaire's somewhat unsympathetic treatment of the reigning King of Poland, Augustus, which he had probably hoped would be overlooked because he had given the more noble role to Stanislas, father of the Queen of France. But if the Garde des Sceaux was unwilling to take risks, Voltaire was able to find more amenable authorities in Rouen. Equipped with the false indication 'Christophe Revis, Basle', the new first edition appeared there in 1731.[2]

It was not until some twenty years later, with the appearance of the *Siècle de Louis XIV*, that Voltaire was to publish another historical work of comparable scale. By that time he had reached his maturity as a historian. The *Histoire de Charles XII* can, therefore, be thought of as the work of an apprentice; all the more so because it differs in a number of essential ways from the later works. In 1731 Voltaire is still far from being the 'philosophic' historian he is later to become.

The *Histoire de Charles XII* was an immediate success,[3] and innumerable subsequent editions testify to its continued popularity. It is certainly the most easily approachable of Voltaire's historical works, being written in a direct and vivid narrative style, devoid of complicated analysis or erudition, and free from all but the most reasonable forms of 'philosophic' propaganda. Based on a relatively small number of sources, many of which are known, it does not appear to present a difficult problem to anyone desirous of analysing its technique.

It is perhaps surprising, therefore, to find critics disagreeing markedly as to its value. Some have denounced it as a sort of prose *Henriade*[4] or as romanesque history akin to that of Courtilz de Sandras.[5] Others have admired its scrupulous documentation.[6] One suggests that through it Voltaire rediscovers the comparative method in modern history and that it enables him to examine

---

[1] *Correspondance* (ed. Foulet), p. 297.
[2] Ibid., p. 303.
[3] Bengesco lists some twelve editions by 1740.
[4] Gandar, 'Voltaire historien', p. 195.
[5] Brunetière, *Études sur le 18e siècle* (Paris, 1911), p. 142.
[6] See the preface to Geffroy's edition of 1847, and Carré, *Consistance de Voltaire le philosophe*, p. 87.

social conditions in various parts of Europe.[1] But Voltaire himself could later dismiss it as 'amusante'.[2]

One reason for this divergence of views is the tendency to examine the *Histoire de Charles XII* in the light of Voltaire's later historical works and theoretical pronouncements. But if some of the seeds of Enlightenment historiography are to be found in the work, they are not its principal feature. In essence it belongs to the humanist tradition. Voltaire has not yet come to reject this tradition and to elaborate a new view of his own.

Something of his state of mind in undertaking the work is revealed by the explanatory letter which he later writes to the *Journal des Savants:*

> Quand je composai cette histoire du monarque le plus singulier qui ait jamais régné en Europe, je ne prétendis faire qu'un simple essai ; je me trouvais en un sens dans la même situation d'esprit où j'étais quand je fis la Henriade. J'avais eu l'honneur de jouir quelques mois à la campagne en 1716 de la société de feu m. Caumartin, l'homme de France qui savait le plus d'anecdotes sur la vie d'Henri IV. . . . De même, me trouvant à la campagne en 1727 avec m. de Fabrice qui avait passé sept années auprès de Charles XII, il me conta des faits si extraordinaires que je ne pus résister à l'envie qu'il m'inspira de les écrire.[3]

In its inspiration then, the *Histoire de Charles XII* is closely allied to the *Henriade*. Both works originate not from any desire to investigate the history of society, but from the fascination exercised by the character of an outstanding individual.[4] Both are primarily conceived as works of art.

The *Discours sur l'Histoire de Charles XII* which Voltaire appended to the first edition of 1731 also provides much valuable information about his aims and his conception of history at this time. Above all, it illustrates the extent to which they conform with those of the humanists of the previous century. The *Histoire de Charles XII* is not an 'histoire de l'esprit humain'—not a social history. It is, as its author tells us, an 'histoire particulière'—the life-story of an individual. Its interest, moreover, derives from the moral instruction to be gained from it. This is clearly implied by

[1] Chase, *The Young Voltaire*, pp. 210–11.
[2] Preface to the *Histoire de Russie*, xvi. 394.
[3] Best, xii. 39 ff.
[4] A tendency to concentrate on the biographical in historical writing is characteristic of much late-seventeenth-century historiography; see Dulong, *L'Abbé de Saint-Réal*, pp. 104–5.

Voltaire's rejection of those episodes of history which contain no such instruction:

> Pour tous les autres princes, qui n'ont été illustres ni en paix, ni en guerre, et qui n'ont été connus ni par de grands vices, ni par de grandes vertus, comme leur vie ne fournit aucun exemple ni à imiter ni à fuir, elle n'est pas digne qu'on s'en souvienne.

More particularly, it is designed, as were so many seventeenth-century histories, with an eye to the moral and political edification of rulers:

> On a pensé que cette lecture pourrait être utile à quelques princes, si ce livre leur tombe par hasard entre les mains. Certainement il n'y a point de souverain qui, en lisant la vie de Charles XII, ne doive être guéri de la folie des conquêtes.[1]

The *Discours* does not mention artistic aims. But we know that Voltaire expressed a desire, after the success of the *Henriade*, to 'réussir en prose', and that whilst he was writing the *Charles XII* he was busy re-reading Quintus Curtius.[2] And an examination of the work itself reveals his concern for artistic form.

In later years, Voltaire frequently draws a parallel between history and drama, suggesting that the former should have the same form as the latter.[3] These views appear surprising, coming from the author of the *Essai sur les mœurs*, for in that work, literary form appears to be a secondary consideration, and dramatic construction is non-existent. But if later works contradict the theory of 'dramatic' history, the *Histoire de Charles XII* is an ideal illustration of it. It possesses, as French classical tragedy should, the three elements of *exposition*, *nœud*, and *dénouement*; the first in the introductory picture of Swedish history and of the childhood of Charles himself; the second in his entry into the war and his campaigns in Denmark, Poland, and Russia; and the third in his tragic death before the walls of Frederickshall.

Of course, the parallel with drama must not be carried too far, for the wide span of the lifetime of an individual demands very different treatment from the twenty-four hours in which the destinies of the hero of classical tragedy are worked out. Voltaire can show both the rise and the fall of his hero; the succession of victories from the miracle of Narva to the drive towards Moscow,

---

[1] xvi. 130–2.   [2] See Gandar, 'Voltaire historien', p. 195.
[3] See pp. 160–1.

followed by the catastrophic defeat at Poltava, the period of exile
and imprisonment in Turkey, and finally, when the wheel of
fortune seemed about to turn again, the stray bullet which brings
the story to an end. Moreover, he has greater freedom in other
ways, too, for the *Histoire de Charles XII* contains a certain
mélange de genres which the dramatist would not have permitted
himself. If there is epic grandeur in the accounts of the great
campaigns, there is more than a suggestion of comedy in the
intrigues of the period of Turkish captivity, and in the cynical
comment of Mégret after Charles's death there is even a dash of
romantic irony.[1]

But the *Histoire de Charles XII* has not only tragic form, it has
also a tragic hero. Like the tragic heroes of antiquity, Charles is
a victim of *hubris*. Voltaire portrays him as a man of extraordinary fearlessness and resolution, but subtly manages to hint at the
obsessional nature of his ideal of glory. Charles's one aim is to
become a second Alexander, and to achieve it he will not hesitate to
sacrifice the welfare of his peoples. Nor will he turn his eyes from
his goal in order to make a realistic appraisal of the means of
achieving it. He is shown to be a skilful and courageous tactician
and a great visionary. But as a strategist he is a failure; and it is
this which leads to his downfall.

Fate and his own nature conspire against him. But he also has a
more tangible opponent in the shape of another individual who,
like himself, is cast in the heroic mould, and who shares with him
the centre of the stage. This is Peter the Great of Russia.

In Voltaire's eyes, the struggle between them is not just a conflict between individuals. As an individual he probably prefers
Charles, for he has some harsh things to say about Peter's in-
humanity. But the conflict is also one between two types of
activity, between two 'philosophies'. And here it is Peter who has
his approval. Peter is a creative and constructive monarch, whereas
Charles can do nothing but conquer and destroy, and finally involves himself and his country in ruin. As Voltaire judges the two
men on the basis of their achievement rather than on their personality, he shows throughout a distinct preference for Peter. Nor
is their any evidence to suggest that he had earlier held a different
view. If the *Histoire de Charles XII* has affinities with the *Henriade*,
this does not mean that Voltaire admires Charles in the same way

[1] 'Voilà la pièce finie, allons souper' (xvi. 350).

as he does Henri IV. From the very beginning he speaks of him as a curious amalgam of greatness and madness.[1] He later sums him up as 'moitié Alexandre, moitié don Quichotte'.[2]

Such a statement suggests that he is interested in the psychological make-up of the king. Yet it is here that the parallel between the *Histoire de Charles XII* and classical drama tends to break down. For if Voltaire has such an interest, he nevertheless shows himself to be but a mediocre practitioner of the art of analysing and explaining human character. If he succeeds in creating a credible picture of Charles, his success is due principally to the wealth of anecdotes on all periods of the king's life which fill the pages of his work. In the light of them, the reader can interpret Charles's character; but he has to do most of the interpretation himself. Where the author intervenes with his personal comments, it is nearly always in order to judge rather than to comprehend or explain. He is often content with the stereotyped formula; phrases like 'puissant génie', 'âme singulière', and 'homme supérieur' are frequent. And the shrewder comments are those which deal with the social and political consequences of a character's action rather than with its motives. The 'philosophical' historian is already beginning to reveal himself.

However, Voltaire's lack of psychological profundity is compensated for by his narrative skill. The *Histoire de Charles XII* is in essence neither a study of character nor a sociological investigation, but a fascinating story of action and adventure. This is true even of the earlier part of the work. But it is particularly true of the account of Charles's misfortunes in Turkey. Throughout Voltaire's accounts of battles, one is able to sense that he has never taken part in one himself. But in the narrower field of political intrigue and counter-intrigue he is both a convincing and an enthralling story-teller.

As an adventure story, and an adventure story concerned with heroic individuals, the *Histoire de Charles XII* is necessarily composed primarily of anecdotes. This is true even of the account of Charles's childhood. But it is even more true of the description of his stay at Bender, for here the narrative becomes a series of colourful, though often questionable, incidents, which have been related to Voltaire by his various informants. There is, for example, the story of the disguise used by Villelongue in order to present a

---

[1] e.g. xxxiii. 241 and 483.   [2] xxxiv. 270.

petition to the sultan, and of his subsequent interview with the
Turkish ruler himself.[1] There is the long account of the intrigue
which Count Poniatowski attempts to conduct with the sultana.[2]
There is the anecdote which explains the enmity of the Ukrainian
ruler Mazeppa towards the czar—an enmity on which Charles is
to base the whole of his campaign in the Ukraine.[3]

Moreover, Voltaire shows a marked preference for anecdotes
with a romanesque flavour. Both the Poniatowski and the Villelongue intrigues fall into this category, and the latter, though
vouched for by Villelongue himself, is the object of the criticisms
of another of Voltaire's informants, Fierville.[4] But a more striking
example is the story of a certain Frederick who was taken prisoner
by the Tartars when Charles was captured at Bender and was torn
to pieces by them because they could not decide which of them
was to be his master.[5] This anecdote, together with another relating
to the presence of a Scots spy at Birzen,[6] is later deleted.

Voltaire is a master of narrative prose and his style is unmistakable. Yet the *Histoire de Charles XII* is not altogether free from
the stereotyped stylistic devices which characterize many of the
humanists. If there are no long harangues in the work, there are a
remarkable number of short direct quotations from many of the
characters.[7] There are letters and documents, such as the text of
the Russian prayer after the defeat of Narva,[8] mostly of very doubtful authenticity. The death of Charles is followed by a lengthy
funeral oration in the grand manner.[9] And, illustrative of another
device beloved by the humanists, there is the 'parallel' of Charles
and Peter:

Les deux plus singuliers monarques qui fussent alors dans le monde:
Charles XII, illustre par neuf années de victoires, Pierre Alexiowitz par
neuf années de peines prises pour former des troupes égales aux troupes
suédoises; l'un glorieux d'avoir donné des états, l'autre d'avoir civilisé
les siens, etc.[10]

Moral reflections, of which the above is but one example, play a
considerable part in Voltaire's narrative. But this is characteristic

---

[1] xvi. 309–10.   [2] xvi. 256–7.   [3] xvi. 237.
[4] See xvi. 310.
[5] *Histoire de Charles XII* (Basle [*sic*], 1732), pp. 334–5.
[6] Ibid., pp. 64–65.
[7] e.g. xvi. 151, 153, 174, 193.
[8] xvi. 177.   [9] xvi. 350–1.   [10] xvi. 245.

of his later work also. More typically humanist is a certain tone
of exaggerated admiration which indicates a striving after effect
rather than a search for truth, as in the following description of
Charles himself:

L'homme le plus extraordinaire peut-être qui ait jamais été sur la
terre, qui a réuni en lui toutes les grandes qualités de ses aïeux, et qui
n'a eu d'autre défaut ni d'autre malheur que de les avoir toutes outrées.[1]

In its moral and artistic purposes, its tendency to biography, its
predilection for the romanesque, and its stylistic devices, the
Histoire de Charles XII shows itself to be a work in the humanist
tradition. If it also has its links with 'philosophic' history, these
are by no means so close as some critics suggest.

One of the main themes of Voltaire's 'philosophic' propaganda
in later years is his opposition to war, and especially aggressive war.
And this theme is equally visible in the *Histoire de Charles XII*.
Indeed, the *Discours* claims that the work's purpose is to cure
princes of the folly of conquests.[2] Yet although the parallel exists,
it would be a mistake to attribute too much importance to it.
Even Bossuet had found it difficult to defend aggression, and
Louis XIV was reported to have died saying that he had loved war
too much. And after the peace of Utrecht, condemnation of war is
common in France. Popular historians like Limiers and Larrey
show a definite dislike of the heroic conqueror without being in
any sense themselves *philosophes*.[3]

The same is true in other fields. When one finds Voltaire indulg-
ing in long reflections on the barbarous execution of the Lithua-
nian patriot Patkul,[4] one tends to hear the voice of the future
defender of Calas or Lally. But in reality, Voltaire's passage is little
more than a summary of a similar one in one of his sources, the
historian Limiers. Again, there are a number of passages criticizing the power of the Roman Church. One, for example, asserts that

Ses ministres n'avaient pas manqué de profiter de toutes les con-
jonctures favorables pour étendre leur pouvoir, révéré par la multitude,
mais toujours contesté par les plus sages.[5]

[1] xvi. 150.   [2] xvi. 132.
[3] See the prefaces to Limiers's *Histoire du règne de Louis XIV* and Larrey's
Histoire de France sous le règne de Louis XIV, especially with reference to the
invasion of Holland.
[4] xvi. 221.
[5] xvi. 205.

Such criticisms appear to link up with the Voltairian aim of crushing *l'infâme*. But to contemporaries they probably appeared as part of an established Gallican tradition, and they were far less extreme in tone than many of the outbursts of Gallicans like Lenglet du Fresnoy.[1] The critics of the *Histoire de Charles XII* accuse Voltaire of practically every sort of misdeed, but not one of them accuses him of irreligion, or even pays any attention to the passages in which he attacks the power of Rome.

The 'philosophic' views expressed in the *Histoire de Charles XII* are, then, views which were widely accepted by many sections of French opinion at the time. Even were this not the case, the expression of such views would not in itself constitute 'philosophic' history, for the latter is not merely liberal or anti-clerical propaganda, but is an attempt to understand and interpret human societies and customs in terms of Enlightenment beliefs about the nature of man and the universe.

There is certainly some evidence to suggest that Voltaire is making such an attempt in the *Histoire de Charles XII*. It is to be found scattered throughout the work in innumerable comments on social and political affairs in the various countries to which Voltaire's hero leads him. But it is found more clearly in a relatively small number of passages in which the author attempts to give a detailed description and explanation of a society. The first book, for example, is devoted almost exclusively to an attempt to situate the two main contestants, Charles and Peter, against their respective backgrounds. Details are given of the geography and climate of Sweden and Russia, of changes in the form of government over recent years, of religious beliefs and institutions. They reveal both an inquiring mind, alert to seize on what is distinctive, and a 'philosophical' critical spirit, ready to censure whatever seems contrary to liberty, tolerance, and common sense.

The second book contains a somewhat similar account of Poland. Here it is the political interest which predominates. Voltaire sees in the Polish constitution the last remnant of a bygone age:

Son gouvernement est la plus fidèle image de l'ancien gouvernement celte et gothique, corrigé ou altéré partout ailleurs. C'est le seul État qui ait conservé le nom de république avec la dignité royale.[2]

[1] See his *Méthode pour étudier l'histoire* (1713), i. 87, 114, and 189.
[2] xvi. 18ı.

And he goes on to examine in detail the relations between the different social classes of the nation, noting that Poland is the one country in which the social contract between king and people appears to be a reality, and contrasting the apparent power of the king with his real weakness when faced with a hostile nobility. He discusses, too, the right of veto possessed by each member of the nobility, the organization of the militia, the power of the Church, and many other matters.

Each country with which he deals is the object of similar scrutiny. Though in some cases, as, for example, that of Turkey,[1] he is relatively brief and superficial, yet his constant interest in social and constitutional questions is clearly visible.

However, the writing of social history is not yet, as it is later to become, his primary aim. Descriptions of social developments are still subordinate to the account of the lives of the two central figures; action still predominates over interpretation. It would, moreover, be mistaken to imagine that the humanists' preoccupation with individuals precluded any interest in social problems. Writers like Fénelon and Lenglet du Fresnoy urge the study of constitutions, forms of government, and customs.[2] But for Lenglet, such studies are, like the study of geography or chronology, a sort of prelude to the study of history proper. If in Voltaire's work they occupy much more space, they still tend to fulfil the same introductory function. If the *Histoire de Charles XII* tends to stretch the bonds of humanist historical form, it is still far from bursting them.

In form and technique, then, the *Histoire de Charles XII* is closer to a humanist narrative history such as Saint-Réal's *Conjuration contre Venise*[3] than to, say, Montesquieu's *Grandeur et décadence des Romains*. However, the besetting sin of historians like Saint-Réal is their cavalier attitude towards their sources. It remains to be seen whether Voltaire is also guilty of this.

In the *Discours sur l'Histoire de Charles XII* he has very little to say about his sources. At first he contents himself with the assertion that

On a composé cette histoire sur des récits de personnes connues qui

---

[1] xvi. 255–6.
[2] For Fénelon's views, see pp. 36 ff., and for those of Lenglet, his *Méthode pour étudier l'histoire*, *passim*.
[3] See p. 30.

ont passé plusieurs années auprès de Charles XII et de Pierre le Grand,
empereur de Moscovie, et qui, s'étant retirées dans un pays libre, longtemps après la mort de ces princes, n'avaient aucun intérêt de déguiser
la vérité.[1]

But the individuals concerned are not named, and the text of the
first edition itself contains hardly any reference to authorities.

However, in answer to the criticisms of Des Roches de Parthenay, Voltaire adds, in the 1733 'Basle' edition, a list of five
people who have supplied him with memoirs.[2] Of these, four—
Fabrice, Villelongue, Fierville, and Poniatowski—had been
attached to Charles during the period of his exile in Turkey. The
fifth, Croissy, had been French ambassador at Stralsund when
Charles was beseiged there in 1715. It will be seen that Voltaire's
direct information refers only to one period of Charles's life.
Moreover, if Fabrice's help is available from the beginning, the
memoirs of other informants may have been slow in arriving.
Villelongue's two long letters are written in February and March
1730.[3] Poniatowski's first contribution may have been a small one,
for in 1741 he sends Voltaire a work containing many criticisms of
minor factual errors in the *Histoire de Charles XII*, and denying
some of the actions attributed to him by Voltaire.[4] Clearly, other
sources must have played a considerable part.

Among these other sources are eyewitnesses like the French
ambassador to Sweden, Brancas,[5] and the ambassador to Constantinople, Des Aleurs;[6] Voltaire acknowledges his debt to them
in the text itself. He also uses earlier published works such as
Cantemir's *Annales turques*,[7] Dalerac's *Anecdotes de Pologne*,[8] La
Mottraye's *Voyages en Europe, Asie et Afrique*,[9] and Perry's
État présent de la Grande Russie.[10] But his greatest debt, in the early
stages of his work, is probably to a book he never mentions, the
Histoire de Suède sous le règne de Charles XII, published in 1720
by the historian Limiers.

[1] xvi. 132. The list which follows did not appear in the first edition.
[2] *Histoire de Charles XII* (Basle [sic], 1733), ii. 225–6.
[3] Best, ii. 110–28 and 129–36.
[4] See ibid. xi. 61, 77, and 95, and see p. 22, n. 1.   [5] xvi. 241.
[6] *Correspondance* (ed. Foulet), p. 298.
[7] See the letter to Cantemir, xxxv. 210.
[8] See xxxiii. 192.
[9] See p. 20.
[10] See Beauvois's review of Danielson's *Voltaire Kaarle XII* in the *Revue historique*, 1879, for references to this and other sources.

There are many similarities between the accounts of Limiers and Voltaire. The Swedish historian Nordberg, in the footnotes to his own *Histoire de Charles XII*, takes a malicious pleasure in pointing out the errors of his predecessors, and on a number of occasions we find him noting the same error in Voltaire and Limiers and nowhere else.[1] The prayer offered by the inhabitants of Moscow after the defeat of Narva is found in identical terms in both writers.[2] Limiers quotes as his source the *History of the Wars of Charles XII* published anonymously in 1715. But it is unlikely that Voltaire took his information from this work, for its author, after relating this incident with considerable scepticism, hastens, as he says, 'to leave this ridiculous stuff'.[3]

Other important anecdotes also come from Limiers. There is the story, later deleted, of the Scots spy sent by Charles XII to gain information about the meeting of Peter the Great and Augustus at Birzen.[4] There are the details of the battle of Narva which are later altered as a result of Nordberg's criticisms. And on more than one occasion, verbal similarities between the two texts suggest direct borrowing.[5]

Such, then, was the approximate extent of Voltaire's sources at the time of the first edition of the *Histoire de Charles XII*. An evaluation of them clearly depends on the standard with which they are compared. It is clear that for a considerable part of his account, Voltaire has done little but copy Limiers. But for other periods, notably that of Charles's exile at Bender, he has made considerable efforts to procure a large number of first-hand testimonies. His documentation is far from measuring up to the high standards demanded by the more erudite historians. But if he is somewhat naïve in accepting doubtful authorities such as Limiers, he nevertheless has some backing for nearly everything he says, and he does not indulge in the type of romantic invention associated with writers like Saint-Réal or Courtilz de Sandras. If his work is in the humanist tradition, it is one of the finest products of that tradition.

Moreover, he does not rest content with the first edition of the *Histoire de Charles XII*. He is constantly seeking further help,

---

[1] e.g. i. 17, 142, and 346, and ii. 152.
[2] *Histoire de Suède*, v. 98 and xvi. 177.
[3] Op. cit., p. 97.
[4] Limiers, v. 103 and *Histoire de Charles XII* (Basle [*sic*], 1732), pp. 64–65.
[5] See Geffroy's edition, p. 52.

C

constantly revising his work in the light of criticism. La Mottraye's *Remarques historiques et critiques sur l'*Histoire de Charles XII *de Voltaire*, which appear in 1732, contain many scathing criticisms. These arouse Voltaire's anger, but he nevertheless profits from them. And two works by Swedish authors, the *Histoire militaire de Charles XII* by Adlerfeld and the *Histoire de Charles XII* of Nordberg, which appear in 1740 and 1742 respectively, are both used by Voltaire for revisions of his own text. And in order to make his account as accurate as possible, he seeks information from many of the participants in the events described, among them King Stanislas of Poland[1] and the Saxon general Schullembourg.[2] By the time of the 1748 edition the majority of the earlier in-accuracies have disappeared.

But it is clear that in 1731 Voltaire had neither developed his conception of a new type of *histoire de l'esprit humain*, nor eluci-dated the sceptical critical method which was also to become characteristic of his later years. During the next twenty years, before the appearance of the *Siècle de Louis XIV*, he is to think about the problems of history as he has not thought before. And one of the stimuli which leads him to undertake this critical revision of his ideas is that provided by the series of attacks to which the *Histoire de Charles XII* is subjected.

The contempt of the critics for Voltaire's first historical work appears to have been directly proportional to its success with the general public. No sooner has the work appeared, than the abbé Des Roches de Parthenay, in the introduction to his *Histoire de Pologne sous le règne d'Auguste II*, accuses it of being little more than an *Henriade* in prose.[3] The evidence he adduces in support of his accusation is not very impressive, for he does little but point out a number of minor errors of fact. But a more redoubtable critic soon appears in the person of La Mottraye, whose *Historical and Critical Remarks* appear in both English and French in 1732.

La Mottraye was himself an eyewitness of the events at Bender, and had published an account of them in his *Voyages en Europe, Asie et Afrique*. Voltaire had read this work and, in the first edition of the *Histoire de Charles XII*, had acknowledged his debt to it.[4] But his debt was not great, for his account differed consider-

---

[1] See xvi. 142.   [2] See xxxv. 506–7.   [3] Preface, pp. xv–xix.
[4] *Histoire de Charles XII* (Basle [sic], 1732), p. 357.

ably from that of La Mottraye, and he obviously placed greater reliance on his other sources. It was doubtless this which roused La Mottraye's anger.

La Mottraye, after a passing word of praise for Voltaire's style, makes a whole series of criticisms of his factual accuracy. His statements about Peter's adviser, Le Fort, his account of the battle of Narva and of Charles's flight after Poltava, are all asserted to be full of error. His accounts of the relations between Poniatowski and the sultana 'appear merely romantick, and deserving a place in the *Turkish Spy* or the *Persian Letters*'.[1] His anecdotes about Russian attempts to corrupt Turkish officials or poison Poniatowski are based on false Turkish propaganda stories.[2] His imaginary conversations are the antithesis of true historical writing:

> Instead of giving out such imaginary intrigues, of making the Sultan, the Viziers, the King of Sweden, the Pachas, etc., say witty or silly things which nobody heard them say . . . you ought to relate material facts and true Circumstances, which you are able to prove to the world.[3]

If this forthright criticism of Voltaire's method is often justified (it is precisely the criticism he himself is later to make of other historians), La Mottraye rarely offers proof that his version of the facts is the correct one. But Voltaire's reaction shows that he himself is at times convinced. In the 1733 edition, for example, he alters his account of Le Fort's parentage, substituting for the earlier version one more in accordance with the statements of La Mottraye.[4] But he is unwilling to alter his account of the battle of Narva or delete his version of the Russian prayer, even though his only authority for these appears to be Limiers. And where he has other sources of information, as he has for his account of events in Turkey, he is even less willing to give way. He defends these authorities in his counter-attack on La Mottraye which is first published in the Amsterdam edition of 1733. And he further revenges himself on his critic by adding a deprecatory footnote to the reference to La Mottraye in the text of the *Histoire de Charles XII*,[5] and later by removing La Mottraye's name altogether.

Further criticisms appear in Poniatowski's *Remarques d'un*

---

[1] *Historical and Critical Remarks*, p. 43.
[2] Ibid., p. 48.
[3] Ibid. p. 50.
[4] Compare the Basle [*sic*], 1732 edition, p. 29 with xvi. 159.
[5] *Charles XII* (Basle [*sic*], 1733), ii. 50.

seigneur polonais of 1741. Voltaire asserts that this work is a pirated edition of a memoir which he had originally received privately from Poniatowski, but its appearance occasions further minor modifications in the text of the *Histoire de Charles XII*.[1] Poniatowski's criticisms, however, were slight compared with those of the Swedish historian Nordberg, whose *Histoire de Charles XII* began to appear in translation in 1742. In his preface Nordberg describes Voltaire as 'Archi-Menteur', an appellation which he attempts to substantiate by listing, in his footnotes, all Voltaire's errors. So bitter, indeed, is Nordberg, that his French translator feels obliged to come to Voltaire's rescue, and on more than one occasion a critical footnote of Nordberg's is followed by a further note by the translator defending Voltaire. It is worthy of note that Nordberg uses the first edition of Voltaire's work as the object of his criticisms, and that more than once, the translator is able to point out that the error to which Nordberg is drawing attention has already been corrected in later editions.[2]

In view of the bitterness of Nordberg's attack, it is not surprising that Voltaire is equally scathing about Nordberg's own work.[3] Indeed, he has good reason to be, for if the work is well documented, it is nevertheless full of useless details and sycophantic in tone. But Voltaire seems to have considerable respect for Nordberg's accuracy. He had been unwilling to alter his account of the battle of Narva when it had been criticized by La Mottraye, but now, faced with the objections of Nordberg, he does so.[4] And it is also on Nordberg's advice that he deletes the story of the Scots spy at Birzen which, like his account of Narva, had been taken from Limiers.[5]

These encounters with various critics have, then, a considerable effect on the text of the *Histoire de Charles XII*. More important, however, is their general effect on Voltaire's conception of history and historical method. How these are influenced may be seen both from his correspondence and from other critical writings.

---

[1] e.g. Poniatowski (p. 67) denies all knowledge of a M. Bru who, according to Voltaire (Amsterdam edition, 1732, ii. 5) was closely linked with him. Voltaire deletes all reference to Bru.

[2] e.g. Preface, p. xiii and ii. 152 and 154.

[3] e.g. xvi. 128 and 517, and xxxvi. 278.

[4] Compare the Basle [*sic*] edition of 1733, p. 42 with xvi. 175. See Nordberg, i. 133, n. *a*.

[5] Ibid., p. 155, n. *a*.

As early as 1732 we find him writing to Bertin de Rocheret in order to complain of the difficulty he has had in choosing between 'des relations absolument contraires', and to admit, as he so signally failed to admit in the *Discours*, that even his original eye-witness accounts often contradicted each other flatly.[1] In 1737, in the *Conseils à un journaliste*, he again refers to the *Histoire de Charles XII*, this time in the tone of one who thinks he has been unfairly criticized. In self-defence he lists all his authorities and asserts that he has treated them impartially.[2] Yet he knows that it is not so much his impartiality as his critical sense that is being called in question. He writes in the same year to Frederick the Great:

Ces messieurs [his sources] ont très bien pu se tromper; et j'ai senti combien il était difficile d'écrire une histoire contemporaine. Tous ceux qui ont vu les mêmes événements les ont vus avec des yeux différents; les témoins se contredisent.[3]

And in a letter to Schullembourg the new sceptical note is even more predominant: 'Moi qui doute de tout, et sur-tout des anec-dotes, je commençais à me condamner moi-même sur beaucoup de faits que j'avais avancés.'[4]

This attitude of greater scepticism and increasing critical aware-ness which results largely from the controversies over the *Histoire de Charles XII*, reaches its climax in the preface which Voltaire writes for the 1748 edition. The first part of this preface has, indeed, nothing whatever to do with the *Histoire de Charles XII*, but is a statement of his attitude of incredulity towards the mira-culous and fantastic elements in the accounts of historians. Here, for the first time, he sets out the critical principles which are to govern his later investigations of ancient and medieval history.[5]

When he turns to the *Histoire de Charles XII* itself, there is a certain note of apology in what he has to say:

Mais comme les témoins ne voient pas tout, et qu'ils voient quelque-fois mal, je tombai dans plus d'une erreur, non sur les faits essentiels, mais sur quelques anecdotes qui sont assez indifférentes en elles-mêmes, et sur lesquelles les petits critiques triomphent.[6]

This defence, however, is not altogether convincing; for so much

---

[1] xxxiii. 254.   [2] xxii. 247.   [3] xxxiv. 270.
[4] xxxv. 506.   [5] See p. 100.   [6] xvi. 128.

of the work consists of the type of anecdote which Voltaire now classes as indifferent. But it indicates that, in another sense, too, his attitude to history has changed. He has become aware that there are such things as 'faits essentiels', and in his correspondence he makes clear what he thinks these facts are. Writing to Frederick the Great to thank him for information about Russia and the career of Peter, he remarks that

> Je n'ai pris de ces détails curieux dont vous m'avez honoré que ce qui doit être connu de tout le monde, sans blesser personne: le dénombrement des peuples, les lois nouvelles, les mœurs publiques.[1]

And in reply to the criticisms of Nordberg, he writes:

> Vous nous dites, après le détail de ces grandes choses, à quelle heure Charles XII fut couronné; mais vous ne dites point pourquoi il le fut avant l'âge prescrit par la loi: pourquoi on ôta la régence à la reine-mère; comment le fameux Piper eut la confiance du roi; quelles étaient alors les forces de la Suède; quel nombre de citoyens elle avait, etc.[2]

Statements like these show that Voltaire has come to look askance on the picturesque anecdote, and to demand a type of history which attempts to analyse the important facts about social developments. His increased scepticism probably owes much to the controversy over the *Histoire de Charles XII*. But his preference for social history dates from the earliest years of that controversy. It is already visible in the *Lettres Philosophiques*, for in his brief excursions into English history in that work, Voltaire has no time for anecdotes, but is interested, above all, in English constitutional developments. During the thirties he is busy collecting material for *Le Siècle de Louis XIV*, and his correspondence shows that, from the very beginning, this work is planned as a history of the new type.[3] The same is true of the universal history, later to be known as the *Essai sur les mœurs*, on which he begins work in the 1740's. It is undertaken to prove to the scientifically minded Mme du Châtelet that history can be as important and as interesting as natural science.[4]

As he tackles the problems which these two works present, Voltaire makes increasing contact with the thought of those of his predecessors who have tried to give a new orientation to history,

---

[1] xxxv. 121.
[3] See pp. 46 ff.

[2] xxxvi. 279.
[4] See pp. 61 ff.

and gradually elaborates his own theory. But it is not until after 1750 that the new works are published. By this time he has reached his maturity as an historian, and from this time onwards his conception of history, though it shows development, shows no fundamental change. It can therefore be treated as a unity.

II

VOLTAIRE AND HIS PREDECESSORS

IN some fields it is comparatively easy to find the sources of Voltaire's views. He himself tells us how much he owes to Locke and Newton or to Racine and Boileau. But no previous historian is the object of similar admiration, and some of those to whom we might expect him to pay homage—Bayle and Fontenelle, for example—are frequently the object of his criticisms. Nevertheless, his own theory probably owes much to these men and to many others. It is important to ascertain the degree of his indebtedness to predecessors in order to be able to measure his own originality.

The humanist historians

The *Histoire de Charles XII* still has many affinities with the seventeenth-century tradition of historical writing. In later years Voltaire becomes much more critical of this tradition. He makes a whole series of criticisms of past historians in general, and though he does not always apply them specifically to the seventeenth-century humanists, these criticisms do refer to weaknesses to which they are particularly prone. He attacks their credulity and lack of critical sense,[1] their national and religious prejudices,[2] their insignificant and useless details,[3] their preoccupation with battles and genealogies,[4] and their falsifications and defamations.[5] He is equally scathing, too, about their harangues, portraits, and other outmoded rhetorical devices.[6]

However, he is by no means entirely consistent in his rejection of humanist standards. He is too much of an artist himself not to be attracted by stylistic merit, even when it is divorced from factual accuracy or 'philosophical' understanding. In consequence, his attitude, especially to individuals, often fluctuates. In his early and middle periods he often tends to judge historians on the basis of their literary merit. Later, he is more concerned with their

[1] e.g. xiv. 182 and 319.
[2] e.g. xxv. 170–1.
[3] e.g. xiv. 202.
[4] e.g. xxxviii. 394 and xii. 72.
[5] e.g. xxvii. 266.
[6] See pp. 161–3.

factual accuracy and their ability to describe and judge society. Finally, in his last years, it is often their attitude to religion which influences him most.

The two best-known authors of histories of France in the seventeenth and early eighteenth centuries were Mézeray and Daniel; and the variations in Voltaire's point of view are clearly illustrated by what he has to say about them. The *Catalogue des écrivains* which accompanied the 1751 edition of the *Siècle de Louis XIV* discusses both authors, and shows a marked preference for Daniel. Mézeray, whose style has something of the freedom of the pre-classical period, is considered to be 'plus hardi qu'exact, et inégal dans son style'.[1] Daniel, who is the subject of a much longer entry, is criticized both for weaknesses of style and diction and for failing to deal adequately with laws and customs. But he is 'instruit, exact, sage et vrai', and his history of France is the best in existence.[2] Such a comment is not surprising, for Daniel was one of the first humanist historians to show the influence of the more erudite seventeenth-century scholars,[3] and his work is distinguished not only by its accurate citation of sources, but also by its author's categorical refusal to follow the humanist fashion of inventing harangues.[4]

In later years, however, Voltaire's attitude changes. He can still criticize both authors, and particularly Mézeray, for their naïve credulity.[5] But as he becomes absorbed in his own 'philosopher's war', the political and religious pronouncements of the orthodox Jesuit become far more blameworthy in his eyes than the fantastic extravagances and the *esprit frondeur* of Mézeray. The *Essai sur les mœurs* contains many attacks on Daniel. His failure to mention the horrors of the Vehmgericht,[6] his condoning of François Iᵉʳ's alliance with the Barbary Turks,[7] his attempt to prove the sincerity of Henri IV's conversion to Catholicism,[8] and the emphasis he places, in his account of Henri's life, on the role of Père Coton[9] are all strongly criticized. When Voltaire comes to annotate Daniel's own *Observations critiques sur l'*Histoire de France *de Mézeray*, he pro-

---

[1] xiv. 105. [2] xiv. 61.
[3] The lengthy preface to the *Histoire de France* is largely devoted to a discussion of critical methods.
[4] Preface, p. lxxix. [5] e.g. xvi. 124–5 and xii. 21.
[6] xi. 260. [7] xii. 270.
[8] xii. 546. See also xxiv. 509.
[9] xii. 538; xli. 402; and xxxviii. 394.

duces further criticisms, asserting, for example, that Daniel takes a special interest in those kings of France who have been illegitimate in order to flatter Louis XIV's own desire to further the interests of his illegitimate sons.[1] His notes are largely a defence of Mézeray, whose work he has now come to prefer; and he later dismisses that of Daniel as 'une sèche et pauvre histoire'.[2]

However, he still admires one part of Daniel's work. This is the *Préface historique* in which Daniel discusses his reasons for beginning his narrative not with the mythical Pharamond, still less with Aeneas, but with Clovis. In the *Commentaire sur l'Esprit des Lois*, Voltaire describes this preface as 'un chef-d'œuvre de bonne critique'.[3] This is not surprising, for he, too, shows no desire to penetrate into the history of the origin of the Franks, but begins his *Essai sur les mœurs* at a point even later than that chosen by Daniel, and one at which he believes it possible to achieve some degree of historical certainty.[4] He may owe a certain debt to Daniel here. Daniel's demand for accurate citation of sources[5] may also have influenced him, for he is to preach similar exactitude himself even though he is very slow to practise it.[6] He may also owe to Daniel (though Bayle is an alternative and probably more likely source) the distinction which both writers make between the main facts, where some degree of certainty is possible, and the details, which are to be thrown to the wolves of historical Pyrrhonism.[7] Despite his avowed hostility, then, he may have profited from those aspects of Daniel's work which show a tendency to break with the humanist tradition.

This begins to appear more likely when we examine his attitude to other writers who share something of Daniel's methodological beliefs without agreeing with his religious ones. If he has little to say about the majority of the seventeenth-century humanists, except to make contemptuous references to the inaccuracy of men like Sarrasin and Maimbourg,[8] he speaks much more frequently of those early eighteenth-century historians who attempt to bridge the gulf between humanism and erudition or who reveal a more liberal attitude in political or religious matters. The two writers for whom he expresses particular approval are Giannone and

[1] xxix. 413.
[2] xxviii. 8. See also xxvii. 289.
[3] xxx. 447.
[4] See p. 65.
[5] Preface, p. li.
[6] See p. 129.
[7] Preface, p. xix. See p. 137.
[8] e.g. xiii. 577; xvi. 307; and xiii. 403.

Rapin de Thoyras. Giannone's criticisms of the temporal power of the Papacy had led to his death in a Papal prison, and this alone would have been enough to arouse Voltaire's enthusiasm for him. But he praises particularly the scholarly accuracy which is characteristic of the *Istoria civile del regno di Napoli*.[1] He never refers to Giannone as a source of his own conception of the 'histoire de l'esprit humain', and certainly the predominantly legalistic way in which Giannone treats the history of Naples is very different from his own method. Yet Giannone's work certainly offers an alternative to the military and diplomatic type of history, and it may well have played its part in forming Voltaire's own views.

Rapin de Thoyras, the Huguenot refugee who, both in his *Histoire d'Angleterre* and in other works, did much to introduce English political ideas into France, is often referred to by Voltaire. In the *Catalogue* of the *Siècle de Louis XIV* the *Histoire d'Angleterre* is described as 'la meilleure histoire qu'on ait de ce royaume, et la seule impartiale dans un pays où l'on n'écrit guère que par esprit de parti'.[2] Voltaire often quotes Rapin,[3] and seems particularly impressed by his impartiality. However, when Hume's *History of England* appears, he has second thoughts about that of Rapin. In his review of Hume in the *Gazette littéraire* of 1764, he remarks that 'Rapin Thoiras, étranger, semblait seul avoir écrit une histoire impartiale: mais on voit encore la souillure du préjugé jusque dans les vérités que Thoiras raconte'.[4] If one is to believe the anecdote of Martin Sherlock, however, this judgement is itself later reversed. He records a conversation with Voltaire in which the latter remarks that 'Hume a écrit son *Histoire* pour être loué; Rapin pour instruire; et l'un et l'autre a atteint son but'.[5] But Voltaire does not explain the reasons for his change of attitude. Nor does he, at any time, give precise reasons for admiring Rapin. In all probability, he does so because he likes his liberal attitude in politics and religion, and approves of his accuracy. For Rapin, too, is influenced by the *érudits*, and the *Histoire d'Angleterre* makes much use of the researches of Rymer.[6] Though the work is in many ways far from Voltaire's 'philosophical' ideal (it opens, for example, with a linguistic proof that the Britons were descended from one of the

---

[1] e.g. xiii. 276 and xxvii. 197.   [2] xiv. 120.
[3] e.g. xiv. 554; xxii. 177; xxxvi. 174; and xli. 402.
[4] xxv. 173.   [5] i. 391.
[6] *Histoire d'Angleterre*, Preface.

grandsons of Noah[1]), it probably had some influence on the development of his own theories.

In general, then, Voltaire appears to approve only of those
humanists who are beginning to break with humanist form and
outlook. But to this generalization there is one outstanding exception—Vichart de Saint-Réal, the author of the *Conjuration des
Espagnols contre la république de Venise* of 1674. Saint-Réal has all
the faults of the least conscientious humanists. He is essentially an
historical novelist rather than an historian.[2] But he is a very able
novelist and the *Conjuration* is an exciting and vivid piece of
writing with affinities with Voltaire's own *Histoire de Charles XII*.
Voltaire's admiration for Saint-Réal's style is great enough to make
him forget his factual inaccuracy. In the *Siècle de Louis XIV* the
Conjuration is the one historical work, apart from Bossuet's
Discours sur l'histoire universelle, that he is prepared to mention in
the same context as Pascal and Racine.[3] And he often praises it
elsewhere.[4] Even when he becomes more aware of its factual inaccuracy and advises the reader in search of strict truth to turn
to Nani's account instead,[5] he still thinks that its errors of fact
are redeemed by its stylistic excellence. In 1769, in the *Défense
de Louis XIV*, he can still assert that: 'On nous a donné depuis
de beaux morceaux d'histoire, mais on mettra toujours à côté de
Salluste la Conspiration de Venise par l'abbé de Saint-Réal.'[6]
Faced with what he regards as a literary masterpiece, Voltaire is
still enough of a humanist himself to forget his normally critical
standards.

Bossuet

Just as many of Voltaire's views on the subject-matter and method
of the historian are elaborated as a reaction against those of the
humanists, so much of his philosophy of history springs from his
conscious opposition to that of Bossuet. In this negative way,
Bossuet's influence on him is an important one.

In a sense it is an anachronism to speak of a philosophy of
history in the seventeenth century. The philosophers have little time
for history. *Libertins* like La Mothe le Vayer tend to be as sceptical

---

[1] *Histoire d'Angleterre*, Preface.
[2] See Dulong, *L'Abbé de Saint-Réal, passim*.   [3] xiv. 546.
[4] e.g. xiv. 131 and xxxiv. 1.   [5] xiii. 113–14.   [6] xxviii. 329.

about it as they are about everything else.[1] Descartes is contemptuous of 'les sciences des livres'[2] and Malebranche is even more
strongly anti-historical.[3]

Yet the Church, which taught that human destiny was controlled by Providence, offered a key to the explanation of history.
And Bossuet's *Discours sur l'histoire universelle* of 1681 was the
clearest and most eloquent formulation of this doctrine. It traced
the history of mankind from the Creation to the accession of
Charlemagne, explaining the rise and fall of empires in terms of
God's purposes for his chosen people and his Church.[4]

Bossuet, however, was not uninfluenced by Cartesian rationalism, and he saw God working not by direct miraculous intervention, but indirectly, through the minds of men. It was the strength
and the weakness of his theory that it could be neither proved nor
disproved by an appeal to facts. What could, however, be criticized
on factual grounds was Bossuet's account of the actual events of
ancient history. For it was based entirely on a literal interpretation
of the Bible, supplemented by Greek and Roman historians, and
had nothing to say about the rest of the ancient world.

In his more concessive moments, Voltaire is willing to recognize
a certain greatness in Bossuet's synthesis of world history. He frequently praises his eloquence[5] and is even prepared to say (though
possibly with his tongue in his cheek) that he began his own *Essai
sur les mœurs* with Charlemagne 'parce que c'est là où Bossuet
s'est arrêté, et que je n'osais toucher à ce qui avait été traité par
ce grand homme'.[6]

But the criticisms are far more numerous. Bossuet is repeatedly
accused of hypocrisy and insincerity,[7] of lying,[8] and of copying
uncritically the fantastic stories of the ancients.[9] These accusations,
particularly that of hypocrisy, are rarely supported by evidence.
Yet they nevertheless appear to be sincere, and seem to result from
Voltaire's inability to believe that anyone could sincerely hold
opinions so totally different from his own.

However, his most frequent criticism is directed against what is

[1] See his *Du peu de certitude qu'il y a dans l'histoire*, 1668.
[2] *Discours de la méthode* (ed. Gilson), p. 12.
[3] See *La Recherche de la vérité*, especially Bk. II, chs. 4 and 5.
[4] See, especially, *Discours* (1681), p. 557.
[5] e.g. xiv. 543 and xxxiv. 1.   [6] i. 9.
[7] e.g. xlv. 461 and xxvii. 321.
[8] xxxiv. 1.   [9] xxvi. 385.

probably in fact the principal weakness in Bossuet's account of history: the smallness of his so-called universe. In *Le Pyrrhonisme de l'histoire* he speaks of

Sa prétendue *Histoire Universelle*, qui n'est que celle de quatre ou cinq peuples, et surtout de la petite nation juive, ou ignorée ou justement méprisée du reste de la terre, à laquelle pourtant il rapporte tous les événements, et pour laquelle il dit que tout a été fait, comme si un écrivain de Cornouailles disait que rien n'est arrivé dans l'empire romain qu'en vue de la province de Galles.[1]

The same point is made in the article 'Gloire' of the *Dictionnaire Philosophique* and in many other places.[2] And the emphasis which, as we shall see, Voltaire gives to India and China in his own account of universal history is doubtless also linked with his desire to refute Bossuet.

The hand of God, which, in Bossuet's universe, controls the destinies of men, is absent from the universe of Voltaire.[3] Yet it is significant that though he tries to develop an alternative theory of causation to that of Bossuet, he never attempts to refute directly the idea of Providence. His own Deism has some affinity with Bossuet's Christianity, and he is sufficiently uncertain about the providential control of events to refrain from attacking it.

The sceptics

If Voltaire looks on Bossuet as an opponent, he regards the sceptics, and particularly Bayle, as allies. Yet the relationship of the Enlightenment in general, and of Voltaire in particular, to the *libertinage* of the seventeenth century is not without its complexities. The picture of the young Voltaire receiving a legacy from the aged Ninon de Lenclos has become the traditional image of a certain continuity of thought. Yet if the *libertins* and the *philosophes* are both opposed to traditional authority, there are, nevertheless, profound differences between them. In Voltaire's belief in enlightened despotism, the demonstrability of deism, or the certainty of the rules of classical taste, there is visible a positive, almost an authoritarian, attitude which is the antithesis of the Pyrrhonism of the *libertins*.

This may help to explain Voltaire's relative silence on the sub-

[1] xxvii. 237.   [2] xix. 268; xlvi. 128; and xlv. 542.
[3] See p. 122.

ject of the earlier *libertins*. He speaks only rarely of La Mothe le Vayer and, in particular, never discusses his *Du peu de certitude qu'il y a dans l'histoire*, though it is an important source of historical Pyrrhonism. Towards Saint-Évremond he is predominantly critical,[1] and though he places his *Réflexions sur les divers génies du peuple romain* high on a list of historical writings he recommends to Fawkener in 1752,[2] he never discusses the work. It may never-theless have influenced him, for the de-mythologizing tone of the opening chapters on early Roman history has affinities with the attitude he himself later adopts.

But he has a much more thorough knowledge of Bayle, with whose work he is acquainted in the 1720's[3] and whose *Dictionnaire historique et critique* is later to become the Bible of the *philosophes* of Potsdam. At the time of the Lisbon earthquake, when he is pre-occupied with the problem of evil, it is to Bayle that he turns for guidance:

La balance à la main, Bayle enseigne à douter.[4]

However, the sympathy he feels for Bayle's philosophical posi-tion is not extended to other aspects of his work. He criticizes his style and disapproves of his predilection for scurrilous anecdotes.[5] His one direct comment on the historian is unfavourable. In the *Essai sur les mœurs* he notes, with reference to one of Bayle's anec-dotes, that he is 'souvent aussi répréhensible et aussi petit quand il traite des points d'histoire, qu'il est judicieux et profond quand il manie la dialectique'.[6]

Yet his debt to Bayle is probably far greater than such a state-ment would lead one to expect. As many of his works, and parti-cularly the *Pyrrhonisme de l'histoire* itself, show, he is profoundly influenced by historical Pyrrhonism. This influence probably comes very largely from Bayle, for Voltaire does not appear to be closely acquainted with, say, Hardouin or Levesque de Pouilly. Moreover, on quite a number of occasions direct parallels can be observed between his views and those of Bayle. It is Bayle who, in the article 'David' in the *Dictionnaire*, first makes the distinction

[1] See the *Lettres à Mgr de Brunswick*, xxvi. 500.
[2] Best. xx. 263.
[3] See Pomeau, *La Religion de Voltaire*, p. 93, and Haxo, *Pierre Bayle et Vol-taire avant les 'Lettres Philosophiques'*.
[4] *Poème sur le désastre de Lisbonne*, ix. 476.
[5] xiv. 38 and 546.
[6] xii. 538.

between the historical and the dogmatic content of the Bible, and claims the historian's right to criticize the former.[1] Voltaire repeatedly does the same thing in works like the *Philosophie de l'histoire*, and goes even farther when he criticizes accounts of miracles on the grounds of their physical impossibility.[2] Again, like Bayle, he is led by his love of tolerance both to criticize intolerant Christians such as St. Bernard, and to defend non-Christians such as Mahomet. His attitude to both men probably owes much to Bayle's articles on them in the *Dictionnaire*.[3]

Both Bayle and Voltaire are pessimistic in their view of history, and Bayle's article 'Manichéens' (Remarque D) shows history as a collection of crimes and misfortunes in much the same way as Voltaire is later to do.[4] This leads Bayle to a feeling of the purposelessness of history revealed in his love of unimportant facts and his emphasis on the way in which insignificant causes lead to great events. If Voltaire does not share the first of these attitudes, he loves to emphasize the disparity between causes and effects.[5] Lastly, he probably derives from Bayle the distinction he often makes between major facts, of which one can be reasonably certain, and the details, about which it is usually wisest to doubt.[6]

These similarities may well lead us to conclude that Cazes's dictum: 'Sans Bayle, Voltaire eût été impossible',[7] is as true in the field of historiography as it is elsewhere. Yet this critical sceptical aspect of Voltaire's writing is not the most important one. In his efforts to write a more social type of history or to establish scientific criteria of historical possibility, in short, in all the positive aspects of his work, Voltaire obtains no help from Bayle. Despite the many similarities, the gulf between the sceptic and the *philosophe* remains a wide one.

Fontenelle

Fontenelle is far more of an eighteenth-century figure than Bayle, not merely because of his longevity, but also because of his belief

---

[1] *Dictionnaire*, v. 409.

[2] See xi. 110 ff., and the articles 'Déluge universel' and 'Inondation' in the *Dictionnaire Philosophique* (xvii. 327 and xix. 475).

[3] Pomeau (*La Religion de Voltaire*, p. 93) suggests that Bayle may be responsible for Voltaire's early hostility to St. Bernard. For Voltaire's attitude to Mahomet, see pp. 83 ff.

[4] See p. 123.

[5] See pp. 107 ff.

[6] See *Œuvres diverses*, ii. 11.

[7] Cazes, *Pierre Bayle*, p. 76.

in progress, his scientific interests, and his unwillingness to rest content with purely sceptical conclusions. Voltaire probably owes much to him, and certainly knows much of his work before his exile in England.[1] But on the whole he is disinclined to admit his debt. At times, as in the *Catalogue des écrivains* of the *Siècle de Louis XIV*, or in a letter to Walpole in 1768, he speaks highly of him.[2] But more often, possibly because he sees in Fontenelle a rival for the leadership of the *philosophes*, he is critical. He objects to his rather precious style, to his Cartesian physics, and to his luke-warmness in the 'philosophic' struggle.[3] He satirizes him in *Micromégas*,[4] and in the article 'Oracles' of the *Dictionnaire Philosophique* he refers not to the *Histoire des oracles* but to its much less well-known source, the learned treatise of Van Dale.[5]

Nowhere, however, does he examine the work of Fontenelle the historian. As Edsall's study of the relations between the two men has shown, he makes no mention of *Sur l'histoire* or of *De l'origine des fables*, though Edsall would like to think that he knew the former work before 1730, and he certainly possessed a copy of the 1724 edition of the latter. This, together with the *Éloge de Leibniz*, would have given him most of Fontenelle's views on history.[6]

However, there is no doubt that he knew the *Histoire des oracles*. In particular, he had absorbed one of its central doctrines, that contained in the famous parable of the Golden Tooth, with its insistence that one should be absolutely sure about the facts before worrying about the causes.[7] In the *Dictionnaire Philosophique*, article 'Conséquence', he relates the miraculous story of the elephant father of the god Fo, and then inquires: 'Mais ton éléphant a-t-il existé . . .? C'est là ce qu'il fallait examiner.'[8] And he repeatedly uses the same argument to reject unauthenticated legends,[9] reiterating Fontenelle's statement that they are 'des fables convenues'.

There are other parallels, too, between the two men. *De l'origine des fables* attempts to explain fables not by the usual method of assuming that all fabulous figures are exaggerations of historical

---

[1] See Pomeau, *La Religion de Voltaire*, p. 93.
[2] xiv. 72 and xlvi. 79.   [3] xiv. 546.
[4] See the edition by I. Wade, pp. 24–26.   [5] xx. 138 ff.
[6] See Edsall, *The Idea of History and Progress in Fontenelle and Voltaire*, especially p. 166.
[7] *Histoire des oracles* (ed. Maigron), p. 30.
[8] xviii. 243.   [9] See p. 138.

characters, but by analysing the animistic way in which the human mind works before it has learnt to reason scientifically. Though there are times when Voltaire adopts the euhemerist interpretation, he also frequently insists, with Fontenelle, that fables cannot be treated as if they were history.[1]

More important, however, are the similarities in the positive field, and here Fontenelle's influence is far more important than that of Bayle. In *Sur l'histoire* he demands the sweeping away of the 'histoire des révolutions, des États, des guerres' and its replacement by 'celle des erreurs et des passions humaines'.[2] Like Voltaire he is interested in causation in history,[3] and like Voltaire he tends, as in the discussion between Fulvie and Hélène in the *Dialogues des morts*,[4] to emphasize the disparity between minute causes and great events. A similar parallel exists, moreover, in the attitude of the two men to the idea of progress. The author of the *Digression sur les anciens et les modernes* is often thought of as one of the principal creators of the concept of progress. But the *Dialogues des morts* insist that human nature is essentially unchanging.[5] Voltaire, too, adopts both these points of view, and never succeeds in reconciling them.[6]

Voltaire's debt to Fontenelle is therefore considerable. But there are still many differences between them. If Fontenelle can speak of 'l'histoire de l'esprit humain' he uses the phrase in a literal and relatively narrow sense. Works like *L'Histoire des oracles* and *De l'origine des fables* seek to investigate the history of the human mind, to show how it first begins to think about the world, and how faltering and uncertain are its first attempts to reason. Voltaire, on the other hand, uses the phrase in its widest possible sense, and he is primarily interested not in the human mind itself but in its products, be they works of art, inventions, or social systems. His attitude is much more that of a historian.

Fénelon and Boulainvilliers

Both Fénelon and Boulainvilliers have been suggested as the principal source of Voltaire's conception of history. Ascoli asserts

---

[1] See Carré's introduction to his edition of *De l'origine des fables*, and see p. 145.   [2] Carré, pp. 3–7.
[3] See the discussion between Charles V and Erasmus in the *Dialogues des morts (Œuvres*, ii. 202).
[4] Ibid., p. 222.   [5] Ibid., p. 191.   [6] See pp. 125 ff.

that Fénelon is Voltaire's master,[1] and Boulainvilliers's biographer Renée Simon attempts to show that all Voltaire's important ideas on history are already to be found in the work of her hero.[2]

Fénelon's views on the writing of history are contained in the eighth section of the *Lettre à l'Académie*. His treatment of the subject is brief, but is nevertheless sufficiently developed to reveal the curious juxtaposition of backward- and forward-looking views which characterizes his attitude in many other fields too. In many ways his views are akin to those of the humanists: he insists on the moral value of history; he regards form and style as of paramount importance, and likens history to epic poetry; he is contemptuous of what he regards as unnecessary erudition and useless details; almost all his examples, and many of his precepts, come from ancient historians.

But if he insists on the moral value of history, he condemns moral didacticism in the historian. He thinks that it is far more important to write the history of nations than that of individuals, and that the historian should study 'il costume'—the customs and habits, the social conditions and institutions of the age and people with which he is dealing. He elaborates on the absurdity of accounts which ignore such variations, emphasizing in particular the importance of a thorough study of the institutions of feudal society.[3]

Almost all these views are also held by Voltaire. He, too, sees a moral value in history, but distrusts moral didacticism.[4] He frequently speaks of the artistic qualities which an historical work should possess, and often compares history with drama.[5] He is consistently hostile to useless erudition,[6] and demands that the historian should describe customs and social institutions.[7] In the *Essai sur les mœurs* and the *Annales de l'empire* he makes a serious attempt to explain feudal society.[8]

Voltaire never speaks of Fénelon's views on history. But it seems very probable that he knew them. He was acquainted with much of Fénelon's work at an early age, and there are echoes of Fénelon in his own works, e.g. in the *Lettres Philosophiques*.[9] Fénelon probably has an important influence on his own views. Yet it is doubtful whether he can be called Fénelon's disciple. Many of the views

---

[1] 'Voltaire historien', p. 501.   [2] *Henry de Boulainviller*, p. 46.
[3] *Lettre* (ed. Cahen), pp. 109 ff.   [4] See pp. 96 ff.
[5] See p. 160.   [6] See p. 134.
[7] See pp. 46 ff.   [8] See pp. 66 ff. and 71 ff.
[9] See Pomeau, *La Religion de Voltaire*, p. 61.

they share are also held by others. Opposition to unnecessary details and erudition, a moral purpose, and a concern for artistic form, are common among the humanists.[1] The demand for a closer study of customs and institutions is being voiced by many people.

Moreover, despite similarities of phraseology, they probably have different attitudes on other issues. Fénelon's interest in the organization of feudal society may well be linked with his political opposition to Louis XIV, and it seems probable that Boulain-villiers's political treatment of the subject, containing, as it does, a strong element of propaganda, corresponds to his ideas more closely than does that of Voltaire. Again, if Voltaire continues to draw parallels between history and drama, his own work, after the *Histoire de Charles XII*, becomes less 'dramatic' and less concerned with artistic effect.

Finally, although Voltaire hints otherwise, there is nothing of the *philosophe* about Fénelon. To a considerable extent he looks back to an idealized past, whether it be the feudal society of the Middle Ages or the Salente of *Télémaque*. Voltaire, on the other hand, looks on the past as something which has been overcome, and is interested in it primarily from the point of view of the present and the future. And the contrast of their attitudes in matters of religion and philosophy is even more complete. Voltaire's critical approach to the orthodox account of ancient history, his attempts to achieve universality, and his ever-present sceptical attitude towards myth and miracle owe nothing to Fénelon.

The similarities between some of the views expressed by Boulainvilliers and those held by Voltaire are, at times, even more striking. The following passage from his *Lettre à Mlle Cousinot sur l'histoire de France*, for example, shows remarkable affinities with the *Avant-propos* of the *Essai sur les mœurs*:

Nos auteurs ne nous parlent que des princes ou de leurs favoris, de quelques événements, de batailles, de traités, etc. . . . croyez-vous que l'on soit bien avancé de savoir la date de quelques événements, le nom des princes, de leurs ministres, de leurs généraux et de leurs maîtresses, si l'on ignore d'ailleurs les ressorts de leurs actions, de leurs gouvernements, si l'on ne s'instruit du génie de chaque siècle, des opinions, des

[1] See the criticism of erudition in Saint-Réal (*Œuvres*, i. 3) and in Cordemoy (*Divers traitez*, p. 35).

mœurs, des idées dominantes, ou pour tout dire, des passions qui con
duisent les hommes ?[1]

And on the subject of ancient history, Boulainvilliers expresses
views which appear equally Voltairian:

J'aurai une attention particulière à faire connaître l'histoire des mœurs,
des opinions, des religions, des différents peuples de la terre. Je mar-
querai autant qu'il me sera possible l'origine des arts, des cérémonies et
des usages chez toutes les nations.[2]

However, to prove that these ideas influenced Voltaire, it would
be necessary to show that he knew them. The *Lettre à Mlle
Cousinot* circulated in manuscript, but there is no evidence that
Voltaire ever saw the manuscript. Moreover, some of Boulainvilliers's views contrast sharply with those of Voltaire. In the field
of ancient history, Boulainvilliers not only wishes to describe
customs but also proposes to 'concilier les miracles, même ceux de
la création et du déluge, avec les idées que nous donne la philosophie naturelle'.[3] Voltaire proposes to show that such a reconciliation is impossible.[4]

However, two of Boulainvilliers's works were published soon
after his death, and were known to Voltaire. Though he does not
speak very favourably of the *Vie de Mahomed* of 1730, he certainly
used the work both for his own play *Mahomet* and for the chapter
on Mohammed in the *Essai sur les mœurs*.[5] Boulainvilliers shows
a relatively sympathetic attitude towards the founder of Islam, and
his insistence that Mohammed was sent to preach the oneness of
God has a certain deistic flavour which would also have pleased
Voltaire. However, Boulainvilliers's philosophy of history is akin
to that of Bossuet:

La terre est un vaste théâtre sur lequel il se passe, de siècle en siècle,
quelque tragédie singulière, sous la direction d'une puissance supérieure,
qui partage à chaque peuple des biens et des maux, des châtiments ou
des récompenses, selon son bon plaisir et selon sa justice.[6]

And he later explains the rise of Islam itself in similar terms,
asserting that God brought it about in order to punish bad

---

[1] See Simon, *Henry de Boulainviller*, p. 48. Compare xi. 157.
[2] Simon, op. cit., p. 49.   [3] Ibid., p. 51.
[4] See p. 87.
[5] See Pomeau, *La Religion de Voltaire*, pp. 147–54, and see below, p. 102.
[6] *Vie de Mahomed*, pp. 1–2.

Christians for their misdeeds.[1] Such views are the antithesis of those of Voltaire, whose own philosophy of history is largely an attempt to provide an acceptable alternative.

With Boulainvilliers's other important work, the *Histoire de l'ancien gouvernement de la France* of 1727, and with the controversy to which it gave rise, we shall deal more fully when we consider Voltaire as a social historian.[2] But in essence it is a work of political propaganda rather than of history, and it uses history in a way which Voltaire explicitly rejects.

If Boulainvilliers and Voltaire use very similar phraseology, they do not, therefore, necessarily hold the same ideas. Phrases like 'l'histoire de l'esprit humain' have become the common coin of all those who are dissatisfied with traditional forms of historical writing. Boulainvilliers's contributions to Voltaire's conception of history is probably an important one. But Voltaire rejects almost as much as he accepts of Boulainvilliers's views.

Bolingbroke

Bolingbroke has been claimed as Voltaire's master more frequently than any other writer.[3] Yet the evidence on which this claim was based was for the most part inconclusive, and some years ago Torrey was to go so far as to describe Bolingbroke's influence as 'fictitious'. If there was, for a time, a fairly close relationship between the two men, it did not appear to have survived Voltaire's visit to England. If in later years Voltaire used Bolingbroke's name more frequently than that of any other English deist, this was no indication of the extent of his indebtedness to Bolingbroke, for he frequently associated the Englishman's name with ideas which were not his at all, and seemed to use it merely as part of the English atmosphere of many of his own deistic pamphlets.[4]

However, the discovery by the editor of the *Correspondence*[5] of a letter from Bolingbroke to Voltaire has reopened the controversy. From this letter it would appear that Bolingbroke exercised

---

[1] *Vie de Mahomed*, pp. 177–8.   [2] See pp. 64 ff.

[3] e.g. Hurn, *Voltaire and Bolingbroke*, p. 25; Black, *The Art of History*, pp. 31–32; Mayr, *Voltaire-Studien*, pp. 12 and 39; and Sonet, *Voltaire et l'influence anglaise*, p. 146.

[4] Torrey, 'Bolingbroke and Voltaire—a Fictitious Influence', and *Voltaire and the English Deists*, pp. 135 ff.

[5] Best. i. 245–8.

a considerable influence over the young Voltaire, introducing him
to Locke and Newton, and even providing him with the idea of
the famous concluding sentence of *Candide*. Yet the question still
remains open. For if we have evidence that Bolingbroke urged
Voltaire to read Locke and Newton long before his exile in England,
we have no evidence that Voltaire actually did so.

The letter does not discuss the problem of history, and Torrey,
in his comparison of the views of the two men, deals only briefly
with the subject, concerning himself mainly with their attitude to
the Bible as history. He notes, too, that before the publication of
Bolingbroke's works (which did not occur till after his death in
1751) Voltaire's own method, both critical and constructive, was
already developed. In itself, however, this is not a conclusive argument. On the one hand, Voltaire may have heard something of
Bolingbroke's views from his own lips. On the other, he may have
known Bolingbroke's written works before their publication.
A private edition of the *Letters on the Study and Use of History*
was printed in France in 1735 and circulated to some of Bolingbroke's friends.[1] And the manuscript of his earlier *Substance of some
Letters to M. de Pouilly* was known to a number of people in the
twenties. Voltaire does not mention either work before its publication. But the possibility of his having known them cannot be ruled
out altogether. No conclusion can therefore be arrived at without
a comparison of the ideas of the two men.

The *Substance* may, however, be dismissed fairly rapidly. It
contains a number of views which show considerable similarity
with those later expressed by Voltaire on subjects such as the in-
acceptability of the Old Testament account of history,[2] the tendency of ancient historians to copy each other,[3] and the rashness of
historians who build up elaborate theories on the basis of superficial linguistic affinities.[4] But these are all relatively minor points
of critical method. And the *Substance* cannot have influenced
Voltaire's work in the 1720's, for it is only in the fifties and sixties
that he begins to write about the problems of ancient and biblical
history. By this time he has innumerable other sources (Spinoza
and the English deists, for example) for his suspicions of the Old
Testament, he has the warnings of almost every critic influenced

---

[1] See Cooke, *Memoirs of Lord Bolingbroke* (London, 1835), ii. 171.
[2] Bolingbroke, *Works*, ii. 474.
[3] Ibid., p. 488.   [4] Ibid., p. 478.

by historical Pyrrhonism to remind him of how the ancients copied each other, and he has contemporary examples on which to base his distrust of linguistic analogies.[1]

Moreover, neither before nor after the publication of the *Substance* does he so much as mention its central argument. Bolingbroke is attempting to show that the Creation, although outside the field of modern human experience, is not outside the field of human reason, and that therefore the universal testimony of early human records in favour of it is evidence which is historically valid. He illustrates the way in which the criterion of conformity to experience can lead to a false conclusion by the story of the Siamese king who was willing to believe that the divine Sommona-Codom had straddled the Bay of Bengal (since this was only an exaggerated picture of something within his own experience), but refused to credit the Dutch ambassador who assured him that, in his country, water turned into a hard, solid substance in winter.[2]

If Voltaire's relationship to Bolingbroke had been in any sense that of disciple to master, one would expect at least a mention of this argument, since Voltaire himself regards the Creation as incomprehensible, and would doubtless have been glad to find an acceptable explanation of it for use in his own battles against the atheists. When he reads the work after its publication, he puts a marker opposite the anecdote about Sommona-Codom.[3] But the fact that he never uses this anecdote and that he never mentions Bolingbroke's argument, suggests that he was not merely unconvinced by it but contemptuous of it. It is clear, at least, that his debt to the ideas contained in this work is negligible.

The case of the *Letters on the Study and Use of History* is, however, more complicated. Not only is this work much longer than the *Substance* but it is devoted entirely to the subject which gives it its title. However, it is not difficult to pick out what is most important in its argument.

History for Bolingbroke is 'philosophy teaching by examples' and its purpose is essentially utilitarian.[4] The English statesman has no time for pure erudition, and even less for its practitioners of whom the best that can be said is that 'they deserve encouragement, however, whilst they continue to compile and neither affect

[1] See pp. 144 ff.
[2] *Works*, ii. 468.
[3] See Torrey, *Voltaire and the English Deists*, p. 147.
[4] *Works*, ii. 177.

wit, nor presume to reason'.[1] His utilitarian purpose, moreover,
demands that the student of history should concentrate on those
ages and aspects of the past which will be of most practical value
to him. To be learned about the distant past is 'ridiculous affecta-
tion in any man who means to be useful to the present age'.[2] The
study of universal history is 'this very wantonness of curiosity'.[3]
History is to be studied from the practical point of view of the
statesman, and not only are distant ages to be excluded, but also
distant countries. The English student should ignore not only
India and China, but also Russia and Turkey: 'they have no relation to the knowledge you would acquire.' In Bolingbroke's own
sketch of European history it is the west European balance of
power which is the *leit-motif* to which all events are subordinated
and the standard by which all are judged.[4] And though he admits
that history could be studied from points of view other than his
own, he implies that the view of, say, the Churchman, would be as
much confined to ecclesiastical matters as his own is to political.

Bolingbroke's opposition to ancient history is based, however,
not only on its lack of utility, but also on its lack of certainty.
Though he rejects the complete Pyrrhonism which he associates
with Bayle, he believes that history has been 'purposely and syste-
matically falsified in all ages' and urges the reasonable man to
'doubt absolutely' when confronted with an unsupported testimony.[5] Ancient history is no more authentic than *Amadis of Gaul*.[6]

Between these views and those of Voltaire there are a number of
similarities. Like Bolingbroke, but unlike Bayle and Fontenelle,
Voltaire is concerned, in his early works, almost exclusively with
modern history. And in the *Conseils à un journaliste* of 1737 he
urges the reader to be content with a slight knowledge of ancient
history, and to concentrate on the period since the Renaissance and
particularly on the history of his own country.[7] He regards ancient
history as a mass of fables and he, too, compares it to *Amadis of
Gaul*.[8] And if he does not think that the historian himself should be
consciously didactic, he nevertheless believes in the moral and
utilitarian purpose of the study of history.[9]

The attitude of the young Voltaire has, then, a definite affinity

[1] Ibid., p. 174.   [2] Ibid., p. 329.   [3] Ibid., p. 195.
[4] Ibid., pp. 253 ff.   [5] Ibid., pp. 213 and 217.
[6] Ibid., p. 212.   [7] xxii. 244.   [8] xxi, 277.
[9] See pp. 96 ff.

with that of Bolingbroke. But as he elaborates his own point of view in the thirties and forties, the difference between his position and that of his English hero becomes more marked. Within the field of modern history his interests are much wider than those of Bolingbroke. In the *Siècle de Louis XIV* he is not just concerned with politics, but is interested in the arts and sciences, in economic developments, and in religious controversies.[1] In the *Essai sur les mœurs* he begins his story at the time of Charlemagne, and his decision to open with a chapter on China is as much a rejection of Bolingbroke's views as it is a criticism of those of Bossuet. Moreover, in later years he becomes increasingly interested in ancient history, and if he still retains much of his scepticism he shows that he no longer accepts Bolingbroke's view that the distant past is unimportant because it is not immediately useful.

If Voltaire only comes to know Bolingbroke's views after the publication of the *Letters* in 1752, their influence on him can only be slight, for by that time he has already elaborated a very different theory of his own. But if he knows these views as a result of conversations in the twenties, it may well be that they provided an important stimulus for his own. This, however, must remain a conjecture, for the evidence is insufficient either to prove or refute it. Moreover, if Bolingbroke urges Voltaire to concentrate on modern history, he is reinforcing an already existing tendency,[2] and the one work which Voltaire produces during the period in which Bolingbroke may have influenced him directly, the *Histoire de Charles XII*, has already been explained in terms of the development of humanist historiography without any need to mention Bolingbroke except as the source of a few facts.

The little Voltaire has to say about Bolingbroke's historical writings confirms this general conclusion. The appearance of the *Letters* brings forth a comment to D'Argental to the effect that 'Ce qu'il y a de plus hardi dans ces *Lettres sur l'histoire* est ce qu'il y a de meilleur',[3] a reference, presumably, to Bolingbroke's hostile comments on the Book of Genesis. When Bolingbroke's *Memoirs* appear, he criticizes their style and their prejudice, and concludes that he cannot conceive how a man who seemed to have 'des vues si grandes' could produce 'des choses si petites'.[4] If in 1722 he admired Bolingbroke's views, by 1752 he has surpassed Bolingbroke

---

[1] See pp. 48 ff.
[3] xxxviii. 205.
[2] See p. 5.
[4] xxxviii. 208.

and developed a much fuller theory of his own. All he can now see in the opinions of his predecessor is their pettiness.

III

Many other sources of Voltaire's ideas can be and have been suggested. Not all the suggestions can be accepted. Hume, for example, has been proclaimed as Voltaire's mentor.[1] But Voltaire's own ideas were already elaborated, and the *Siècle* and the *Essai* already published, before he had ever heard of Hume,[2] and though he later comes to admire him, and uses his work as the source of a number of facts about English history, there is no evidence of any subsequent influence of Hume's ideas on his. On the other hand, his critical method may well owe more than a little to Fleury, whose *Discours sur l'histoire écclésiastique* of 1691, which contains a lengthy statement of critical principles, is the object of his praise.[3] He may equally have profited from a handbook of historical studies like Lenglet du Fresnoy's *Méthode pour étudier l'histoire* of 1713, of which he also speaks approvingly.[4] Doubtless there are many other sources too. For there is nothing profoundly original in Voltaire's views. He draws to himself all the different currents of historical thought, and forms of them his own synthesis. Yet if he is not original, he is individual. The synthesis he evolves is distinctively his own, and no predecessor or contemporary succeeds, as he does, in realizing in practice the greater part of his theory. This practice itself must now be examined.

[1] See Zerffi, 'Voltaire in his Relation to the Study of General History',
[2] He first speaks of Hume's work in 1758 (xxxix. 512).
[3] xiv. 71. Fleury's attitude to the Middle Ages and the Crusades is reminiscent of Voltaire's; see the *Discours sur l'histoire ecclésiastique*, pp. 200–1 and 244.
[4] Letter to D'Argenson, 1743 (xxxvi. 228).

III

SOCIAL HISTORY

IN the *Histoire de Charles XII* the description of society, though
not without importance, was secondary to the account of the
life and adventures of the hero himself. We have already seen
that in the controversies which follow the publication of the work,
Voltaire comes to lay increasing stress on the social aspects of
history. But whilst he is engaged in these controversies, he is also
engaged in compiling material for the *Siècle de Louis XIV*. And
from the beginning he insists that this work is going to be a history
of a new type—the history not of an individual but of an age. In
his letters about the *Siècle* he attacks the traditional preoccupation
with military matters:

> Les batailles données, les révolutions des empires, sont les moindres
> parties de ce dessin; des escadrons et des bataillons battants ou battus,
> des villes prises et reprises, sont l'histoire de tous les temps.[1]

And he proposes to replace them with something very different:

> Une écluse du canal qui joint les Deux-Mers, un tableau de Poussin,
> une belle tragédie . . . sont des choses mille fois plus précieuses que
> toutes les annales de cour et que toutes les relations de campagne.

Similar statements occur frequently in his correspondence.[2] And
he elaborates his ideas in a number of his published works. The
Nouvelles considérations sur l'histoire of 1744 are a manifesto of the
new attitude. Voltaire expresses his interest in questions of military
and economic strength and political and social organization, and
concludes:

> En vain je lis les annales de France: nos historiens se taisent tous sur
> ces détails. Aucun n'a eu pour devise 'Homo sum, humani nil a me
> alienum puto'. Il faudrait donc, me semble, incorporer avec art ces
> connaissances utiles dans le tissu des événements. Je crois que c'est la
> seule manière d'écrire l'histoire moderne en vrai politique et en vrai
> philosophe.[3]

[1] xxxiii. 513.
[2] xxxiii. 506. See also xxxiii. 515, 474, and 483.   [3] xvi. 140.

In the 1754 preface to the *Essai sur les mœurs*, he again expounds his own views, this time in a criticism of Puffendorf.

Je me souviens que quand nous commençâmes à ouvrir Puffendorf qui avait écrit dans Stockholm, et à qui les archives de l'État furent ouvertes, nous nous assurions d'y trouver quelles étaient les forces de ce pays, combien il nourrissait d'habitants, comment les peuples de la province de Gothie s'étaient joints à ceux qui ravagèrent l'empire romain, comment les arts s'introduisirent en Suède dans la suite des temps, quelles étaient ses lois principales, ses richesses, ou plutôt sa pauvreté: nous ne trouvâmes pas un mot de ce que nous cherchions.[1]

The breadth of his interests may be judged from these and many similar quotations, as well as from the innumerable questions on political, social, religious, and economic matters which he puts to his Russian correspondent Schouvalow, when he is writing the *Histoire de Russie*.[2] But it is best seen in the historical works themselves.

In some ways these are less 'revolutionary' than a perusal of Voltaire's theoretical views might lead one to expect. His interest in social questions does not lead him to abandon narrative history and to substitute for it a type of sociological inquiry analogous to, if different from, that of Montesquieu. He recognizes that history divorced from the narrative of events ceases to be history and becomes something else. Moreover, he lacks the necessary information for writing a totally new type of history. The amount of new material he introduces is small, and the changes he effects in the nature of historical writing result almost as much from his exclusion of lengthy accounts of battles, genealogies, &c., as from his inclusion of new material on the arts, sciences, and economic and social matters. According to the standards of his times, his historical works are short. The two thin volumes of the first edition of the *Histoire Universelle* seem insignificant beside the eighteen tomes of Hardion's work on the same subject, and the *Siècle* is far shorter than many earlier histories of Louis XIV such as those of Limiers and Larrey. Voltaire's originality lies in selection rather than in original research.

[1] xxiv. 42.
[2] See especially xxxix. 243.

Le Siècle de Louis XIV

Nearly twenty years elapsed between the time when Voltaire began work on the *Siècle*[1] and its publication in 1751. It is not surprising that he could assert of the work, in 1735, that 'c'est l'ouvrage de toute ma vie'.[2] If he lived long enough to disprove that statement, the *Siècle* has one thing in common with many other works that take a lifetime to write: its purpose changes as its author grows older, and its final form is far from corresponding to its original plan.

When Voltaire first began work on the *Siècle* he had probably two aims. The first, to depict the development of the arts during a period in which they had reached one of their highest peaks. The second, to point the contrast between this greatness and the relative decadence which had succeeded it.[3] In so far as he had this second purpose in mind, he envisaged the *Siècle* as a sort of counterpart to the *Lettres sur les Anglais* which he was writing at the same time. The *Lettres* criticized the France of Louis XV by comparing its bigotry and stupidity with the tolerance and enlightenment of contemporary England. The *Siècle* was to serve a similar purpose by emphasizing the achievement of the age of Louis XIV, the enlightened patron of the arts, and contrasting it with the artistic decadence and political inertia of the France of Louis XV.

To attain this end, Voltaire adopted a method of presentation which constituted one of the most novel features of the work. He rejected the purely chronological approach and replaced it with an analytical one, giving to his description of the age the form of a pyramid. At the base of the pyramid came the ordinary narrative of political and military events which occupies the first part of the work. In the centre came the description of society—the chapters analysing social, economic, legal, and ecclesiastical affairs. Finally, at the apex, came the artistic achievement which constituted the real culmination of the age, and to which five or six chapters were to be devoted.

---

[1] The first direct reference occurs in a letter to Thiériot in May 1732 (xxxiii. 265). However, an urgent demand which Voltaire makes in 1729 for the loan of Lelong's *Bibliothèque historique de la France* (xxxiii. 185) suggests that work on the *Siècle* may have begun as early as this.   [2] xxxiii. 502.

[3] This is suggested, for example, by the threat implied in his statement that 'Les louanges que je donne à Louis XIV avec toute l'Europe, ne deviendront la satire de Louis XV que si Louis XV ne l'imite point'. For further evidence see the edition of the *Siècle* by Bourgeois, Introduction, pp. v–viii.

Such was the original plan of the *Siècle* as expounded in a letter to Dubos in 1738.[1] It was a necessary consequence of a desire to stress artistic achievement, for this aim could hardly have been realized by a chronological presentation, since the closing years of Louis's reign were years of relative artistic decadence as well as being years of famine, military defeat, and increasing despotism. But once adopted, it tended, by its very nature, to compel Voltaire to discuss problems rather than merely recount events. It also involved a complete break with the narrative technique of the *Histoire de Charles XII*.

The plan of the *Siècle* has often been criticized.[2] But the criticisms refer to the version finally published in 1751. And in the intervening years Voltaire's plan had altered considerably. The *Siècle* of 1751 contained only two chapters on the arts[3] and these no longer concluded the work. Their place had been taken by the chapters on ecclesiastical affairs, which had been expanded,[4] and the work now ended on a satirical note with the chapter on the 'Disputes sur les cérémonies chinoises'. The spectacle of these dissensions contrasted with the general laudatory tone of the rest of the work, and the 'architectural' unity of the whole was destroyed.

It is not hard to discover the reason for this change. Though it was not until he arrived at the safety of Ferney that Voltaire opened his deistic campaign, much of the preparatory work for the assault on *l'Infâme* had already been undertaken at Cirey.[5] The closing chapters of the *Siècle* are a manifestation of this greater interest in religious questions, though their moderate and balanced tone is far removed from that of the later deistic pamphlets.

During the twenty years of work on the *Siècle*, Voltaire's attitude to the age of Louis XIV has undergone significant changes of which he himself never appears explicitly aware. His interest in the arts is tending to diminish,[6] and his interest in 'philosophy' to

[1] xxxv. 29.
[2] See Grimm, *Correspondance littéraire*, ii. 254; Bourgeois, op. cit., Introduction, p. xxvii; and Quignard, 'Un Établissement de texte: *Le Siècle de Louis XIV* de Voltaire', p. 324, n. 1.   [3] Later expanded again to four.
[4] The letter to Dubos (xxxv. 29) suggests two chapters. These later become five.
[5] See Wade, *Voltaire and Mme du Châtelet, passim*.
[6] It is significant that the arts play a less important part in the *Essai sur les mœurs*. Voltaire claims to have 'lost' a folio of documents dealing with art history, though a few of them crop up later in other works. See Caussy, *Supplément aux Œuvres de Voltaire*, i. 21–23.

increase. But if the age of Molière and Racine is one of the four
great periods of history from the artistic point of view, the age of
Jansenism, the repeal of the Edict of Nantes, and the Cévennes
revolt is hardly an ideal for the *philosophe*. Though Voltaire never
condemns the age of Louis XIV, his early enthusiasm is tempered.
At one time he can remark that 'on a beaucoup écrit dans ce siècle;
on avait du génie dans l'autre'.[1] But in the later *Épître à Boileau*,
where he characterizes the seventeenth century as the

> Siècle de grands talents bien plus que de lumière,[2]

he shows his awareness of its want of 'philosophical' enlightenment.

But it is the artistic unity of the *Siècle*, and not its value as
a social history, which suffers from these changes. The latter,
indeed, is probably increased.

The first part of the *Siècle* is devoted to a narrative of events;
not surprisingly, war and diplomacy occupy the most important
place. But even here, Voltaire's originality is visible. The introductory chapter attempts to pick out the salient features of the age
of Louis XIV and to compare it with the other three great ages of
human history.[3] The following chapter, 'Des États de l'Europe
avant Louis XIV', is a brief survey of Europe in which political,
economic, sociological, and artistic considerations are all to be
found. Thus, Voltaire discusses the constitution of the German
empire, the power of the emperor, the religious differences, the
relative poverty before the influx of Huguenot refugees, and the
undeveloped state of the arts. He outlines the political and hints
at the economic causes of the rise of the Dutch republic, traces the
economic poverty of the Papal States to the weaknesses of ecclesiastical government, and discusses the military strength and the
'philosophical' backwardness of France.[4] And throughout the
narrative of events in subsequent chapters, he is constantly linking
particular happenings with the deeper themes of social and
economic development, describing, for example, Colbert's industrial policy[5] or the economic exhaustion resulting from the War
of Spanish Succession.[6]

But it is in the later chapters devoted to specific topics that the

[1] xv. 434.   [2] x. 398.   [3] xiv. 155–9.
[4] xiv. 160–73.   [5] xiv. 286–8.   [6] xiv. 388.

historian of society reveals himself fully. The first of these, dealing with 'Gouvernement intérieur', &c.,[1] describes the achievements of Louis XIV and Colbert in many fields. Voltaire shows how the king has reformed legal procedure by interesting himself personally in the dispensation of justice; how he, with the help of Colbert, has reduced taxation, improved roads, encouraged commerce, and founded the companies trading with the Indies. He compares Colbert with Sully, and finds in the former 'des vues beaucoup plus étendues', illustrating this with descriptions of Colbert's industrial achievement; the foundation of the cloth industry at Abbeville, the reorganization of the silk industry, the creation of new manufactures of mirrors, carpets, and tapestries. From these he turns to the improvements in Paris itself: the establishment of street lighting, paving, the reorganization of the city's police; and the description of these is followed by a section devoted to the great architectural monuments of the age: Versailles, the Louvre, the Invalides, Saint-Cyr, and the Languedoc canal, 'le monument le plus glorieux par son utilité, par sa grandeur, et par ses difficultés'.

Voltaire proceeds to examine Louis's legislative achievements: a new 'ordonnance civile', a new 'code des eaux et forêts', a new series of statutes on manufactures, on criminal and commercial law, &c. He expatiates on the benefits derived from the abolition of the duel, and examines in some detail the various reforms initiated in the army and the navy.

His account is not purely descriptive, for he has criticisms to offer too. He argues, for example, that if Louis had spent more on embellishing Paris and less on Maintenon and Versailles, he would have turned his capital into 'la plus magnifique ville de l'univers'. And though he admires Louis's legal reforms, he notes that judges in civil lawsuits have still to choose between a hundred different customs. These are a remnant of feudalism, 'des décombres d'un bâtiment gothique ruiné', which Voltaire would be glad to see dismantled altogether.

Yet despite such criticisms, he is principally concerned with emphasizing the greatness of what has been achieved—especially by the king himself. All these reforms have led to a decline in the 'esprit de faction, de fureur et de rébellion' which had possessed the citizens of France from the time of François II onwards. A new and more civilized spirit has developed and spread from the

[1] xiv. 497 ff.

nobility to all classes: 'On s'aperçoit aujourd'hui jusque dans le
fond d'une boutique, que la politesse a gagné toutes les conditions. Les provinces se sont ressenties avec le temps de tous ces
changements.'

The following chapter, 'Finances et Règlements',[1] is devoted
mainly to an exposition and justification of the economic policies
of Colbert. And here Voltaire leaves the field of pure description
and enters that of controversy. The opposition to Colbert, and the
glorification of Sully in contrast to him, were characteristic of the
main trend of economic thought in the eighteenth century, which
culminated in the doctrines of the Physiocrats.[2] To them Colbert
represented mercantilism and *dirigisme*, whereas they advocated
freedom of trade; he represented a predominantly industrial and
commercial policy, whereas they insisted on the primary importance of agricultural prosperity; he advocated protection, whereas
they demanded the breaking down of all artificial barriers, especially to the trade in grain.

In the second half of the eighteenth century Voltaire is one of
the very few writers who still defends Colbert.[3] But he has authorities for his view. He probably owes more than a little to Melon,
whose *Essai politique sur le commerce* of 1734 is one of the last works
by an economist to express unstinting praise of Colbert. Like
Voltaire, Melon is an admirer of Colbert's industrial organization[4]
and an apologist of 'le luxe',[5] and his description of the fluctuations
in the value of money may be the source of Voltaire's.[6] But a more
immediate source is Forbonnais, whose *Recherches et considérations
sur les finances de France* of 1758 leads Voltaire to undertake an
extensive rewriting of the whole of this chapter.[7] Forbonnais is
by no means an uncritical admirer of Colbert, and in particular,
attacks his refusal to introduce freedom of trade in grain.[8] But his
richly documented work gives a very thorough picture of the
economic history of the period 1595 to 1721, and in particular he
devotes over 300 pages to an exposition of Colbert's policies and

---

[1] xiv. 518 ff.
[2] See Weulersse, *Le Mouvement physiocratique en France*.
[3] He is later (1773) to be championed again by the socialistic writer Pechméja;
see Lichtenberger, *Le Socialisme au XVIIIe siècle*, pp. 267–9.
[4] Op. cit., p. 37.   [5] Ibid., pp. 122 ff.   [6] Ibid., pp. 154 ff.
[7] See Quignard, 'Un Établissement de texte: *Le Siècle de Louis XIV* de Voltaire', p. 328.
[8] Op. cit. i. 291–2.

their results. Compared with such a work, Voltaire's discussion of Colbert in the *Siècle* is very slight. Its argument, moreover, is not very convincing.

Voltaire opens his discussion with a categorical but unsupported denial of the accusations of Boisguillebert, whose *Détail de France* had largely inaugurated the opposition to Colbert.[1] He has already described many aspects of Colbert's policy in earlier chapters, and here he tries to defend him by insisting that he really had the interests of agriculture at heart, emphasizing the importance of his decrees against financial speculators, and suggesting that he would himself have removed the restrictions on trade in grain, had not the *Parlement* been strongly opposed to any such measure, and had not the onset of war made further reform impossible and necessitated recourse to the help of the financiers whom Colbert himself detested. This defence fails to carry conviction, for it is a defence not of Colbert's actual policy, but of the policy which Voltaire imagines Colbert would have followed had the circumstances been more favourable. But he cannot prove that his interpretation of Colbert's intentions is correct. In other matters, however, such as industrial organization, he is able to adduce evidence to show that Colbert's policies brought positive results and that he has been unjustly criticized.

Colbert's successors are more harshly dealt with. Voltaire describes the growing impoverishment of the country, the increasing need to borrow capital, the devaluation of the currency, and the sale of offices to increase revenue, as a series of misfortunes. But these, he insists, resulted from the war and the famine of 1709, not from the ambitious building programmes or the luxurious spending of Louis XIV. Against Fénelon and other opponents of extravagance, he asserts that 'le luxe' increases prosperity by encouraging industry.[2]

The final section of this chapter compares the economic state of the country under Louis XIV with that under Louis XV. Although government revenue has decreased, the actual wealth of the country has increased; industry and agriculture, the real sources of prosperity, have developed, and with the adoption of

[1] Voltaire also attributes Vauban's *Dîme royale* to Boisguillebert; a confusion which probably arises because Boisguillebert's work was published under the title of *Testament politique du maréchal de Vauban.*
[2] xiv. 519–29.

English financial practices, such as the use of paper money, could be developed still further. The middle classes in particular have enriched themselves, whereas the aristocracy, dependent on fixed *rentes* or income from property, has become poorer. The peasantry though still poor (Voltaire does not wish them otherwise) have been freed from want. All these developments lead to an optimistic conclusion:

Aujourd'hui l'industrie a ouvert mille chemins qu'on ne connaissait pas il y a cent ans. Enfin, de quelle manière que les finances de l'État soient administrées, la France possède, dans le travail d'environ vingt millions d'habitants, un trésor inestimable.[1]

To judge from Voltaire's own statements, the great originality of the *Siècle* was to have consisted in the treatment accorded to the arts and sciences. And though the space these subjects occupied in the published version was less than had originally been intended, yet the presence of these four chapters in a general history itself constitutes a minor revolution in historical writing. It is another question, however, whether their achievement lives up to their promise.

Perhaps the most striking feature of the chapter on the sciences is its brevity. In the *Lettres sur les Anglais*, English science, in the persons of Bacon and Newton particularly, had been the subject of thorough study, and at Cirey, Voltaire had increased his scientific knowledge.[2] Yet only a hint of these interests is to be found in this chapter and in the chapter 'Des beaux-arts en Europe' which, despite its title, also deals, in part, with scientific developments. This may result partly from Voltaire's hostility to some of the scientist-philosophers of the seventeenth century—particularly Pascal and Descartes. Yet one might have expected that, as the purpose of the *Siècle* became less 'artistic' and increasingly 'philosophical', Voltaire would have expanded his treatment of those scientists, from Galileo to Newton, who were the object of his admiration. This has not happened. Instead, it is the chapters on religious affairs which have been expanded. One might say that the *Siècle* has been rewritten with a desire to 'écraser l'Infâme' rather than to 'répandre la lumière'.

[1] xiv. 529–33.
[2] As is shown, for example, by the *Éléments de la philosophie de Newton* (xxii. 400 ff.).

The chapter on sciences,[1] then, contains comparatively little information. Voltaire begins by remarking that the early years of the century, characterized by the civil wars, the Inquisition, the condemnation of Galileo, &c., gave little hint of the progress which was later to be made. After a passing word of praise for Galileo and Bacon, he turns to Descartes. His exposition here is in keeping with his usual predominantly critical attitude towards Descartes. Though he calls him 'le premier des mathématiciens', he does not attempt to show how he deserves this title, but instead makes sweeping (and unjustified) generalizations about Descartes's ignorance of experimental method: 'Un homme qui dédaigna les expériences, qui ne cita jamais Galilée, qui voulut bâtir sans matériaux, ne pouvait élever qu'un édifice imaginaire.'

Voltaire then proceeds to list some of the scientific discoveries of the age, and follows these with a brief account of the foundation of the Royal Society and the Académie des Sciences, of Colbert's patronage of men like Huygens and Roemer, and of the voyages of discovery. The growth of the scientific spirit has also, he remarks, led to the decline of superstition—of belief in witchcraft and astrology and of trial by ordeal. It has resulted in a more tolerant and humanitarian outlook.

Si on a dit que les peuples seraient heureux quand ils auraient des philosophes pour rois, il est très vrai de dire que les rois en sont plus heureux quand il y a beaucoup de leurs sujets philosophes.

The arts are dealt with more fully in the following chapters. But here another weakness becomes visible. One critic has remarked that some of Voltaire's judgements are 'so full of personal bias as to be virtually grotesque'.[2] This is not altogether fair, for the bias is not just personal, but is characteristic of Voltaire's age. But it is none the less surprising to find that the only merit of Amyot, Marot, Montaigne, and Régnier is 'une certaine naïveté'.[3] Voltaire suggests that the perfection of classical literature is the result of a long process. But so contemptuous is he of everything that precedes classicism, that he gives the impression that the classical masterpieces arise practically out of nothing.

His extensive treatment of classical literature itself,[4] however, affords some compensation for his contempt for what went before.

[1] xiv. 534 ff.
[2] Black, *The Art of History*, p. 67.
[3] xiv. 540.
[4] xiv. 540–52.

In his survey of the history of prose writing and of religious
and legal oratory he is primarily interested in the development of
clarity and elegance of style, though he does not exclude other
considerations. He criticizes the artificiality which he still finds in
the work of Balzac and Voiture, and sees in La Rochefoucauld,
and still more in Pascal, the first real masters of the language. The
Lettres provinciales receive the highest praise as a work of art. The
Pensées, however, so often the object of Voltaire's criticisms, are
not mentioned.

He proceeds to praise the work of Bourdaloue, Massillon, and
Bossuet, admiring their oratory, though regretting the artificiality
which results from having to preach to a specific text. And he finds
the same oratorical power in Bossuet's *Discours sur l'histoire universelle*, though hinting that he has less regard for the historical
accuracy of this work than for its literary qualities. Then he discusses Fénelon's *Télémaque*, stressing particularly its relevance to
the political problems of Louis XIV's time, and La Bruyère's
Caractères, in which he finds 'un usage tout nouveau de la langue',
but one which he does not consider to infringe the classical rules.
He ends with brief praise of three works; Fontenelle's *Pluralité des
mondes*, the style of which he admires, though not without expressing doubts as to its suitability for philosophical subjects; Bayle's
Dictionnaire which is 'le premier ouvrage de ce genre où l'on puisse
apprendre à penser'; and Saint-Réal's *Conjuration de Venise* which
he considers to equal and perhaps to surpass Sallust.

In his discussion of poetry, Voltaire deals principally with the
three great dramatists. He sees in Corneille the real creator not
only of modern drama, but of the classical language, and suggests
that he may have had a profound influence on prose style also. He
expresses his admiration for *Le Cid* and *Cinna*, but makes it clear
that he prefers Racine for the regularity of his dramatic construction, the purity of his style, and his knowledge of the human heart.
Molière is dismissed fairly briefly, though Voltaire expresses
approval of his satires of contemporary foibles, and particularly of
preciosity.

Other poets are dealt with even more briefly. Boileau is praised
primarily as a didactic poet, and La Fontaine criticized for his
archaic style. Voltaire makes an effort to be fair to his personal
enemy J.-B. Rousseau, though only succeeds in damning him with
faint praise. The chapter ends with a number of general reflections

on the development of language and on the atmosphere necessary
for literary achievement in which Voltaire concludes that there is
bound to be a period of decline after an age of genius, since its
immediate successors are reduced 'ou à imiter ou à s'égarer'.[1]

Compared with this chapter, the next two are again brief. The
chapter on the arts other than literature contains little more than
general expressions of approval of a number of artists, among them
Lulli, Poussin, and Lebrun. Once again it reveals a systematic
disparagement of all the achievements of the sixteenth century.[2]
The chapter on the fine arts in the rest of Europe[3] is only a little
more ambitious. For his literary examples Voltaire turns mostly
to England, but his attitude to Milton (who receives the fullest
treatment) is here, as elsewhere, unsympathetic. Only Addison's
Cato, a dull but 'correct' tragedy, receives unqualified praise.

From it Voltaire turns to English philosophy. But he speaks only
briefly of the achievement of Locke and Newton in terms similar
to those he uses elsewhere. And of philosophy in other countries
he has even less to say. A paragraph on Leibniz speaks admiringly
of his erudition and mathematical genius, and, surprisingly, contains little trace of the criticisms Voltaire so often makes elsewhere.[4] The Italian arts and sciences are dismissed in two short
paragraphs containing little more than a list of names.

If the presence of these chapters in a general history is of great
importance, their intrinsic value is less outstanding. Voltaire tries
to cover a vast field in a small space. Yet it is the nature of his
comments rather than their brevity which is at fault. Except when
he is dealing with classical literature, his judgements are either
completely colourless, like his praise of seventeenth-century
painters, prejudiced, like his views on Descartes, or narrow-
minded, like his contempt for sixteenth-century literature. The
idea of introducing artistic and cultural achievements into the
narrative of history was excellent. But its successful accomplish-
ment demanded greater insight and broader sympathies than
Voltaire himself possessed.

In contrast, the chapters dealing with ecclesiastical affairs, which
replace those on the arts as the final chapters of the work, are
among the best examples of Voltaire's historical writing. It is
no doubt true that they are introduced largely because of his

[1] xiv. 552–4.   [2] xiv. 555–8.   [3] xiv. 559–64.
[4] See Barber, *Leibniz in France*, pp. 174 ff., for a study of Voltaire's attitude.

increasing hostility to the Church. But it is equally true that he is determined to appear as unprejudiced as possible, and these chapters show a far greater concern for impartial and measured comment than do his judgements on many other subjects. Compared with the violent criticism of the Church to be found in the introductory chapter of the *Siècle* in its first form,[1] they are the height of moderation.

Voltaire's approach to the religious disputes of the reign of Louis XIV[2] is essentially a social one. He is not interested in theological questions or in the spiritual differences between the various sects. He begins with a discussion of ecclesiastical revenues, criticizing not their magnitude, which he does not appear to find excessive, but the inequality of their distribution. In his comparison of Protestantism and Jansenism he is particularly concerned to find out why the former should lead to civil war, whereas the conflicts produced by the latter have been much less harmful. Again, when he comes to discuss Gallicanism, it is the social manifestations of the movement—and particularly the political struggle over the 'droit de régale'—which absorb his attention. And if at times he is content to ascribe religious differences to that mysterious and undefinable factor 'custom', he also points out the connexion between religious beliefs and other social developments, asserting, for example, that the financial crisis resulting from Law's 'system' was the main reason for the appeasement of the religious quarrels in the 1720's.

His moderation is most apparent in his criticism of the repeal of the Edict of Nantes. His condemnation is based not on moral principles, nor on a theoretical belief in tolerance, but on the economic harm done to France by the Protestant exodus. So mild is it that even the *philosophes* protest,[3] and in the 1753 edition he feels the need to intensify it a little by introducing a quotation from Christine of Sweden criticizing the *dragonnades*.[4] Protestantism itself he regards principally as a social movement associated with the democratic spirit and with opposition to imperial despotism in Germany. In France, if it had been left alone, it would probably have died a natural death.

[1] See Caussy, *Supplément aux Œuvres de Voltaire*, i. 277.
[2] xv. 1 ff.
[3] See Grimm, *Correspondance littéraire*, iii. 336.
[4] See Caussy, op. cit., p. 284.

As an historian of different aspects of society, Voltaire, in the *Siècle*, appears to have both his triumphs and his failures. But if instead of criticizing his work in the light of our own ideals, we compare it with that of some of his predecessors, its originality is more strikingly revealed.

Among the works which Voltaire consulted when writing the *Siècle*, were the three histories of Louis XIV by Limiers (1717), Larrey (1718), and La Hode (1737). There is little in these works to indicate any tendency to a more social type of history. None uses an analytical method, and none shows the preoccupation with historical explanation which Voltaire exhibits. Limiers expatiates on the difficulty of reconciling the telling of the whole truth with 'ce qu'on doit aux têtes couronnées', but what he is really interested in is justifying the 'histoires galantes' of the king and other figures which play a prominent part in his work. If anything, he would prefer the history of Louis himself to that of his century, and regrets the relative absence of information on Louis's private life.[1] And his subsequent narrative confirms the impression made by these remarks in his preface. He thinks that the fact that Louis XIV 'vient au monde avec ses dents' is worthy of a place in a chapter-heading, and devotes much space to Louis's *amours*, some twenty pages to a description of the king's marriage, and almost half as much to an account of his coronation.[2] The rest of the narrative is taken up, for the most part, with lengthy relations of diplomatic and military events. And Larrey and La Hode, though less concerned with 'histoires galantes', show no significant development from this approach. The two things which Larrey claims to be most proud of in his work are, on the one hand, 'les deux grands jours de la Royauté, celui de la Majorité et celui du Sacre', and, on the other, 'd'avoir fait un récit exact des Négotiations de la fameuse Assemblée de Westphalie'.[3]

The characteristic preoccupations of Voltaire are absent from the works of these earlier writers. This is most noticeable in the case of the arts. There is not an absolute lack of reference to cultural developments; where the king himself is directly involved they are often discussed. Limiers, for example, describes the 'plaisirs de l'isle enchantée' and mentions certain material achievements

---

[1] Limiers, *Histoire du règne de Louis XIV*, preface.
[2] Ibid., ii. 264–83 and 1–7.
[3] *Histoire de France sous le règne de Louis XIV*, preface, pp. xxvii–xxviii.

like the repaving of Paris.[1] Larrey describes the construction of
the royal palaces, and also that of the 'canal des Deux-Mers'.[2]
But both are interested in the spectacular rather than in artistic or
scientific achievement. In their treatment of the king's minority,
neither so much as mentions Corneille or Descartes. And in the
field of social and economic history they have not very much more
to say. Limiers does discuss Colbert's policies, but he does so
within the space of one page.[3] Larrey, in his own summary of the
most important features of his work, makes no mention of economic
developments. It is only in the work of La Hode that financial
questions are beginning to occupy more space. In his history of the
Regency he devotes considerable space to an exposition of Law's
system, and attempts to explain its failure.[4]

Some signs of progress are seen in a writer closer to the
philosophes, who is frequently consulted by Voltaire. Président
Hénault's *Abrégé chronologique de l'histoire de France* first appeared
in 1744 and was one of the most successful historical works of the
century. In it one finds, as one might expect from a lawyer, a
greater interest in legal and constitutional matters and in the role
of the *Parlements*. Hénault, too, separates his chronological
narrative from the discussion of the significance of each historical
period, thus approaching Voltaire's analytical method. Yet his
chapters on the seventeenth century are still devoted mainly to
accounts of diplomacy and battles, and anecdotes of court and
nobility. The arts and sciences are almost ignored. There is, it is
true, a short eulogy of Descartes,[5] but Corneille is not mentioned,
and Racine's name only figures because he had conferred on him
the dignity of *historiographe du roi*.[6] And Hénault contrives to deal
with the repeal of the Edict of Nantes in one line, and to speak
briefly of Colbert without attempting any assessment of his
policies.[7]

When Voltaire's work is compared with such as these, the
originality and extent of his achievement is clearly visible. He has
introduced a great deal of new material and a totally new emphasis.
Where he fails is in his attempt to integrate it into a new kind of
history. The most serious general criticism which can be levelled

[1] Op. cit. iii. 4–5.
[2] Op. cit., preface, p. xvii.
[3] Op. cit. ii. 350.
[4] *Vie de Philippe d'Orléans*, especially ii. 3.
[5] Op. cit. ii. 693–4.
[6] Ibid., pp. 768 and 801.
[7] Ibid., pp. 788 and 782.

against his work is that his picture of the age is a static, not a developing one. If he describes its greatness, he does not account for it. To enhance the achievement of Louis he minimizes that of Mazarin. He describes the Fronde as a sort of comic-opera rebellion.[1] Though he states that many years are necessary for the perfection of taste and language,[2] and thus, by implication sees classicism as the culmination of a process of evolution, he repeatedly seems to go out of his way to deny this evolution. And his desire to emphasize the personal achievement of the king causes him to treat as peculiar to Louis's reign processes which are taking place throughout the century. Thus he emphasizes the growth of social intercourse during the later years of the century[3] but says not a word of the importance of the *salons* before 1650. Louis XIV and Colbert have, he suggests, played a great part in forming Racine, but he will not allow Richelieu any similar influence on the formation of Corneille.[4] In consequence, if the *Siècle* offers an excellent account of what happened, it hardly attempts to explain why it happened.

Yet the idea of development is not absent from the *Siècle*. The development which is depicted is not, however, that which leads up to, but that which follows on after the age of Louis XIV. Had Voltaire written a work entitled 'The Origins of modern France', many of the discussions of economic or artistic development in the *Siècle* could have found a place in it without much need of alteration. Voltaire is deeply concerned with the problems of his own times and can never refrain from referring to them. And the fact that he does so much to describe the changes between the seventeenth and eighteenth centuries compensates, to some extent, for his failure to show how the age of Louis XIV itself came into being.

The Essai sur les mœurs

Like the *Siècle*, the *Essai* developed over a long period. It was in the 1740's that Voltaire began work on a universal history with the intention of convincing the sceptical Mme du Châtelet that history could be as interesting and as significant as natural science. Though chapters of the work appeared in the *Mercure* in the forties, and an unauthorized edition of the first part was published by Néaulme

[1] e.g. xiv. 192. [2] xiv. 552. [3] xiv. 516.
[4] xiv. 548.

in 1753, it was not until 1756 that the first complete edition
appeared. In 1763 a revised edition included the *Siècle de Louis
XIV* and chapters dealing with more recent events which were
later to be separated from the main work and become part of the
Précis du Siècle de Louis XV. Two years later the survey of universal
history was completed with the writing of *La Philosophie de
l'histoire*, and in 1769 this work was added as the Introduction to
the *Essai* itself. Moreover, it was not only the scope of the work
which was increased; the treatment of the main period (from the
accession of Charlemagne to that of Louis XIV) was also constantly being expanded.

The task Voltaire set himself in this work was one of far greater
magnitude than that of writing the *Siècle*. Moreover, he was in
some ways ill equipped for it. His reliance on second-hand sources,
only partial in the *Siècle*, became almost total in the *Essai*. He had
no knowledge of the technical disciplines of the medieval historian,
and was, moreover, exiled from the main sources of information.
Again, he was not, as in the case of the *Siècle*, undertaking a labour
of love. He had little sympathy with any aspect of the Middle
Ages, and it was with them that the greater part of the *Essai* was
concerned. All this led to a greater detachment and at times a
certain superficiality. Yet it had its advantages. In the *Essai*
Voltaire is not constantly involved in comparisons with his own
times; he has no 'hero' like Louis XIV, whose personal achievement he must emphasize. If this often leads him to dismiss things
he does not understand as 'sottises du genre humain', it also leads
to a more realistic appraisal of many of the factors determining the
course of events. Again, in dealing with the distant past, his
interests are in some ways wider than when he treats more recent
happenings. Details of many social customs (changes in dress, for
example), which are not thought necessary in the *Siècle*, are included in the *Essai*.

The *Essai* contains a wealth of information on innumerable
aspects of the social life of the period it covers. Here, our discussion
must be restricted to some of the more important features.

The history of the arts occupies a far less important place than
in the *Siècle*. On the whole this is not to be regretted, for what
Voltaire does say about them often serves to emphasize his lack of
comprehension. Speaking of Persian architecture, he compares it
with Gothic, remarking that 'Toutes les figures sont aussi lourdes

et aussi sèches que celles dont nos églises gothiques sont encore malheureusement ornées'.[1] And after reading such a judgement, one is relieved to find that Voltaire has practically nothing to say about medieval art. The French Renaissance of the twelfth century is unknown to him. It is only with the arrival on the scene of Dante and Petrarch that he begins to show signs of interest, but he finds the *Commedia* 'bizarre', and insists that Petrarch is inferior to Ariosto and Tasso.[2] However, he includes translations of passages from both the earlier poets, as well as from the Persian Sadi. It is therefore all the more surprising that when he comes to speak of Renaissance art, which he admires, he has practically nothing to say. Indeed, he devotes to the subject less than half the space allotted to the art of the previous two centuries, and contrives to deal with painting, architecture, and music without mentioning the name of a single artist, and in terms of the broadest generality. Literature—particularly the poetry of Ariosto and Tasso—is treated somewhat more fully. But here again, Voltaire's classical prejudices are in evidence. He dismisses the drama of the Spanish Golden Age because it is not 'regular' and asserts that the mediocrity of Shakespeare is proved by the fact that he has never been appreciated outside his own country.[3]

The arts—the fine arts, at any rate—clearly have a minor role in the *Essai*. Other aspects of the history of society, however, receive fuller and more valuable treatment. Yet on one subject Voltaire is silent. As, in the eyes of many contemporaries, it was a subject of great importance, his silence is itself of great significance in characterizing his attitude to history.

The question of the origin of the Franks and the nature of the Frankish conquest of Gaul was the object of probably the most important historical controversy of the eighteenth century. And the matter was far from being one of purely academic interest. Even the apparently harmless discussion as to whether the Franks were of Trojan, Gaulish, or Germanic origin proved sufficiently dangerous to involve one of the contesting theorists, Fréret, in a sojourn in the Bastille.[4]

The problem of the nature of the Frankish conquest, however,

[1] xi. 197.   [2] xii. 57–64.
[3] xii. 245–7. The *Essai sur l'histoire générale* also contained a chapter (ch. xlii) on seventeenth-century painters, &c., which was later added as an appendix to the *Catalogue des écrivains* of the *Siècle*. See J. Seznec, 'Falconet, Voltaire et Diderot'.   [4] See Thierry, *Œuvres*, iv. 33–35.

had more important political implications. Boulainvilliers's *Histoire de l'ancien gouvernement de la France* of 1727 revived a controversy which had raged in the sixteenth century. The work analysed the history of the Franks and of their conquest of Gaul in an attempt to prove that the original form of government in France was that of a conquering Germanic aristocracy, equal among themselves, but keeping the defeated Gallo-Romans in serfdom. Boulainvilliers wished to show that this was the natural form of government for France, and to suggest that any deviation from it, towards either greater despotism or greater democracy, was therefore 'unnatural' and likely to end in disaster.[1]

By implication, Boulainvilliers's work criticized the aspirations of both the *Tiers État* and the monarchy, and it is not surprising that his conclusions did not go unchallenged. In 1734 the abbé Dubos published his *Histoire critique de l'établissement de la monarchie française dans les Gaules*. This work, more scholarly and less obviously partial than that of Boulainvilliers, set out to prove that the Frankish invasion was not a simple conquest, but that it had taken place at the request of the Roman governors and as a result of diplomatic negotiations and formal treaties. The essential administration of Gaul was unchanged by the conquest; there was no enslavement of the vanquished; and feudal society only came into existence some four centuries later.

Dubos does not, as Boulainvilliers had done, attempt to draw a political lesson from his account. Nevertheless, his work may be taken as the reply of the monarchy to the claims of Boulainvilliers and the nobility, since in it the French kings are shown to be the legitimate heirs of the Roman emperors. Such, at any rate, is the view of Montesquieu, who, in the *Esprit des Lois*, himself enters the controversy. He remarks of the two works that 'l'un semble être une conjuration contre le Tiers-État, et l'autre une conjuration contre la noblesse', and proceeds to subject both to criticism.[2] But whilst he insists that Boulainvilliers has failed to prove his main contention, since he has produced no evidence to show that the Franks reduced the Gallo-Romans to a state of slavery, his attack is directed principally against Dubos. The latter's work is, he asserts, 'un colosse immense qui a des pieds d'argile', since, for all its erudition, it contains no proof of the thesis Dubos

[1] See preface and i. 36 ff.
[2] *Esprit des Lois*, Bk. XXX, chs. 10 ff.

is attempting to maintain. He agrees with Dubos, however, in regarding Feudalism as a later development, resulting partly from Frankish customs, and partly from conditions which arose when the Franks had settled in Gaul.

Finally, the democratic interpretation of the conquest comes from the pen of the abbé Mably. In his *Observations sur l'histoire de France* of 1765, Mably stresses the spirit of democratic equality to be found among the Franks, much as Boulainvilliers had done. But he proceeds to assert, if hardly to prove, that after the conquest of Gaul, the Salic law was, as it were, 'thrown open' to the defeated Gauls.[1] Thus France was originally a democracy, and only later did feudalism bring a decline from this happy state, mainly as a result of the greed of kings and bishops. Mably can almost see *Liberté, Égalité, Fraternité* inscribed on the banners of Clovis.

The controversy between the *romanistes* and the *germanistes*, and among the latter, between the extreme aristocratic thesis of Boulainvilliers and the more liberal one of Montesquieu, continues throughout the century. It finds considerable expression, for example, in the *Encyclopédie*. The Encyclopedists themselves are all *germanistes*, but Boucher d'Argis tends towards the views of Boulainvilliers, whereas Diderot and Jaucourt adopt the point of view of Montesquieu.[2]

The *Essai sur les mœurs* begins, nominally, with Charlemagne. Voltaire's ostensible reason for this is that he is beginning where Bossuet left off.[3] But as he is really hostile to Bossuet's conception of history, and as he is later to rewrite the history of the period Bossuet had treated, one may doubt whether this reason was the real one. Moreover, in the opening chapters of the *Essai*, Voltaire does, in fact, go back quite a long way before A.D. 800, not only in speaking of the Far East, but also in order to trace the gradual decline of the Roman empire and the rise of the Papacy.[4] Yet he refuses to enter into either of the controversies which preoccupy his contemporaries.

For this he has two reasons. The first is his attitude of suspicion towards the accounts classical historians give of the migration of peoples. They are mostly, he says, 'des fables que tous nos auteurs copient'. In the circumstances he is willing to content himself with

[1] *Œuvres*, i. 151.
[2] See Hubert, *Les Sciences sociales dans l'Encyclopédie*, pp. 116–21.
[3] xi. 158.   [4] *Essai*, chs. 8–14.

the generalization that 'tous ces peuples coururent au pillage les uns après les autres'.[1] In the *Commentaire sur l'Esprit des Lois*, he defines his attitude even more clearly:

> Je n'entrerai point dans la discussion de l'ancien gouvernement des Francs, vainqueurs des Gaulois; dans ce chaos de coutumes toutes bizarres, toutes contradictoires; dans l'examen de cette barbarie, de cette anarchie qui a duré si longtemps, et sur lesquelles il y autant de sentiments différents que nous en avons en théologie. On n'a perdu que trop de temps à descendre dans ces abîmes de ruines, et l'auteur de l'*Esprit sur les Lois* a dû s'y égarer comme les autres.[2]

His second reason for refusing to take part in the controversy is explained in the article 'Histoire' of the *Dictionnaire Philosophique*:

> On fait quelquefois aujourd'hui un usage un peu bizarre de l'étude de l'histoire. On déterre des chartes du temps de Dagobert, la plupart suspectes et mal entendues, et on en infère que des coutumes, des droits, des prérogatives qui subsistaient alors doivent revivre aujourd'hui. Je conseille à ceux qui étudient et raisonnent ainsi de dire à la mer: Tu as été autrefois à Aigues-Mortes, à Fréjus, à Ravenne, à Ferrare; retournes-y tout à l'heure.[3]

This is an important declaration, for it serves to characterize a significant feature not only of the *Essai* but of Voltaire's historical writing as a whole. Although the purposes of the liberal propagandist are almost everywhere apparent in his work, he uses history as a source of examples, never as a source of authority. The lessons of the past can be used in shaping the future, but the fact that something existed in the past is no reason for allowing it to continue in the future. Still less should one attempt to return to the past simply because it is the past. Voltaire's history of social institutions never contains propaganda of the type Boulainvilliers and his successors indulge in.

'Je voudrais découvrir', he writes, 'quelle était alors la société des hommes, comment on vivait dans l'intérieur des familles, quels arts étaient cultivés.'[4] And towards this aim he directs the greater part of his energies. He succeeds even in giving some sort of picture of the Carolingian age, remarking on a number of its customs, describing contemporary dress, and illustrating the scientific

[1] xi. 241.
[2] xxx. 441.
[3] xix. 356.
[4] xii. 53.

poverty of the times with an account of the admiration afforded
to a striking clock given to the Emperor by the Caliph. But the
description of the later Middle Ages is much more complete.
Clothing is described; the inventions of the age—spectacles,
windmills, clocks, paper, the compass—are all commented on.
Certain customs and institutions, such as tourneys, duels, and the
orders of chivalry, are discussed at some length.[1]

In particular Voltaire makes a real effort to understand, at
least in its general outlines, the nature of feudalism itself. He tries
to show how the monarchy gradually ceased to be elective and
became hereditary. He explains how the nobility came into
existence, deriving their origin from their employment rather than
from the land, how later the *noblesse de robe* appeared, and how
even the *bourgeoisie* were at times ennobled.[2] Yet if he tries to
understand feudalism he does not attempt to sympathize with it.
He describes the general evolution of feudal society in the following terms:

> Celui qui n'avait pu se saisir que de deux ou trois bourgades rendait
> hommage aux usurpateurs d'une province; et qui n'avait qu'un château
> relevait de celui qui avait usurpé une ville. De tout cela s'était fait cet
> assemblage monstrueux de membres qui ne formaient point un corps.[3]

And he is horrified to find that a vassal who has suffered injustice
at the hands of the king has the right to demand armed help from
his own vassals. Such a law, he asserts, should be called 'Ordonnance pour faire la guerre civile'. No people could have chosen
such a form of government of their own free will.[4]

He is even more shocked at some of the primitive forms of
justice he finds in medieval times; judicial combat, trial by water,
&c.[5] Yet towards the positive legislation of the Middle Ages he is
often more sympathetic. He praises the laws of Saint Louis, on
the policing of Paris, on commerce, and on the Gallican Church,
asserting that they would have made France a flourishing country
had it not been for the folly of the Crusades.[6] He discusses the
creation of the *Parlement de Paris* by Philippe le Bel, seeing in it
a significant weakening of the feudal system. He examines the
functions of the *Parlement* itself, listing the gradual increase in its

[1] xii. 54–55, 130–4, 142–52. [2] xii. 134–41.
[3] xi. 348. [4] xi. 411 and xii. 128–30.
[5] xi. 291. [6] xi. 504.

rights, and giving details of its procedure. He applauds the admission of the *Tiers État* to the counsels of the nation and the abolition of duelling; both achievements of Philippe.[1] Here, and in subsequent chapters, he is concerned to show how society has developed, and how institutions have changed accordingly. As he approaches modern times, the amount of information he gives increases. At the same time it is his range rather than his depth which is remarkable. He never enters into a really detailed discussion of any of the problems he is dealing with, and his comments on much-disputed issues such as the origins of feudalism tend to remain superficial. Yet considering the field it covers, the *Essai* has just the right balance of narrative and explanation to hold the interest of the reader.

The *Essai* is not without its heroes. Alfred the Great of England is depicted as a truly great monarch.[2] Henri IV of France is treated with the admiration one would expect from the author of the *Henriade*. And even a pope, Alexander III, finds his way into the list of the great benefactors of the human race as a result of his decree freeing Christians from serfdom.[3] Yet the heroes are relatively few, and the barbarians and tyrants omnipresent. Voltaire has become more pessimistic since the *Siècle*. He delights in pointing out that the greater part of medieval history is a long story of crimes and horrors. 'Qu'on juge des mœurs des peuples par celles des princes', he says, and proceeds to give a list of the crimes committed by Clovis and his successors. If other historians speak of the magnificence of Dagobert, all Voltaire knows about him is 'qu'il avait à la fois trois épouses, qu'il assemblait des conciles, et qu'il tyrannisait son pays'.[4] The popular figure of Charlemagne suffers little better at his hands.[5] And in the same spirit he treats the alternate crimes of popes and emperors throughout the Middle Ages and, later, the similar barbarities of Catholic and Protestant.

One result of this approach is that his treatment of the economic aspect of history becomes more detailed. He is delighted to be able to show that the Crusades were not the result of lofty religious motives, but of a desire for plunder,[6] and he is equally pleased that he can attribute the Fronde or the English Revolution to similar

---

[1] xi. 515 and xii. 74–80.
[2] xi. 309.
[3] xii. 553–4 and xi. 406–8.
[4] xi. 269–70.
[5] xi. 257–61.
[6] xi. 442 and 459.

causes.[1] But important as such extra-historical motives are, Voltaire is also concerned with economic history for its own sake.

Examples of his interest are to be found in the earliest parts of the *Essai*. Thus, a chapter is devoted to 'Commerce, finances, sciences' in the time of Charlemagne; and in it the military and economic organization of feudal society is examined. The growth of commerce with the East, and the early development of the Italian towns are commented on. There is a long discussion of the difficulty of assessing the real value of money, and the need for taking into account the weight of silver in coins, and the variations in purchasing power.[2] Above all, emphasis is placed on the development of industry and commerce:

La seule ressource du genre humain était dans les villes que les grands souverains méprisaient. Le commerce et l'industrie de ces villes a réparé sourdement le mal que les princes faisaient avec tant de fracas.[3]

The development of the English woollen industry and of the cities of Italy and Flanders illustrates this. And the revival of France, Voltaire suggests, owes far more to a financier like Jacques Cœur than to the Maid of Orleans.[4]

Agricultural prosperity is also considered important. With reference to the recovery of France after the Hundred Years War, Voltaire notes that 'un pays riche par ses denrées ne cesse jamais de l'être quand la culture n'est pas abandonnée'.[5] And yet the organization and progress of agriculture are never examined as those of commerce and industry are. Voltaire's silence shows his lack of sympathy with the physiocrats.[6]

Passing references to the importance of economic factors are found throughout his narrative. Thus, for example, after noting the prodigious expenses of Charles V, he remarks: 'Il ne faut pas mépriser de tels détails qui sont la source cachée de la ruine des États comme des familles.' Or again, he asserts that the construction of a fleet of 1,200 ships to invade England 'montre qu'il y avait alors plus de bois de construction et qu'on n'était pas sans industrie'.[7] And more modern economic problems also interest him, even when he cannot find a solution to them. He is very much aware of the price revolution in western Europe which

[1] See p. 124.   [2] xi. 274–6.   [3] xii. 22.
[4] xii. 53.   [5] xii. 52.
[6] See also *L'Homme aux quarante écus* (xxi. 305 ff.).
[7] xii. 36–37.

results from the influx of bullion from the New World, and puzzled
as to why Spain, which should have gained so much from it,
seems, in fact, to have gained nothing.[1] As a corollary, perhaps, he
shows considerable interest in colonial settlements, discussing the
value of colonies to the parent nation. It is probably in part the
apparent failure of Spanish colonialism which leads him to set
little store by colonial expansion, and to regard as meaningless
the struggle of England and France for the 'quelques arpents de
neige' of Canada.[2]

The role of economic motives in Voltaire's conception of causation in history will be discussed later. But from the above examples,
the important place which economic facts occupy in his narrative
can be clearly seen. More than his predecessors, and more than
many of his contemporaries, who are often involved in abstract
political theorizing, he succeeds in giving to economic developments a place in the narrative of history not too far removed from
that which they occupy today.

Other works

To none of his other works does Voltaire devote the same amount
of time and effort as he does to the *Siècle* and the *Essai*. Moreover,
they are all, in part at any rate, written to order. The *Annales de
l'Empire* are ordered by the Duchess of Saxe-Gotha 'comme on
commande des petits pâtés'.[3] The *Histoire de Russie* is commissioned by the Russian court.[4] The *Précis du Siècle de Louis XV*
consists partly of chapters written when Voltaire was *Historiographe du roi* and in which courtly flattery is all too obvious, and
the *Histoire du Parlement de Paris* is closely linked with the
ministerial campaign against the *Parlement* in the late sixties, and
may have been written at the government's request.[5]

Yet all these works exhibit Voltaire's continued interest in social
history. The *Histoire du Parlement* relates the history of an institution, the nature of which has changed as society has developed.[6]
Voltaire no doubt insists on this partly because of his lack of
sympathy with the *Parlement* and his desire to show that because

[1] xii. 381. See also xxii. 262.
[2] xii. 406–7 and 410–12. See also xli. 48.
[3] xxxviii. 149.   [4] See xxxix. 182.
[5] See xv. 439–41.   [6] See especially xv. 445.

that body bears a similar name to, and has in the past exercised some of the functions of the English legislative assembly, it does not follow that the *Parlement* in its present form has any right to speak for the nation. But such a propagandist purpose does not detract, in this case, from the historical value of the work, for Voltaire is perfectly fair to the *Parlement*, and is, indeed, far less critical of it than he is in some of his other writings.[1] Propaganda plays a larger part in the *Précis du Siècle de Louis XV*. In particular, the chapters dealing with the War of Austrian Succession which were written during Voltaire's period of favour at court are full of flattery, especially of Voltaire's own protector and hero, the maréchal de Richelieu.[2] And the final chapter, 'Des Lois', is propaganda of a different sort, for it is not a study of the legislation of Louis XV, but a plea for legal reform taken largely from the *Commentaire sur le livre des délits et des peines* of 1766, in which Voltaire expresses his approval of the criticisms of Beccaria. And yet even in this work, there are many passages attempting to explain aspects of the social and economic history of the time. In particular, the chapter on Law and his system shows both impartiality and understanding. Voltaire's own fortune owed much to the Paris brothers, to whom it fell to attempt to restore the situation after Law's downfall. Yet he makes every effort to be just to Law, emphasizing that the financier gained little, personally, from his system.[3] And he is sympathetic towards the principle of the system itself—the attempt to stimulate trade through the creation of credit resulting from the circulation of paper money. He blames the failure of the scheme not on Law, but on the public who indulge in an orgy of financial speculation. In a passage reminiscent of Montesquieu's observations in the *Lettres persanes*, he describes the evil effects of the system.[4] Yet he never discusses the actual details of Law's scheme, and, like most contemporaries, he is probably uncertain as to the actual causes of its failure.

The *Annales de l'Empire*, although covering much the same period

[1] e.g. the first edition does not discuss the Lally case (one of Voltaire's grievances against the *Parlement*) although it is discussed at length in the *Précis*.

[2] See the indignant criticisms of Grimm, *Correspondance littéraire*, iii. 142. But Voltaire may be merely repeating the account of Richelieu's part in the battle which he has received from D'Argenson. See the latter's letter in Best. xiv. 37.

[3] xv. 165 and 168, n. 2. [4] xv. 163.

as the *Essai sur les mœurs*, amplify considerably what Voltaire has
to say in the *Essai* on the subject of feudalism. The criticisms in
particular are more thorough, and more forcefully expressed.
Voltaire regards feudalism as anarchical and incompatible with
human progress. In the first place it leads inevitably to war. 'La
plus grande partie de l'Allemagne est ravagée par cette guerre
civile, effet naturel du gouvernement féodal', he remarks.[1] But
even as an organization for war it is unsatisfactory, since it breeds
'l'indépendance des chefs, et par conséquent la désunion, le désor-
dre, et l'imprudence'. It is largely to these causes that the failure
of the Crusades is attributed.[2]

The wretchedness of life in feudal times forms the subject of a
long descriptive passage in the section devoted to the Emperor
Henry V.[3] So critical, indeed, is Voltaire that he even tries to
present feudalism as something worse than what has gone before:
'C'est à l'empire de Charles le Chauve que commence le grand
gouvernement féodal, et la décadence de toutes choses.'[4]

At the same time, he attempts to put greater emphasis on the
main characteristics of feudalism. He repeatedly insists on the
elective nature of the early empire.[5] He traces the way in which
rights of succession are established, and hereditary fiefs gradually
appear.[6] He interprets the long struggle between Empire and
Papacy not only as a struggle between Church and State (here his
sympathies are all with the State) but also as a struggle between
Italian nationalism and German oppression. And here he strives
to give even the popes their due, presenting them as Italian
patriots and approving their attempts to destroy the imperial
power and increase the temporal power of the Papacy.[7] This
temporal power, which elsewhere is so often criticized, here becomes almost an object of admiration:

Jules II meurt après avoit fondé la véritable grandeur des papes, la
temporelle: car pour l'autre, elle diminuait tous les jours. Cette grandeur
temporelle pouvait faire l'équilibre de l'Italie, et ne l'a pas fait.[8]

This failure is ascribed to the weaknesses of priestly government,
and particularly to the amount of nepotism in Rome.

[1] xiii. 328.   [2] xiii. 314 and 328.   [3] xiii. 306.
[4] xiii. 256.   [5] e.g. xiii. 277, 280, 377.   [6] e.g. xiii. 226, 273.
[7] xiii. 222–4 and 274. See also the *Doutes sur quelques points de l'histoire
de l'Empire* (xxvi. 37).
[8] xiii. 474–5.

Generally, however, the papacy is favourably treated in the *Annales*, especially where it can be seen as representing Italian patriotism. Thus, when John XII asks for Hungarian help against Otto I, Voltaire remarks approvingly; 'C'est ce qu'il fallait faire auparavant', and when he is deposed, nominally for scandalous behaviour, he concludes that he 'le fut en effet pour avoir voulu, ainsi que tous les Romains, détruire la puissance allemande dans Rome'.[1] And Adrian IV receives even more fulsome praise:

Ce pape est un des grands exemples de ce que peuvent le mérite personnel et la fortune . . . il avait d'autant plus d'élévation dans l'esprit qu'il était parvenu d'un état plus abject.[2]

Whilst of the role of the clergy in general, Voltaire has this to say:

C'est une consolation pour le genre humain qu'il y ait partout des hommes qui puissent au nom de la divinité, inspirer des remords aux princes.[3]

When he comes to deal with the Reformation, he searches once again for social causes. If, as in the *Essai*, he finds them partly in economic needs and motives,[4] he also discovers a more spiritual cause in the Protestants' desire for a return to the more simple faith of the early Church, a desire which they share with earlier reformers such as Vaudois, Albigensians, and Lollards.[5]

There are considerable differences, then, between the *Annales* and the *Essai*. What the former loses in the relative poverty of its detail, it sometimes makes up in the greater emphasis placed on salient facts and lines of development, as well as in its broader sympathies.

The *Histoire de Russie* was also a commissioned work, but in this case Voltaire had himself solicited the commission. As early as 1745 he had written to the French ambassador in St. Petersburg, trying to interest the empress in the work,[6] but it was not until 1757 that a definite proposal arrived from the Russian ambassador in Paris.[7] The first part of the *Histoire de Russie* appeared two years later.

Its composition, however, was not without incident. Voltaire

---

[1] xiii. 274. [2] xiii. 316–17.
[3] xiii. 242. See also xiii. 252.
[4] See xiii. 479, with reference to Luther.
[5] xiii. 236. [6] xxxvi. 359. [7] xxxix. 182.

had been put into contact with the Russian Schouvalow, who was to supply him with all the information he required. His letters to Schouvalow are full of demands for information on Russian trade, manufactures, finance, law, &c. But not all these inquiries are answered. Schouvalow often delays his information, and the delays are accentuated by the fact that his letters have to cross a war-torn Europe. Moreover, after the appearance of the first volume of the work he annoys Voltaire by sending, not further information, but the criticisms of the German historian Müller.[1] As a result, Voltaire's enthusiasm for his subject wanes, and though he per-severes with his task, something of his dissatisfaction may be seen in a letter to Mme du Deffand[2] and more particularly in the cynical comment which, according to Chamfort, he made in reply to one critic: 'Mon ami, ils m'ont donné de bonnes pelisses, et je suis très frileux.'[3]

Nevertheless, the *Histoire de Russie sous Pierre le Grand* does offer a picture of Russian society. Its very title shows that Voltaire is primarily interested not, as in the *Histoire de Charles XII*, in an individual, but in a nation. He himself asserts that '*L'Histoire de Charles XII* était amusante, celle de Pierre Ier est instructive'.[4] If the contrast between the two works is not so great as this statement suggests, this is because he has much information on and is deeply interested in Peter's life and character. But this interest remains secondary to the account of Peter's social achievements.

The plan of the *Histoire de Russie* has some affinities with that of the *Siècle de Louis XIV*, for the chapters describing social changes are to some extent separated from the rest. The opening chapter contains a geographical survey of Russia, with some remarks on the various races of its inhabitants. Here, Voltaire is obviously relying largely on travellers' accounts, and there is nothing signifi-cantly new in his comments. But the second chapter, which deals with the more recent history of European Russia, contains more information. The details of the census of 1747 are quoted at some length, and Voltaire discusses whether the population has fallen since the appearance of smallpox in Russia, and criticizes the waste of man-power resulting from the large number of monastic

[1] See xli. 316.
[2] He complains, among other things, that the reader of the *Histoire de Russie* 'se trouve dans un monde inconnu' (xli. 16).
[3] Chamfort, *Maximes et pensées* (Porrentruy, 1946), p. 143.
[4] xvi. 394.

establishments. He speaks at some length of forms of dress, and relatively briefly of the form of government, which he compares to that of the Turks. He then launches into a long discussion of religion, religious disputes, and civil wars.[1]

The concluding chapters of the book are also devoted mainly to social developments. To a greater extent than in the case of the *Siècle*, however, the developments which are described are those brought about primarily by the activity of the king himself. A chapter is devoted to social reforms: the establishment of schools, the abolition of mendicity, the standardization of weights and measures, the development of industries.[2] Another deals with the stimulation of commerce, and particularly of trade with China.[3] A third is devoted to Peter's legal reforms, and a fourth to his reforms of religious usages. If Voltaire tends, as in the *Siècle*,[4] to see these reforms from the point of view of the reforming monarch, and to ignore changes which were not the result of his direct intervention, the work nevertheless does show the extent to which its author's interest in social developments has progressed since the *Histoire de Charles XII*.

Voltaire's original contribution to the knowledge of the history of society is not, perhaps, an outstanding one. In their own spheres, the medievalists, the economists, and the jurists have all penetrated deeper than he. But the role he gives in general history to the arts and sciences, to economic and constitutional changes, to accounts of customs and inventions, and to the life of the ordinary man, is vastly more important than that afforded to them by most earlier historians who are concerned with war, diplomatic intrigue, and colourful incident. He is attempting to achieve an aim which is also that of many contemporaries. But unlike most of them, he goes far towards translating theory into practice.

[1] xvi. 392–427.   [2] xvi. 593–6.   [3] xvi. 596–600.
[4] xiv. 600–7.

IV

UNIVERSAL HISTORY

VOLTAIRE'S dissatisfaction with his predecessors' failure to describe and explain what was most interesting in the development of a society is paralleled by his disapproval of those 'universal' historians whose universe was, in reality, but a small corner of the globe, and who confined history within the narrow temporal limits imposed by a literal interpretation of the Bible.[1] But if the *Essai sur les mœurs* attempts, from the beginning, to offer an alternative view, this alternative is only fully developed in the last period of Voltaire's life. This is the Ferney period, the period in which his advocacy of deism and his opposition to catholicism are at their most outspoken. In many of his writings at this time deist propaganda and historical investigation are inextricably mixed, and works like the *Philosophie de l'histoire* or the *Fragments historiques sur l'Inde* often lack the impartiality of the *Siècle* or the *Essai*. But they nevertheless contain views of great importance.

One of Voltaire's greatest achievements is his success in replacing Bossuet's picture of the history of the world with one which, in its general outlines, is that of historians of the present day. There are, of course, many blank patches in his picture. If he feels that Asia is as important as Europe, he knows relatively little about Asian history; and if he senses that the development of civilization took a vast amount of time, he can only conjecture as to the stages of that development. But in extending the bounds of history both spatially and temporally, he does much to prepare the way for later historians who are to explore the new territories which he has charted.

Cosmopolitan history

In many ways Voltaire seems remarkably well equipped for writing a more cosmopolitan type of history free from the national prejudices for which he justly reproaches many of his predecessors. Though he is essentially French, bonds of sympathy attach him to

[1] See p. 32.

most of the countries of Europe. He admires the republican liberties of the Dutch and the Swiss, and the constitutional monarchy and philosophic spirit of the English.[1] But he is equally filled with admiration for the achievement of the enlightened despot like Frederick the Great or Peter of Russia.[2] Moreover, if his first-hand knowledge is limited to Europe, his enthusiasms range far beyond. His opposition to orthodox Christianity leads him to look sympathetically at Islam, China, and India, and to find (or to think he finds) there, the realization of many of his 'philosophic' ideals. And if he has no time for Rousseau's glorification of natural man, he can, nevertheless, go out of his way to defend the morals of 'savages',[3] and can, as in *L'Ingénu*, use primitive man to satirize civilized society.

These advantages, however, are not without compensating drawbacks. Fénelon's ideal historian 'n'est d'aucun temps ni d'aucun pays'.[4] If Voltaire goes far towards complying with the second of these conditions, he is far from complying with the first. He sees the pure flame of natural religion behind every form of primitive cult, and discovers the *philosophe* beneath the robes of the Chinese mandarin or the Indian Brahman. He attaches universal validity to the beliefs and standards of his own time, and searches for their equivalent throughout the world with little concern for national and racial variations. He is much less concerned with oriental architecture or Islamic poetry[5] than with showing that both Chinese and Mohammedans are really tolerant deists.

In consequence, what Voltaire actually says about distant civilizations is often coloured by prejudice. What is most significant and most original in his account is the importance he attaches to them. Though the *Essai* begins ostensibly with the Emperor Charlemagne, its opening chapter is devoted to the history of China. And this is the case with the very first version of the *Essai*, as it is published in the *Mercure* in 1745.[6] Voltaire wishes to emphasize the relativity of the problems of medieval Europe by beginning with the description of a civilization which is both more distant and more ancient.

---

[1] See xxxiii. 74; xiii. 457; and x. 364; and the *Lettres Philosophiques*.
[2] See p. 75.
[3] e.g. xi. 18 ff. and xvii. 262.
[4] *Lettre à l'Académie*, p. 111.
[5] See xi. 197 and xii. 62.
[6] *Mercure*, April 1745, pp. 5 ff.

This opening chapter may therefore be considered as a reply to Bossuet and his disciples. But it is not merely this. For Voltaire proceeds, both in the *Essai* and in other works, such as the concluding chapter of the *Siècle*, the *Fragment sur l'histoire générale*, and the *Lettres chinoises, indiennes et tartares*, to give a picture of Chinese civilization and history which is not without its intrinsic importance.

The development of his knowledge of China can be measured by a comparison of the chapter of the *Histoire Universelle* of 1753 with the chapters of the final version of the *Essai*. The chapter in the *Histoire Universelle* is brief and consists purely of a certain amount of general information drawn almost exclusively from the *Description de la Chine* of the Jesuit P. du Halde,[1] with no attempt at chronological presentation. But by the time he writes the final version, Voltaire has consulted a great many authorities and arrived at the stage where he can say that China is 'enfin mieux connue de nos jours que plusieurs provinces de l'Europe'.[2]

The opening chapter of the *Essai* contains much varied information. Voltaire discusses the achievements of Chinese astronomy and its bearing on the early historical records of China, examines the population statistics, describes the Great Wall, and gives details of finances and of industries. He speaks of the Chinese development of the compass and of the government and legal system which reward the virtuous as well as punishing the wicked.[3] And in the following chapter he turns to religious matters, describing the doctrine of Confucius in glowing terms. He considers Confucianism to be the pure religion of the *lettrés* and contrasts it with the superstitious beliefs of the populace. Yet he knows little of what these beliefs are, for though he appears to be describing some of the more superstitious aspects of Buddhism, the very name of Buddha is unknown to him. He concentrates on the religion of Confucius and on defending the Chinese government against the accusation of atheism, and giving evidence of official belief in the Divinity.[4]

A further chapter at the end of the *Essai* completes Voltaire's picture of China. In it he describes in greater detail the actual

[1] See Pinot, *La Chine et la formation de l'esprit philosophique en France*, p. 168.
[2] xxvii. 1. For details of his knowledge of historians of China, see Rowbotham, *Voltaire, sinophile* and Engemann, *Voltaire und China*.
[3] xi. 165–75.
[4] xi. 176–81.

form of Chinese government. He expresses his admiration for the series of sovereign courts that rule the country (an admiration in marked contrast to his usual preference for concentrated power), and is pleased to learn that Chinese mandarins have to pass examinations to arrive at positions of authority. He describes the Mongol invasions which temporarily destroyed this happy state of affairs, and then discusses the impact of Christianity, contriving to suggest that it might well have had the same effect if its propagation had not been halted.[1]

Throughout his treatment of China, both in the *Essai* and elsewhere, Voltaire's eulogistic purpose is evident. Of the administration of China he remarks that 'l'esprit humain ne peut certainement imaginer un gouvernement meilleur'. And this enthusiasm is probably a deliberate reaction against those who have put forward the opposite view. Montesquieu, in particular, had accused China of being a despotism.[2] Even in the first chapter of the *Essai*, Voltaire had attempted to defend the Chinese against 'les imputations vagues qu'on trouve dans l'*Esprit des Lois* contre ce gouvernement'.[3] He is later to defend not only the government but the nation as a whole against the author of the *Histoire de l'expédition de l'amiral Anson* who speaks of them as being contemptible, faithless, and lazy.[4]

However, it is Chinese religion which is the principal object of his admiration. A portrait of Confucius adorned the walls of Ferney, and Voltaire makes every effort to portray Confucianism as a sort of tolerant deism. He reduces Confucius's teaching to a moral code 'which consists in being just' and quotes passages in support of this view. But he is only able to prove the purity of Confucianism by the device of asserting that whatever is enlightened in China belongs to the Confucian mandarins, and whatever is stupid or superstitious belongs to the people. Such a division had already been made by some of the missionaries, but others (even some of the usually pro-Chinese Jesuits) had produced highly critical accounts which Voltaire ignores.[5] Moreover, later works sometimes show that he is not unaware that China is not quite the paradise depicted in the *Essai*. If in the *Essai* he praises the Chinese annals for their freedom from superstitious fables, in

---

[1] xiii. 162–8.
[2] *Esprit des Lois*, Bk. VIII, ch. 21.
[3] xi. 174.
[4] xv. 317.
[5] See Rowbotham, p. 1062.

the *Lettres chinoises* he quotes one such fable himself.[1] If in the *Essai* he says relatively little about ancestor-worship, in the *Lettres chinoises* he advances it as one of the main causes of the stagnation of modern China.[2]

Even if the idealizing tendency predominates, and Voltaire becomes sufficiently pro-Chinese to abandon his classical standards to the extent of expressing a liking for pagodas, he is never entirely blinded by his own propaganda. In particular, he is very much aware of the absence of progress in modern China, and is constantly seeking the reason for it. He usually explains it by an appeal to a sort of race psychology, but he also suggests more definite causes: the difficulties of the language and script, the backwardness of the educational system, the predominance of ancestor worship, and the Tartar conquest.[3] Even in the description of his 'philosophical' utopia, he never closes his eyes to the facts completely.

Voltaire's interest in India develops somewhat later, partly, no doubt, because, in the 1740's, he appears to have very little information except that furnished by the accounts of travellers such as Bernier, and the relatively unsympathetic description of Indian religion by P. Lalane.[4] The *Histoire Universelle* devotes only a small section of a chapter to India, and gives little more than a general picture of the human geography of the peninsula.[5] At this time, Voltaire is undecided as to whether India or China is the older civilization. He is later to decide definitely in favour of India.[6]

The greater interest in India which characterizes his later years has two causes. His reading of the work of Dow and Holwell[7] and his knowledge of the *Ezour-Veidam* (a theological work to which he attributed great antiquity, but which was in fact probably an eighteenth-century compilation of Christian and Brahman themes)[8]

[1] xxix. 455.   [2] xxix. 470.
[3] xi. 173 and 487; xv. 76; and xxix. 228.
[4] See Pomeau, *La Religion de Voltaire*, p. 157.
[5] i. 26–31. The account of China occupies twenty-five pages.
[6] Compare *Histoire Universelle*, p. 27 with xi. 49 and 183.
[7] It is from Holwell's *Événements historiques intéressants relatifs aux provinces de Bengale et à l'empire de l'Indostan* (trans. 1768) that he obtains information about the Shastabad. On both men, see xxix. 166 and 479.
[8] The manuscript was given to Voltaire by M. de Modave and later presented to the Bibliothèque du Roi: see xi. 192, n. 2, and xxvi. 391 ff. On the real nature of the *Ezour-Veidam*, see Pomeau, p. 360.

stimulate his interest in Indian religion. And his attempt to re-
habilitate the memory of Lally leads to an interest in Lally's
campaigns and in modern Indian history. His longest work on
India, the *Fragments historiques sur l'Inde*, is almost entirely devoted
to these two subjects.

A propagandist purpose is not absent from Voltaire's treatment
of Indian religion, whether it be to illustrate the universality of the
moral law,[1] or to show how much Christian theology is derived
from Indian mythology.[2] Moreover, he is led astray by the fraudulent *Ezour-Veidam*. Yet there is much of interest in what he has
to say. Following the accounts of travellers like Catrou, Bernier,
and Tavernier, he describes the races and peoples of India and
their customs.[3] He attempts, as in the case of China, to explain
the stagnation of the country in modern times, and attributes this,
too, in part, to the Tartar conquest.[4] But he sees more important causes in Indian religion and climate. The former, with its
emphasis on transmigration of souls and its consequent abhorrence
of bloodshed, has led to an unmilitary civilization, and this tendency has been intensified by the warm climate and the abundance
of nature's gifts. As a result, the Indians have repeatedly been
conquered.[5]

One fact in particular seems to contradict the picture which
Voltaire gives of the Indians—the self-immolation of widows. He
is himself aware of this contradiction, but is unable to explain it.
He notes signs of similar fanaticism among the Brahmans, and remarks that 'Il semblerait qu'une nation chez qui les philosophes et
même les femmes se dévouaient ainsi à la mort, dût être une nation
guerrière et invincible'.[6] But the opposite is the case. The contrast
between this fanaticism and the extreme gentleness which otherwise characterizes the Brahmans is equally inexplicable. It is probably largely because of sutteeism that Voltaire does not place his
Indian Brahmans on the same level as the Chinese mandarins.[7]
In face of direct evidence that the Indian priests both encourage
and indulge in such fanatical customs, he cannot make an absolute
distinction between the wise *philosophes* and the ignorant and
superstitious *peuple*.

[1] e.g. xi. 190. The ancient Indians, like all other peoples, recognized the
Supreme Being (xi. 54 and xv. 326).
[2] e.g. xi. 190 and *Lettres chinoises* (xxix. 479 ff.).   [3] xii. 368–73.
[4] xi. 185.   [5] xi. 50.   [6] xi. 188; see also xxix. 484.
[7] He is later to criticize the Brahmans even more sharply; see below, p. 90.

When he deals with Indian history of the seventeenth and eighteenth centuries, Voltaire's account becomes more complete— far more complete, indeed, than his account of any period of Chinese history. This is especially the case in the *Précis du siècle de Louis XV* and the *Fragments historiques* where he is dealing with the campaigns of Lally.[1] But even when he is engaged in the defence of Lally, he has other interests too. He discusses the nature of Indian government and concludes that it is essentially the same as feudalism in Europe.[2] He repeatedly contests Bernier's statement that there is no private property in India, asserting that such a situation is impossible because it is contrary to human nature, and suggesting that Bernier has been led astray by some purely symbolical form of homage.[3]

The third of the important non-European civilizations with which Voltaire deals in the *Essai* and elsewhere is that of Islam. Here, of course, the subject is not a new one. It is his sympathetic attitude to Islam which is relatively new. Indeed, this seems to strike contemporaries more than what he has to say about India or China. In 1759 there appeared a *Critique de l'Histoire Universelle de M. de Voltaire au sujet de Mahomet et du Mahométisme*.[4] Even earlier, Grimm remarks in the *Correspondance littéraire* that the wits were saying that Voltaire would end up by having himself circumcised in Constantinople.[5]

The author of the *Chanson de Roland* had proclaimed that

Paien unt tort e chrestiens unt dreit,

and it was only towards the end of the seventeenth century that this view came to be regarded as an over-simplification. Bayle's article 'Mahomet' in the *Dictionnaire* was one of the more important steps in the gradual development from hostility towards sympathetic understanding. Boulainvilliers's *Vie de Mahomed* of 1730 set out to stress the deistic aspect of Islamic beliefs and to show that Mahomet was far from being a barbarous impostor.[6]

---

[1] See especially xxix. 130–53.   [2] xiii. 156 and xv. 355 ff.
[3] xii. 371 and 438.
[4] Voltaire replies to this in the *Lettre civile et honnête* of 1760 (xxiv. 141–9).
[5] ii. 310.
[6] See especially pp. 267–8. For details of other stages in the development of the interpretation of Mahommedanism, see Hazard, *La Crise de la conscience européenne*, iii. 24–26.

Boulainvilliers drew a very favourable picture of the Arabs, insisting that except 'du côté des dons de la grâce' they were far more admirable than the Jews, and praising many of their customs—especially those adopted by Mahomet himself.[1]

Voltaire's first work dealing with the founder of Islam is the play *Mahomet* of 1741. Here he appears profoundly hostile, though in fact he is using Mahomet as a convenient symbol of fanaticism whilst really wishing to attack examples of it nearer home. When he comes to write the *Histoire Universelle* his attitude becomes much more favourable, and he comes much closer to the point of view of Boulainvilliers, whose work is one of his principal sources.[2] His account, moreover, is free from the occasional reassuring professions of orthodoxy which characterize the work of the earlier writer. His description of Mahomet and his rise to power is not devoid of criticism; understandably, he finds him something of a hypocrite: 'Après avoir bien connu le caractère de ses concitoyens, leur ignorance, leur crédulité, et leur disposition à l'enthousiasme, il vit qu'il pouvait s'ériger en prophète.'[3] However, it is characteristic of his increasingly apologetic tendencies that he later adds a further interpretation which stresses conscious hypocrisy much less:

Il est à croire que Mahomet, comme tous les enthousiastes, violemment frappé de ses idées, les débita d'abord de bonne foi, les fortifia par des rêveries, se trompa lui-même en trompant les autres, et appuya enfin, par des fourberies nécessaires, une doctrine qu'il croyait bonne.[4]

To the Koran itself Voltaire devotes a whole chapter of the *Essai*. Here again, his attitude is mainly sympathetic. It is true that he finds some passages incoherent and others absurd or anachronistic. But he also discovers 'des morceaux qui peuvent paraître sublimes'. And he defends many Islamic customs, asserting, for example, that polygamy was universal in the East, and that, by reducing the permitted number of wives to four, Mahomet gave proof of austerity rather than voluptuousness. He likewise defends polygamy as being appropriate to a hot climate, and, on similar grounds, approves of Mahomet's prohibition of wine and pork.[5]

[1] *Vie de Mahomed*, pp. 36 and 166–8.
[2] See Pomeau, *La Religion de Voltaire*, pp. 153–4.
[3] *Histoire Universelle*, i. 36. See also xi. 204.   [4] xi. 205.
[5] xi. 216–20. See also the *Dictionnaire Philosophique* article 'Mahométans' (xx. 20) and the *Défense de mon oncle* (xxvi. 375–6).

His treatment of the subsequent history of Islam is equally favourable. He speaks of the rapid development of the arts and sciences, and remarks that 'dès le second siècle de Mahomet, il fallut que les Chrétiens d'Occident s'instruisissent chez les Musulmans'. In particular he frequently contrasts Moslem tolerance with Christian intolerance. His account of the fall of Constantinople seems to have been written with an eye to illustrating this theme, and he also stresses it in remarking that the modern Turkish governor of Moldavia and Wallachia is always a Greek Christian.[1] And the Turks, like the Chinese, are also defended against the accusations of despotism which had been made by Montesquieu.[2]

Voltaire deals with other countries from Japan to Peru, but he knows much less about them than he does about China, India, and Islam. These three accounts characterize most fully his attempt to write a more cosmopolitan form of history. They have, moreover, certain common features. In all of them the purely historical purpose is mingled with a propagandist one. Their praise of Eastern religions is always contrived to imply criticism of Christianity. Yet it is equally clear that this purpose is only one of the *raisons d'être* of these chapters, and that there is also a real attempt to understand these civilizations for their own sakes and for the light they throw, by contrast, on European civilization. If Voltaire does not always succeed, his failure is due as much to lack of information as to his propagandist purpose. And he certainly does succeed in producing a universal history more truly universal and more modern than that of any of his predecessors.

The remote past

As many of his critical writings show, Voltaire was deeply influenced by the wave of historical Pyrrhonism of the early years of the century. This led him, in his early historical writings, to choose modern subjects, where some degree of certainty could be achieved, and to assert that pre-Renaissance history, and above all, ancient history, were best left alone.[3] He has not altogether abandoned

[1] *Histoire Universelle*, i. 53; xii. 103 and xvi. 521. See also the article 'Religion' (xx. 343).
[2] e.g. xii. 110 and xiii. 139. See *Esprit des Lois*, Bk. V, ch. 14.
[3] *Conseils à un journaliste* (1737), xxii. 244.

this view in the *Dictionnaire Philosophique*.[1] But other interests made it impossible for him to heed his own advice. The Voltaire of Ferney, who hoped to 'écraser l'Infâme' could not go far towards achieving this aim without criticizing the Bible from an historical point of view. The Voltaire who wished to oppose Bossuet had, sooner or later, to give his own explanation of the events which formed the subject-matter of the *Discours sur l'histoire universelle*.

Voltaire began to undertake this task in the earliest versions of what was to become the *Essai sur les mœurs*. The chapters on India and China do not merely refute Bossuet by reminding him that there are civilizations outside the Middle East and Europe, they also insist that these civilizations are older than those of the Middle East. But it is not until the safety of Ferney is reached that the campaign against *l'Infâme* really begins in earnest. Much of the biblical criticism which Voltaire produces in these last years is, in fact, historical criticism. But it is historical criticism of a very narrow kind, and is full of obvious prejudice. More interesting than this negative criticism is his attempt to construct a new positive account of the early history of the human race.

This account is contained principally in the *Philosophie de l'histoire* of 1765, which in 1769 becomes the Introduction to the *Essai sur les mœurs*. The work is one of deist propaganda in which the choice and, at times, the distortion of the facts for polemical purposes is clearly visible.[2] Yet if one discounts the propaganda and prejudice, one is left with a residue which contains some of Voltaire's most important views on history.

To estimate the significance of the *Philosophie de l'histoire* it is necessary to look at some of the views it is attempting to refute. To begin with, the orthodox view of history was very far from dead. Calmet's *Histoire universelle, sacrée et prophane* of 1735, Hardion's work, under the same title, of 1754, and the English *Universal History from the Earliest Account of Time to the Present* of 1737, all follow in the footsteps of Bossuet. Calmet asserts that the chief merit of his work is the amount of space he has devoted to the Old and New Testaments, and he is sufficiently sure of his chronology to be able to provide a single table of dates, starting

[1] e.g. xix. 354.
[2] The propagandist purpose is admitted in a letter to Damilaville in 1764 (xliii. 273).

with the Creation (4000 B.C.), and including happenings like the foundation of Egypt (2229 B.C.), that of China (1952 B.C.) and 'Prométhée, premier roi de Thessalie' (1571 B.C.). He traces the descent of the Persians and the Greeks from the grandsons of Noah, and puts forward a theory of the control of history by 'le doigt de Dieu' which is the same as Bossuet's.[1] Hardion's work follows a similar pattern, relying on the biblical account, and only expanding it by a euhemerist treatment of mythology. Thus he devotes an appreciable amount of space to the war of Jupiter and Saturn. After his defeat by Jupiter, 'Saturne, obligé de quitter la Grèce, passa en Italie auprès de Janus qui régnait dans cette contrée'. He was finally driven into Sicily, 'où il mourut dans une extrême vieillesse'.[2] The anonymous English *Universal History* is likewise based on 'the only authentick and genuine History of Creation, that which has been left to us by Moses',[3] and if this work, in its later chapters, is somewhat more universal than most histories of the time, its first volume does not so much as mention China or India.

Even some of those closer to the *philosophes* show a similar attitude to ancient history. Voltaire's friend and collaborator Jacob Vernet produces, in 1753, a brief *Abrégé d'histoire universelle* which, in its interest in the arts and sciences, shows affinities with (and probably a debt to) Voltaire's own *Essai*. But in his brief treatment of ancient history, Vernet follows the account of the Bible closely.[4] Turgot, too, despite his originality in other fields, is equally orthodox in his treatment of, for example, the Flood and the Dispersal of Peoples.[5]

But the *philosophes* grouped around the *Encyclopédie* were, like Voltaire, more consciously dissatisfied with tradition. The *Encyclopédie* offers, scattered throughout its pages, an alternative view of the origins of civilization. This view, however, was much less revolutionary than the Encyclopedists themselves imagined. In a penetrating study,[6] Hubert has shown that their social views were often governed, though unconsciously, by what he calls 'biblical categories'; patterns of thought drawn from the Bible. This is visible, for example, in their belief in monogenesis. Not only did

[1] Calmet, preface.   [2] Hardion, i. 53.
[3] See the preface. In one way this work is less dogmatic than that of Calmet, for it includes a table of ninety-eight possible dates of the Creation.
[4] *Abrégé*, pp. 5–7.   [5] *Œuvres*, ii. 598.
[6] *Les Sciences sociales dans l'* Encyclopédie, pp. 26, 96–97, and 158.

the conviction that the human race had a single origin dominate the anthropological thought of men like Diderot and Jaucourt, but it also controlled their historical views, causing them to seek for a similar single origin for all human civilization. They were convinced that they had found this origin in Egypt.

This view not only dominates the *Encyclopédie* but is found elsewhere too. Mably, for example, extols Egypt as 'cette contrée heureuse où la philosophie est née'.[1] And writers like Mairan and De Guignes show how Egyptian influences have spread to the rest of the world and especially to China.[2]

It is against this background that the *Philosophie de l'histoire* and works like the *Défense de mon oncle* which complement it must be judged. It is immediately obvious that Voltaire's work is intended to combat the orthodox Christian point of view. What is less obvious is the extent to which it also criticizes many ideas advanced by other *philosophes*. Voltaire's synthesis is a very personal one.

The *Philosophie de l'histoire* does not begin at the beginning—with the Creation. For as early as the *Traité de métaphysique* Voltaire had asserted that we could have no knowledge about the process of Creation,[3] and he never alters this view. Instead, the opening chapter contains a discussion of geology. And here, already, he is in the midst of controversy, for the chapter is concerned mainly with the existence of sea-shells in areas far removed from the sea. Voltaire refuses to believe that the sea could ever have covered the Alps or the Pyrenees, asserting that such an idea is contrary to all the laws of gravity and hydrostatics.[4]

His attitude may originate in a desire to demonstrate the absurdity of the story of the Flood. But he opposes not only the orthodox interpretation of the presence of these shells, but also that of men like Buffon and Maillet, who suggest a period in the earth's history in which it was wholly covered by water.[5] Voltaire continually attacks this theory, suggesting that the shells are not sea-shells at all, or, more facetiously, that they have fallen from

---

[1] See his *De l'étude de l'histoire*, in Condillac, *Œuvres*, xxi, pp. 4–5.
[2] See pp. 143–4.   [3] xxii. 197.
[4] xi. 5.
[5] Maillet, *Telliamed ou entretien d'un philosophe indien avec un missionnaire français sur la diminution de la mer* (1748), and Buffon, *Théorie de la Terre* (1749). Voltaire later attempts to refute Maillet's evolutionary theories (xxvii. 156–7).

the hats of passing pilgrims.[1] In the *Défense de mon oncle* he insists
on his inability to believe that water ever covered the whole earth,
for, if so, 'Notre globe n'aurait été habité que par des poissons . . .
il est difficile de comprendre que des marsouins aient produit des
hommes'.[2]

Voltaire's reiteration of this view, particularly in his last years, is
linked with his defence of deism and final causes against the
mounting tide of materialist thought. Nevertheless, the sight of the
anti-Catholic Voltaire firmly rejecting the concept of evolution is
not without its dramatic irony. Moreover, just as here he comes
into conflict with Buffon, so, in the following section of the
Philosophie de l'histoire, entitled 'Des différentes races d'hommes',
he clashes with the Encyclopedists. He rejects emphatically the
monogenesis of the human race: 'Il n'est permis qu'à un aveugle de
douter que les Blancs, les Nègres, les Albinos, les Hottentots, les
Lappons, les Chinois, les Américains, soient des races entièrement
différentes.' These differences, moreover, cannot be the result of
climate, for Negroes, when they are transported, keep their colour,
and Albinos, who inhabit the same continent, are completely
different.[3]

In many other places, Voltaire is equally categorical in his rejection of monogenesis, as, for example, when he ridicules Lafiteau's
suggestion that the colour of the Red Indians resulted from the fact
that some of the males had painted themselves red and then shown
themselves to their pregnant wives who, deeply impressed, had
proceeded to produce Red Indian offspring.[4] His final pronounce-
ment on the subject is to be found in the *Fragment sur l'histoire
générale*, and here he shows somewhat greater caution:

> Cette vérité est si démontrée aux yeux qu'elle nous a paru démontrée
> à l'esprit: non que nous osions, avec saint Thomas, dire que l'Être
> Suprême, agissant de toute éternité, ait produit de toute éternité ces
> races d'animaux qui n'ont jamais changé parmi les bouleversements
> d'une terre qui change toujours. Il ne nous appartient pas de nous
> perdre dans ces profondeurs: mais nous avons pensé que ce qui est a du
> moins été longtemps.[5]

From this question Voltaire turns, in the *Philosophie de l'histoire*,

[1] *Des singularités de la nature*, xxvii. 145–6.
[2] xxvi. 406.   [3] xi. 5–6. See also xxvi. 402–4.
[4] xxvi. 404. See Lafiteau, *Mœurs des sauvages amériquains*, p. 32.
[5] xxix. 233.

to matters more truly historical. And again he is involved in controversy, but this time mainly with the Church. The chapter 'De l'antiquité des nations' attempts to show the immense length of time necessary for the formation of a civilization and the immense age of certain existing civilizations, thus making the chronology derived from a literal reading of the Bible appear absurdly inadequate. The formation of a society, or even of a language, demands endless time and favourable geographical and climatic circumstances. Even peoples like the North American Indians, who are still at a primitive level of civilization, must have been in existence for countless years.[1]

But Voltaire has not much information to offer as to how this gradual process of civilization took place. In the following chapters, which deal with early man, he is preoccupied with moral and religious problems. Other aspects of the development of society, even those which interest his contemporaries, like the problem of the origin of language, or that of the origin of society, receive only the briefest mention, and do not have chapters devoted to them as do 'La connaissance de l'âme' and 'La religion des premiers hommes'. In following out the aims of the propagandist, Voltaire almost forgets those of the historian.

Moreover, the picture he gives of the development of religious beliefs is far from being a clear one. It is, indeed, less clear than the orthodox view which sees in the development of idolatry a gradual degeneration of the original knowledge of God common to all men.[2] For Voltaire, primitive religion is 'quelque espèce de culte grossier'—polytheism, totemism, or animal-worship. This tends to become, as with the Jews, a sort of monotheism restricted to the tribe or people. This is followed, in the case of a developing nation like the Egyptians or the Romans, by polytheism which, in its turn, when rational philosophic thought appears, becomes monotheism again. Voltaire concludes of thinkers like Cicero that 'ils étaient tous revenus, par la raison, au point dont les hommes sauvages étaient partis par instinct'.[3]

This is a very complicated form of development. Moreover, it will be seen that it comes to a contradictory conclusion, since

[1] xi. 8–10. See also xx. 236–7.
[2] See Lenglet du Fresnoy, *Méthode pour étudier l'histoire, Supplément* (1739), pp. 52 ff.
[3] xi. 11–14.

primitive man, according to the first part of Voltaire's account, had started out, not from monotheism, but from some 'culte grossier'. The contradiction doubtless springs from that between Voltaire's own realism (leading him to suppose that primitive peoples have a primitive religion) and his deism, which leads him to a desire to show that all religions are essentially 'pure' in origin. On the whole, it is the latter tendency which is predominant, for despite the rather pendulum-like pattern of development which he has traced here, he is, on most occasions, concerned to show that even religions which may on the surface appear idolatrous or polytheistic are in reality monotheistic.[1] In his attempt to show that monotheism is no monopoly of the Jews, he is led to presuppose a primitive universal monotheism which he has earlier rejected.

A similar conflict of views is to be found when Voltaire comes to compare different religions with one another. On the one hand, he emphasizes that positive religions, with their different customs, divide people who would otherwise be united by the moral law.[2] But, on the other hand, the section 'Des usages et des sentiments communs à presque toutes les nations anciennes' insists on the similarity between religious practices everywhere. The worship of heavenly bodies, of certain animals, the development of dreams into prophecies, the conception of the devil; all these are common to all peoples.[3]

He is equally inconsistent in his attitude to theocracy. In the Essai he depicts that of the Indian Brahmans as a sort of Golden Age, but in the Philosophie de l'histoire he finds that it is theocracy which 'pousse la tyrannie aux plus horribles excès où la démence humaine puisse parvenir'.[4]

All these contradictions arise from the duality of Voltaire's purpose. On the one hand, he wishes to attack organized religion, and particularly Judaism and Christianity. On the other, he wishes to extol natural religion based on a universal code of morality and the worship of the Supreme Being. His efforts to disentangle the one from the other are not altogether successful. In consequence he tends to examine any given religion (as, for example, the Indian) first from one point of view and then from the other, and to come to opposing conclusions. The result, on the whole, is not a happy one.

[1] e.g. the article 'Religion' (xx. 349) and Zadig (xxi. 61 ff.).
[2] xi. 54.   [3] xi. 16-18.   [4] xi. 18-4 and 327.

From this criticism of the Christian view of primitive man Voltaire turns, in the section entitled 'Des Sauvages', to attack another opponent—Jean-Jacques Rousseau. He refutes the view of natural man propounded by Rousseau, asserting (as he has maintained from the time of the *Traité de métaphysique*)[1] that 'nous sommes, si je ne me trompe, au premier rang (s'il est permis de le dire) des animaux qui vivent en troupe'. Of this fact man's present social nature is sufficient proof, for human nature cannot have altered in fundamentals.[2]

When he comes to deal with specific countries, it is with those of the Middle East that he begins. He is concerned to demonstrate their antiquity, noting, for example, that Chaldean astronomical observations go back to the time which, according to biblical chronology, is that of the Flood. Then he proceeds to show that the Chaldeans and the Persians are really worshippers of the Supreme Being. The same is true of the Arabians and of the Phoenicians, whose Supreme Being has the added distinction of being the original of the Jewish Jehovah. And when he deals with India and China, religious questions are again his main concern. He discusses transmigration and the doctrines of the Brahmans, speaks of the teaching of Confucius, and again defends the Chinese against the accusation of atheism.[3]

When he turns to Egypt, however, it is to enter again into historical controversy. Though he does not indicate whom he is attacking, he attempts to destroy the idea of Egypt as the mother of civilization. And if this attack is aimed partly at Bossuet, it is aimed more obviously at those of the *philosophes* who espouse this view.

Voltaire's main argument against the primacy of Egyptian civilization is geographical. The nature of the Nile floods, he asserts, would make cultivation and even habitation of the Nile valley impossible until some method had been found for controlling the waters and building houses which could withstand them. These tasks would necessitate an already advanced degree of technical skill. In consequence, it is highly unlikely that civilization should first develop in Egypt when areas like the Ganges delta offered incomparably more favourable conditions.

[1] xxii. 221.
[2] xi. 20–21. See also the article 'Homme' (xix. 378 ff.).
[3] xi. 28–59.

This is the only positive argument which Voltaire offers. He follows it up, however, with a series of criticisms designed to bring Egyptian civilization into disrepute. Egyptian history is full of fabulous stories such as that of Thebes with its hundred gates (a favourite target of Voltaire's scorn) or the story of the conquests of Sesostris. Egyptian monuments are 'sans goût et sans proportions'. The pyramids are 'élevées par le despotisme, la vanité, la servitude et la superstition'. Egyptian religion alone escapes this general condemnation, for Voltaire descries in it the worship of the Supreme Being, and he quotes an inscription on a statue of Isis to prove his contention. But the wisdom and conservatism which Bossuet and many others had seen as characteristic of the Egyptians find no place in Voltaire's account. He deliberately stresses the opposite view:

ce qu'on doit surtout remarquer de l'Égypte, et de toutes les nations, c'est qu'elles n'ont jamais eu d'opinions constantes . . . . Il n'y a d'immuable que la géométrie, tout le reste est une variation continuelle.[1]

The section devoted to Greece administers the *coup de grâce* to the Egyptians. The Greeks themselves assert that their civilization came from Egypt. But as the Egyptians were no sailors, it seems far more probable that it came from Phoenicia. And this opinion is strengthened by the fact that the Greek alphabet is of Phoenician origin.[2]

Voltaire's treatment of Greece reveals, perhaps more clearly than anything else, the polemical purpose of the *Philosophie de l'histoire*. The age of Pericles is one of the four great periods of human history listed in the Introduction to the *Siècle de Louis XIV*. One might have expected, therefore, that the nature and origin of Greek civilization would be of primary importance to an historian attempting to trace the development of culture. But in practice Voltaire dismisses this culture even more briefly than he does that of the Renaissance in the *Essai*. The achievements of Greek philosophy, science, and art are hardly mentioned. Plato receives a brief mention, but only in order to be rejected as incomprehensible and valueless in comparison with Locke. It is in the religion of the Greeks alone that Voltaire is really interested, and he examines

[1] xi. 59–67. Voltaire may owe something of his scepticism to Fréret. See Fréret's letter to him on the subject of the formation of the Nile delta (Best. xii. 168).

[2] xi. 72.

Greek religion in order to extract from it evidence in support of
toleration and deism. The multiplicity of sects and priestly casts,
he asserts, allowed freedom of thought and toleration to develop
in Greece. The intolerance shown towards Socrates was unique,
and was immediately repented of.[1]

Jupiter, needless to say, turns out to be the deist Supreme Being.
And Bacchus has the distinction of a chapter to himself—one
which is ostensibly concerned with refuting Huet's contention
that Bacchus was really Moses, but in which Voltaire contrives to
suggest that probably Moses was really Bacchus.[2]

In the following sections of the *Philosophie de l'histoire*, which
deal with the history of the Jews, all attempt at impartiality is
abandoned. These chapters resemble a long atrocity story in which
vilification is only interrupted here and there in order to give
place to sarcastic mockery. If these sections have their significance
as manifestations of the spirit of critical deism, their value as
historical interpretation is nil.[3]

Lastly, Voltaire turns to Rome. But here, as in the case of
Greece, it is not with the intention of extolling cultural achievements. The Augustan age is not even mentioned. The early
history of Rome is reviewed unsympathetically, for Voltaire sees
in the early Romans little but an exceptionally ruthless band of
barbarians. He comments on the slow growth of the Roman
empire, compared with the swiftness of the conquests of Alexander.
But once again, he is primarily interested in religion. He stresses
the extent to which the Romans tolerated different cults, and
suggests, of course, that they, or at any rate the most enlightened
of them, were worshippers of the Supreme Being. And he attributes the fall of Rome to the rise of Christianity. Instead of defending their empire against the barbarians, the Christian Romans
concentrated on massacring each other in their quarrels over the
more abstruse points of theology.[4]

What has Voltaire achieved in this study of early human history?
His achievement clearly does not lie in his facts. The facts on
which he builds his edifice are known to all his contemporaries.
At times, indeed, he indulges in a rather high-handed simplifica-
tion of them, as when he argues that Mesopotamia is rather small

[1] xi. 76–77 and 106–10.   [2] xi. 80–81.
[3] xi. 110 ff.   [4] xi. 145 ff.

to contain two empires, and suggests, therefore, that Babylon and Nineveh are probably two capitals of the same state.[1] The value of the work lies rather in its negative aspects—in its sweeping away of any chronology based on a literal interpretation of the Bible, and its refusal to substitute the dogmas of the Encyclopedists for those of Bossuet. It lies in the creation of the outline of human history as it really is.

Voltaire fails, however, to fill in the outline. For the details he gives are not those of the arts and sciences, of customs and industry and commerce, but only those which further the aims of the deist propagandist. Rousseau's avowedly imaginative *Discours sur l'inégalité* gives a far more acceptable picture of the origins of society than does Voltaire's ostensibly factual account. Though the *Philosophie de l'histoire* achieves much, yet its achievement falls short of that which Voltaire's theory of history might have led us to expect. The propagandist has got the better of the historian.

[1] xi. 31.

V

THE PHILOSOPHY OF HISTORY

THE phrase 'philosophy of history' has come to have two narrow and widely divergent meanings: the first, that of an epistemological inquiry into the nature of historical truth; the second, speculation as to the 'meaning' or 'goal' of history or the pattern behind historical development. But there are other problems, too, problems associated with the purpose of the study of history, with historical change and causation, with determinism and free will, which, in the eighteenth century at any rate, cannot be dissociated from the first two. Voltaire is interested in them all.

The purpose and nature of history

One of the main features distinguishing modern historical writing from that of the seventeenth century is that history has become an end in itself rather than a medium of moral instruction. The desire to point a moral lesson had unfortunate effects on seventeenth-century historical writing. In the eighteenth century, traditionally minded historians like Rollin or Calmet insist on the moral purpose of history as much as did their predecessors, and Bolingbroke, when he coins his famous phrase 'history is philosophy teaching by examples' shows the same attitude. In 1769 Mopinot publishes his *Morale de l'histoire*, a veritable compendium of the moral lessons of history.

Nor can it be said that the *philosophes*, as a body, show a new approach to history. Diderot and D'Alembert both insist on its moral purpose.[1] When Rousseau, in the *Discours sur l'inégalité*, announces his intention of leaving the facts on one side, he appears to be aiming at creating a new type of 'history', based not on the study of the past, but on the projection of one's own personality back into an imagined past. In reality, Rousseau is not as contemptuous of 'the facts' as his statement suggests. But the way in which this approach can diverge completely from history proper is

[1] For Diderot's views, see xli. 77. For those of D'Alembert, see the *Discours préliminaire de l'Encyclopédie*, p. 45.

illustrated by the abbé Millot's *Histoire philosophique de l'homme* (1766), an imaginative essay on human nature from which historical fact is almost completely excluded.

This unhistorical attitude of what may be termed the 'left wing' of the *philosophes* is best illustrated by Mably who, far more than Rousseau or Millot, is an historian in the proper sense of the term. The *Observations sur l'histoire de France* appears to be a well-documented study of the origins of French society, but Mably's attempt to show that this society was originally democratic make his work one of polemic rather than history.[1] In his *De l'étude de l'histoire*, he insists that history must be a school of morals and politics,[2] and in his *De la manière d'écrire l'histoire* he appears more concerned that the historian should proclaim the 'Natural Law' than that he should ascertain historical fact.[3] History is subordinated to the moral and political instruction of the people just as, in the seventeenth century, it had been subordinated to that of princes. If it has become more social, it has not become more objective.

Voltaire, too, repeatedly insists on the moral and practical value of the study of history. In the article 'Histoire' of the *Dictionnaire Philosophique* he asserts that 'Les exemples font un grand effet sur l'esprit d'un prince qui lit avec attention', and proceeds to give illustrations.[4] These lessons of history are often purely utilitarian, as, for example, in the case of the statement asserting that 'La France non entamée sous Louis XIV montrera évidemment l'utilité des places frontières qu'il construisit', or in the example of the Maréchal de Saxe profiting from having read accounts of the battles of Crécy, Poitiers, &c. But more often the lesson is moral. Thus 'le jugement de la postérité est le seul rempart qu'on ait contre la tyrannie heureuse',[5] 'la consolation du genre humain est d'avoir des annales fidèles qui, en exposant les crimes, excitent à la vertu',[6] or again, 'les papiers publics . . . effrayent le crime, ils arrêtent la main prête à le commettre'.[7]

Similar statements are found throughout Voltaire's work.[8] And his practice often confirms his theory. The condemnation of the killing of Patkul in the *Histoire de Charles XII*,[9] of the devastation

---

[1] See p. 65.
[2] This work of Mably's is published in vol. xxi of Condillac's *Œuvres*.
[3] Op. cit., p. 14.
[4] xix. 357.
[5] xii. 485.
[6] xxxviii. 176.
[7] xxiv. 554.
[8] e.g. xiii. 506 and xxxiv. 569.
[9] xvi. 222.

of the Palatinate in the *Siècle*,[1] or of Peter's judicial murder of his son in the *Histoire de Russie*,[2] all illustrate his desire to point a moral. In the *Essai* there is similar condemnation of, for example, the Pope's approval of the Norman conquest of England,[3] the rebellion of the sons of Louis the Pious,[4] or the cowardly weakness of the English Parliament under Richard III.[5] And equally, there is the praise of benefactors of the human race like Alfred the Great, Alexander III, or Henri IV.[6]

Voltaire appears, then, to believe in the moral purpose of history as do the historians of the previous century. However, there are significant differences between his attitude and theirs. Firstly, although he can still speak of the instruction of princes, his attitude, like that of most of the *philosophes*, is more social than that of an earlier age. He wishes to instruct the human race as a whole, and the vices he castigates and the virtues he applauds tend to be social rather than personal. Louis XIV is one of his heroes not because of his personal character (which is not portrayed as particularly noble or sympathetic) but because of his social achievements. The same is true to an even greater extent of Peter the Great. Because of this, and because his interest in psychological investigation is limited, Voltaire's moral purposes do not tend to restrict him to *histoires particulières* and the moral problems of individuals.

Moreover, if he believes wholeheartedly in the moral value of history, he also believes not only that the historian should strive for impartiality[7] but also that he should avoid deliberate moralizing. The reader should draw a moral lesson from history, but it is not the historian's task to draw it for him. 'Notre objet', he writes in the *Essai*, 'est de peindre les hommes plutôt que de les juger.'[8] The article 'Histoire' asks: 'Quelle serait l'histoire utile ?', and answers, 'Celle qui nous apprendrait nos devoirs et nos droits sans paraître prétendre à nous les enseigner.'[9]

In practice Voltaire is far too interested in moral problems generally and in the 'philosophic' struggle against the Church in particular to achieve the degree of impartiality which in theory he desires. In works like the *Philosophie de l'histoire* it is only too clear that he is subordinating the facts to his propagandist purposes. Yet such works are the exception. In the major historical works, as

[1] xiv. 268–9.   [2] xvi. 571 ff.   [3] xi. 367.
[4] xi. 295.   [5] xii. 214.   [6] See p. 68.
[7] xxxiii. 351.   [8] xi. 216.   [9] xix. 354.

we have seen, though he can never refrain from moral and social comment, he makes a real effort to present the truth impartially.

Moreover, if his theoretical views are predominantly traditional, they are not wholly so. In a relatively early work, the *Nouvelles Considérations sur l'histoire* of 1744, he draws an analogy between natural science and history:

> Peut-être arrivera-t-il bientôt dans la manière d'écrire l'histoire ce qui est déjà arrivé dans la physique. Les nouvelles découvertes ont fait proscrire les anciens systèmes. On voudra connaître le genre humain dans ce détail intéressant qui fait aujourd'hui la base de la philosophie naturelle.[1]

And it is not unreasonable to see in Voltaire's own social history an attempt to achieve this aim.

In the article 'Histoire' of the *Dictionnaire Philosophique* history is defined as: 'Le récit des faits donnés pour vrais, au contraire de la fable, qui est le récit des faits donnés pour faux.'[2] The definition is trite enough, but not without significance. In the first place, the emphasis on the word *récit* has some importance. Voltaire defines history not as the events of the past themselves, but as the story, the narrative of these events. In an age given to analysis and theorizing he never forgets that the historian's first task is to narrate what happened. In works like the *Siècle* he compromises between chronological narrative and analytical investigation. But he does not juxtapose events from different countries or different ages in order to illustrate a general truth about human history as Montesquieu does in the *Esprit des Lois*. Nor does he, like Turgot in the *Discours sur les progrès de l'esprit humain*, write a general account of historical trends ignoring the individual human beings who make them. He is an historian rather than a sociologist.

Again, the phrase 'les faits donnés pour vrais' suggests a certain lack of assurance as to whether the facts actually are true. Like most contemporaries, Voltaire has been influenced by 'le Pyrrhonisme de l'histoire'. If the worst effects of this crisis of doubt have passed, this is because historians have become used to living with doubt, not because they have found a new certainty. Diderot notes regretfully that 'le traité de la certitude historique' has never been written.[3] Attempts to provide one, such as De Crousaz's refutation

---

[1] xvi. 138.   [2] xix. 346.
[3] *De la poésie dramatique*, p. 147.

of Bayle in his *Examen du pyrrhonisme ancien et moderne* (1733), have met with little success.

Voltaire, therefore, is unwilling to believe in historical certainty. The article 'Vérité' explains his position:

Les vérités historiques ne sont que des probabilités.

Si vous avez combattu à la bataille de Philippes, c'est pour vous une vérité que vous connaissez par intuition, par sentiment. Mais pour nous qui habitons tout auprès du désert de Syrie, ce n'est qu'une chose très-probable, que nous connaissons par ouï-dire. Combien faut-il de ouï-dire pour former une persuasion égale à celle d'un homme qui, ayant vu la chose, peut se vanter d'avoir une espèce de certitude?

Celui qui a entendu dire la chose à douze mille témoins oculaires n'a que douze mille probabilités, égales à une forte probabilité, laquelle n'est pas égale à la certitude.[1]

Similar views are expressed in the article 'Histoire'[2] and again in the *Fragment sur l'histoire générale*, where Voltaire asserts that the word 'certain' 'ne doit guère être employé qu'en mathématiques, ou dans ces espèces de connaissances: je pense, je souffre, j'existe, deux et deux font quatre'.[3]

This refusal to believe that history can offer truth of an order comparable with the truths of mathematics re-echoes that of Descartes. Descartes had concluded that the study of history was of little value. It seems surprising that Voltaire, for whom the study of history is of great value, should, nevertheless, start from the same sceptical premiss as Descartes, especially since, in other fields, he has so many criticisms to offer of Cartesian rationalism. But these criticisms largely repeat objections already made by others. And in the field of history no one has yet offered a satisfactory refutation of Descartes's view.

In practice Voltaire is not disheartened by his belief that historical truth can only be approximate. In the heat of controversy, he soon forgets all about it. Yet its influence, and that of historical Pyrrhonism in general, may be detected in another aspect of his theory. When he formulates his views on the criticism of historical testimony, he does so in a predominantly negative way. He can offer few reasons why a given testimony should be accepted, but formulates many criteria according to which it may be rejected. Many of these are concerned with documentary criticism, with

[1] xx. 560. [2] xix. 358. [3] xxix. 248.

the corroboration of evidence, &c. They will be examined later. But others have a philosophical basis. They are first clearly formulated in the preface to the 1748 edition of the *Histoire de Charles XII*. Here Voltaire enunciates three principles.[1] The first:

Je ne crois pas même les témoins oculaires, quand ils me disent des choses que le sens commun désavoue;

the second:

Défions-nous aussi de tout ce qui paraît exagéré;

and the third:

Cette défiance qu'il faut avoir sur les faits particuliers, ayons-la encore sur les mœurs des peuples étrangers; refusons notre créance à tout historien ancien et moderne qui nous rapporte des choses contraires à la nature et à la trempe du cœur humain.

The first and last of these principles are the most important. The first is often used by Voltaire to reject accounts based on some physical or geographical impossibility; but, more important, he uses it as the basis of his attack on miracles. The miraculous is contrary to common sense. It is also, according to Voltaire's metaphysics, contrary to the laws of God.[2] In consequence, no amount of historical evidence can make a miraculous account acceptable. The article 'Histoire' attacks the article 'Certitude' by the abbé de Prades in the *Encyclopédie*. It is, says Voltaire,

un grand paradoxe de dire qu'on devrait croire aussi bien tout Paris qui affirmerait avoir vu ressusciter un mort, qu'on croit tout Paris quand il dit qu'on a gagné la bataille de Fontenoy. Il paraît évident que le témoignage de tout Paris sur une chose improbable ne saurait être égal au témoignage de tout Paris sur une chose probable. Ce sont là les premières notions de la saine logique.[3]

The *Conseils raisonnables à M. Berger* express similar views and urge that one should doubt all facts 'qui ne sont point dans l'ordre de la nature', taking as an example the miracles of the *diacre* Pâris, which have been 'recueillis par un magistrat, signés par un nombre prodigieux de témoins oculaires', but which are nevertheless false, ridiculous, and universally despised.[4]

This distrust of the miraculous is, of course, not new. It is found in the English deists, and in Bayle and Fontenelle. Nor do

[1] xvi. 125–6.   [2] xi. 94.   [3] xix. 359.
[4] xxvii. 41. See also the article 'Certitude' (xviii. 117).

all the Catholic apologists accept the point of view of De Prades. Père H. Griffet, for example, in his *Traité des différentes sortes de preuves qui servent à établir la vérité de l'histoire* (1769) attacks the miraculous and fabulous elements not only in ancient historians but also in modern ones like Maimbourg and Dom Calmet. He wishes to accept only those examples of the miraculous which can be given some sort of rational explanation. But for Griffet, of course, 'les prodiges qui tiennent à la religion' are certain. The difficulty, as Voltaire shows with his example of the miracles of the *diacre* Pâris, is to know which are the miracles 'qui tiennent à la religion'. Griffet's work is of no help here.

And Voltaire's criticisms are much more thoroughgoing than those of Bayle and Fontenelle who, whilst attacking individual miracles, do not (possibly because they dare not) attack the concept of the miraculous itself. Voltaire too often finds it wise to pay lip-service to the miraculous; but always in terms in which the underlying irony is clearly apparent.

The other principle, that of refusing to accept anything 'contraire à la nature et à la trempe du cœur humain', has more complex implications. Observation can tell us much about the nature of our contemporaries. But to apply the results of this observation to men very distant from us in time and space involves the assumption that human nature does not change. To some extent every historian must make this assumption. But Voltaire makes it and applies it in the most narrow and rigorous way.

This has important results. On the whole, Voltaire is lacking in psychological imagination, in the ability to conceive how men can act and think in a way radically different from his own. This is illustrated, for example, by his tendency to conclude that his opponents, particularly in the sphere of religious belief, are all hypocrites. He seems genuinely unable to believe that Bossuet, Rollin, or Fleury could be serious in uttering statements which to him are manifestly absurd, and therefore concludes that they must have been deliberately lying.[1] And if contemporaries cannot be thought sincere when they make statements which do not accord with the principles of eighteenth-century rationalism, how much less can accounts of the past be believed? Faced with a movement like the Crusades, Voltaire has two reactions: he either searches for 'rational' motives such as a desire for plunder, or he throws up

[1] e.g. xxxiv. 1; xlv. 461; xxvii. 239.

his hands in horror dismissing the whole thing as some vast epidemic of lunacy.[1] And where the evidence for an event contrary to 'human nature' is less overwhelming, he will refuse to accept it as he frequently does in the case of accounts of ritual prostitution in the temples of Babylon.[2] Had the evidence of Sutteeism been a little less strong, one suspects that he would have denied the very possibility of its existence.

This natural lack of psychological and historical imagination is reinforced by Voltaire's philosophical belief in the uniformity of human nature and human values. The result is most clearly seen in the field of aesthetics, where all art is evaluated by narrow classical standards. Not only is he unwilling to admire, say, a Gothic cathedral, but he cannot really believe that the people of the thirteenth century could have been so foolish as to do so. And his moral and religious standards are almost as absolute as his aesthetic ones. The search for a universal moral law or universal belief in the Supreme Being constantly restricts what little sense of historical relativism he possesses.

It has been seen that Voltaire's views on historical certainty re-echo those of Descartes. But that his view of human nature should be equally Cartesian is more surprising. For Voltaire often proclaims himself the disciple of Locke, and often, with Locke, criticizes the concept of 'innate ideas' which they both attribute to Descartes. Yet the difference between 'innate ideas' and the concepts of a universal morality and an unchanging human nature in which Voltaire believes, is a very slight one.

The work of Locke appears to offer the historian a philosophical foundation for greater relativism—for a less dogmatic conception of human nature. For if human personality is formed by experience, as Locke insists, then, as the experience varies, so, too, will human nature. Condorcet is later to construct his theory of progress around this doctrine. But Locke himself appears unaware of the historiographical implications of his work.[3] So, too, do Condillac and all Locke's disciples before Hume. And Voltaire is no exception.

[1] e.g. xi. 463 and xxviii. 559–65.
[2] e.g. xvii. 512–14; xvi. 126–7; and xxvi. 371–4.
[3] Collingwood (*The Idea of History*, p. 71) suggests that Locke's description of his method as the 'historical plain method' indicates that he was aware of these implications. But 'historical', here, probably merely means descriptive; see O'Connor, *John Locke*, p. 29.

Moreover, it is precisely on this question of a universal morality that Voltaire ventures to offer his one criticism of Locke. In *Le Philosophe ignorant*, whilst agreeing that there is no such thing as an innate idea, he nevertheless insists that all men have an idea of what is just and unjust and concludes that there is a universal morality created by God and taught by all the sages. In this revealed sense of justice he sees the causes of phenomena which a more thorough-going sensationalist would explain in terms of environment and education.[1]

Hence if it would be an exaggeration to call Voltaire's view of history Cartesian, it is nevertheless true to say that it accords more completely with Descartes's views than it does with the more original aspects of those of Locke. But in view of the parallel Voltaire draws between history and the physical sciences it is perhaps reasonable to draw a similar parallel in the case of his own theory, and to suggest that his own conception of human nature may be called Newtonian. It is with Newton that he asserts that 'natura est semper sibi consona'.[2] It is largely from Newton that he derives his view of a universe governed by unchanging natural laws, and of God as the Great Engineer behind the universal machine. As this concept of an ordered physical universe excludes the miraculous, the freak of nature, so does its transposition into the field of human history exclude similar aberrations. The laws of human conduct are as immutable as the laws of gravity. Man always was and always will be what he is.

Voltaire's view is an attempted application of the spirit of eighteenth-century science to history. Its strength lies in the substitution of scientific criteria for unscientific ones, and in the consequent rejection of the miraculous and the fantastic. Its weakness is that of eighteenth-century science.[3] Voltaire's universe is a static one without evolution or development. Just as his view of natural history is falsified by his opposition to the idea of evolution, so his view of human history is falsified by the search for unchanging principles of reason and behaviour.

However, Voltaire is anything but a systematic thinker. If his theory should have led him to a sort of 'Newtonian' historiography, it is only in a few places, like the *Philosophie de l'histoire*, where

[1] xxvi. 82–85.   [2] xxvi. 85.
[3] More particularly, of early eighteenth-century science; that of Newton rather than Diderot.

lack of imagination and a propagandist purpose combine with the theory, that he produces work in which this search for uniformity is predominant. His observation and realism, always in conflict with his rationalism, make him aware of the diversity of human motives and actions. If at times he loses patience with them, he often makes a real effort to explain them, and it is only rarely that he suppresses them.

Causation and development

For Bossuet, as for traditional Christian historiography, the course of history was controlled by God and revolved around God's chosen people and his Church. Such a view was, of course, unacceptable to the deist Voltaire. But to refute Bossuet he had to offer some alternative theory of causation.

Perhaps the simplest alternative would have been to produce a deist version of Bossuet's theory, in which the Supreme Being takes the place of Bossuet's Jehovah, and 'la Raison' and 'la Saine Philosophie' take the place of the Jews and the Church. Did not Pope's famous line:

God said 'let Newton be', and all was light

point the way?

It is to Voltaire's credit that he refuses to make this simple transposition, though we shall see one occasion on which he comes close to it. But instead he attempts the much harder task of constructing a pattern of historical causation for himself, a pattern from which the finger of God is absent. The extent to which he succeeds has been a matter of some controversy. One critic can assert that it was Voltaire who 'brought to history the modern conception of causation';[1] another that 'he is neither consistent nor profound',[2] and a third that his philosophy of history is 'infiniment mesquine'.[3] And probably all these judgements contain some measure of truth.

When Voltaire rejects the views of Bossuet, he finds no ready-made alternative theory of causation available. But two alternative attitudes exist, even though neither deserves to be called a theory.

[1] Brailsford, *Voltaire*, p. 83. H. Sée also considers Voltaire's conception of history to be 'déjà vraiment scientifique' (*Les Idées politiques de Voltaire*, p. 260).
[2] Black, *The Art of History*, p. 37.
[3] Bourgeois, in his edition of the *Siècle*; Introduction, p. xliv.

The first is implicit in the majority of the humanist historians. This is what may be termed the 'great men' conception of history; the tendency to look upon historical development as essentially the outcome of the impact of a succession of geniuses on their environment. It is a conception which the humanist historians borrow from their classical masters who, for example, pictured their communities as being founded and legislated for by men like Romulus or Lycurgus. And it is still common in the eighteenth century. It is prevalent in the *Encyclopédie*,[1] and one can see how it influences even the more 'democratic' thinkers from the example of Rousseau's discussion of the role of the Legislator in the *Contrat social*.

The alternative view has even less claim to be called a theory. It arises partly as a reaction against the 'great men' view of history, partly as a reaction against the determinism of Bossuet. It is the insistence on the disproportion between causes and effects and the search for examples which show how apparently insignificant causes can have important results. Pascal's remark about the effect of the length of Cleopatra's nose on the course of history is perhaps the most famous instance of the application of this 'theory'. But many others, including Bayle, Fontenelle, and even Montesquieu are attracted by it.[2] It is not surprising that someone attempts to systematize this most unsystematic approach to history. In 1758 Richer produces an *Essai sur les grands événemens par les petites causes*, a lengthy compilation of stories which illustrate this principle. Richer does not take himself too seriously, asserting that his aim is to entertain rather than to instruct.[3] Nevertheless, it is understandable that this view can have a certain serious appeal to writers who are opposing, as Voltaire is, some form of historical determinism.

The *Histoire de Charles XII* is a work in the humanist tradition, in which narration is more important than explanation. But in so far as he does attempt to explain causes, Voltaire relies, on the whole, on the 'great men' view of history, interpreting the struggle of Sweden and Russia largely in terms of the personalities of Charles and Peter the Great.

The *Siècle de Louis XIV*, however, had a much more 'philosophical' purpose—that of showing that what mattered in history was not the kings and their battles, but the cultural and scientific

[1] See Schargo, *History in the Encyclopédie*, pp. 173–7.
[2] See pp. 36 and 112.   [3] Op. cit., *Avertissement*.

achievements of an age. Such a purpose calls not merely for an exposition of these achievements, but also for an explanation of them. From the point of view of a coherent theory of causation and development, however, the *Siècle* is the least satisfactory of Voltaire's works. If he is seeking a theory of his own, he has not yet found it. Instead he borrows from the two existing theories. The resulting compromise is far from satisfactory.

One of the principal aims of the *Siècle* is to show the greatness of the achievement of Louis himself.

Il commença par mettre de l'ordre dans les finances. . . . Tous les arts furent encouragés, et tous employés à la gloire du roi et de la France.[1]

Il fit voir qu'un roi absolu, qui veut le bien, vient à bout de tout sans peine. Il n'avait qu'à commander, et les succès dans l'administration étaient aussi rapides que l'avaient été ses conquêtes.[2]

These are but two examples of a frequently expressed view. If other individuals also contribute to the greatness of the age, their achievements, Voltaire insists, would have led to nothing without the controlling genius of the king.[3]

This view is not, in itself, unreasonable. It seems more so that Voltaire should attribute the French Renaissance entirely to François Ier and assert of his attempt to introduce Renaissance arts that 'il fut trop malheureux pour leur faire prendre racine en France, et tous périrent avec lui'.[4] But most unreasonable is his systematic disparagement of Louis's predecessors. Richelieu and Mazarin are ignored or criticized. The cultural achievements of the sixteenth and early seventeenth centuries are passed over in silence. And that this silence is deliberate is suggested by a comparison of the account given in the *Siècle* with the more equitable one which appears in the *Essai*.[5] Except for Colbert (another of Voltaire's heroes), no one is allowed to share Louis's glory.

English history, too, is explained in terms of the deeds of outstanding individuals. With reference to Cromwell, Voltaire remarks that 'du caractère d'un seul homme dépend souvent la destinée de l'État'.[6] And the revolution of 1688 is equally the result of the personalities of the monarchs:

Il est à croire que la fortune eut peu de part à toute cette révolution

[1] xiv. 226.   [2] xiv. 243.   [3] xiv. 512.   [4] xiv. 158.
[5] See the notes to pp. 5–6 of Bourgeois's edition of the *Siècle*.
[6] xiv. 215.

depuis son commencement jusqu'à sa fin. Les caractères de Guillaume et de Jacques firent tout. Ceux qui aiment à voir dans la conduite des hommes les causes des événements, remarqueront que le roi Guillaume, après sa victoire, fit publier un pardon général: et que le roi Jacques vaincu, en passant par une petite ville nommée Galloway, fit pendre quelques citoyens. . . .[1]

If this view of the role of great men leads to some distortion of the facts, the distortion is increased by the fact that side by side with it, and in complete contrast to it, is found the view that the great events in history result from minute and trivial causes. According to the first theory man, or at any rate the great man, is master of his destiny. According to the second he is the plaything of uncontrollable and unpredictable forces. Whether these forces are called chance or destiny does not, perhaps, greatly matter. They are called chance during the period in which Voltaire believes in Free Will. When he comes to proclaim himself a determinist, they are called destiny. But as this determinism is entirely unforeseeable, it is only after the event that one can see why a particular happening was inevitable.

The *Siècle* contains many examples of this insistence on the irrationality of historical processes. The change in English policy associated with the fall of Marlborough is, Voltaire asserts, entirely due to the quarrel of the Duchess of Marlborough with the queen:

Quelques pairs de gants d'une façon singulière qu'elle refusa à la reine, une jatte d'eau qu'elle laissa tomber en sa présence, par une méprise affectée, sur la robe de Mme Masham, changèrent la face de l'Europe.[2]

The chance discovery which leads to the French victory over Eugène at Denain serves 'à prouver par quels secrets et faibles ressorts les grandes affaires de ce monde sont souvent dirigées'.[3] The success of Louis XIV's Spanish policy and the failure of his invasion of Holland are similarly due to insignificant causes: the first to unforeseen developments in the line of succession to the Spanish throne, the second to the failure to hold the apparently unimportant sluice-gates at Muiden.[4] And in a similar way both the Fronde and the English Revolution are represented as beginning

[1] xiv. 303–4.
[2] xiv. 402. But he later contradicts this view; see Bourgeois, op. cit., p. 414, n. 1.
[3] xiv. 408.
[4] xiv. 323 and 255.

'pour un peu d'argent'.[1] The motives of the Fronde, in particular, are portrayed as trivial. La Beaumelle, often superficial in his criticisms of the *Siècle*, for once goes to the heart of the matter when he notes that:

Ce que l'auteur dit des causes des guerres civiles est moins d'un historien exact que d'un homme qui veut attribuer les plus grands événements aux plus petits principes.[2]

And when allied with determinism, this theory of causation can give rise to a peculiar form of fatalism which Voltaire advances, if rather tentatively, with reference to the Stuarts:

Si quelque chose justifie ceux qui croient une fatalité à laquelle rien ne peut se soustraire, c'est cette suite continuelle de malheurs qui a persécuté la maison de Stuart pendant plus de trois cents années.[3]

These two types of causation are in constant conflict in the *Siècle*. But opposed as they are, they nevertheless have one thing in common: they are both 'catastrophic' in the sense that both maintain that important changes in the course of history are brought about not by slow development of societies, institutions, &c., but by sudden events or actions impinging on society, as it were from outside. In its reliance on them, the *Siècle* exhibits a weakness which has been considered typical of eighteenth-century historiography.[4]

The *Siècle*, however, does not rely exclusively on this type of explanation. Voltaire also attempts to explain social phenomena in terms of the development of societies. The discussion of the reasons for the artistic decline after the classical era is an example. And the final chapters, those dealing with religious affairs, tend to show a growing interest in the causes of social movements. Despite Voltaire's prejudices in this field, his comparison of Protestantism and Jansenism is, as a piece of historical explanation, far superior to his examination of the Fronde. And, as has already been shown,[5] he links religious developments with social, political, and economic ones in a real attempt to comprehend historical development as a unity.

On the whole, the *Siècle* fails to offer a satisfactory solution to the problems of causation in history. But it is significant that its last

---

[1] xiv. 184.   [2] *Siècle de Louis XIV* (Frankfort, 1753), i. 78, n. *n*.
[3] xiv. 306–7.
[4] Collingwood, *The Idea of History*, p. 80.   [5] See pp. 57–58.

chapters (which were, of course, the last to be written) show an advance on the rest of the work. For if Voltaire has not achieved a consistent view of causation in the *Siècle* as a whole, it would be wrong to assume that by rewriting the work and adding the final chapters he had destroyed one. This is the view Bourgeois adopts in the Introduction to his edition.

L'*Essai sur les Mœurs* [he writes] a fait du tort au *Siècle de Louis XIV*. Ce cadre nouveau a déformé un tableau conçu d'une manière infiniment plus large. La philosophie de l'histoire telle que l'a dès lors formulée Voltaire, est infiniment mesquine.[1]

Even if one were to ignore the more valuable parts of the work and accept the last part of this judgement, the first part would remain unacceptable. It is true that Voltaire's changed conception of the work destroys its 'architectural' unity. But there is no evidence to indicate that the version of the *Siècle* which was more or less complete in 1738 was any more satisfactory in its explanation of historical causation than the final version. Certainly the arts and sciences were to form the culmination of the work. But this does not mean that their growth was to be explained historically in a more satisfactory way. It merely means that they were to appear last and be treated at greatest length.

The hastily written *Annales de l'Empire* is a work of which Voltaire himself speaks slightingly.[2] On its appearance Grimm notes that it is 'le premier ouvrage de M. de Voltaire, dont on n'ait daigné parler ni en bien ni en mal à Paris'.[3] Most modern critics have been less reticent, and have criticized the work for its stylistic negligence, its factual inaccuracy, and the extent to which it is a rehash of material compiled for the *Essai*.[4]

These criticisms are not unjustified. Yet as an inquiry into historical causation, the *Annales* may be said to begin where the *Siècle* left off. As an attempt to explain, and not merely describe, the development of a society, it is a greater success than the earlier work, and it is probably more consistent even than the later *Essai*.

The importance of the treatment of feudalism and the Papacy in the *Annales* has already been discussed. What remains to be

---

[1] Op. cit., p. xliv.   [2] e.g. xxxviii. 144, 149, 208.
[3] *Correspondance littéraire*, ii. 324.
[4] e.g. Brailsford, *Voltaire*, p. 96; Morley, *Voltaire*, p. 301; and Gooch, 'Voltaire as Historian', pp. 201-2.

emphasized, however, is the extent to which, in this work, Voltaire attempts to subordinate details to a single central theme.

> On voit [he writes] dans tout le cours de cette histoire deux grands desseins soutenus pendant huit cents années: celui des papes, d'empêcher les empereurs de régner dans Rome, et celui des seigneurs allemands de conserver et d'augmenter leurs privilèges.[1]

This central theme offers an attempted explanation of all the major developments of the times. Feudal society springs from the clash between the German magnates and the emperor, and the constant struggle between Church and Empire from the designs of the Papacy and from Italian patriotism.[2] In fitting events into this general pattern, Voltaire is largely subordinating the 'catastrophic' forms of causation to those which arise from the very nature of the society in which the events are taking place. He still likes to emphasize the disparity between small beginnings and important results. But he is more prepared to see these small beginnings as the occasions rather than the causes of the results, as in the following comment on the origins of the Reformation.

> En Allemagne, les augustins, qui avaient été longtemps en possession de prendre cette marotte à ferme [i.e. the sale of indulgences], furent jaloux des dominicains, auxquels elle fut donnée: et voici la première *étincelle* qui embrasa l'Europe.[3]

Similarly, the role of great men is more limited in the *Annales*:

> Othon tâche de se rendre despotique, et les seigneurs des grands fiefs de se rendre indépendants. Cette grande querelle, tantôt ouverte, tantôt cachée, subsiste dans les esprits depuis huit cents années. . . .

Here the limitations within which the individual emperors work are characterized. Voltaire emphasizes that the same struggles and the same conditions are to be found in all feudal societies, noting, for example, that it is a similar quarrel which has given rise to the mixed government which characterizes modern England.[4]

Significant, too, is the importance given to economic motives in the *Annales*. This is particularly visible when religious movements are being discussed. Voltaire has little sympathy with and little understanding of the Crusades or the Reformation. But the attempt to explain them on economic grounds at least contributes more to

---

[1] xiii. 597.　　　　　　　　　　[2] xiii. 222–4.
[3] xiii. 479. My italics.　　　　　[4] xiii. 268.

the understanding of them than does the tendency, visible in the *Essai*, to dismiss them as 'sottises du genre humain'. In the *Annales* the First Crusade is explained by emphasizing the greed of the Crusaders, and relating how they began with a massacre of wealthy German Jews.[1] Similarly, the non-religious aspects of the religious wars are emphasized. Voltaire stresses the amount of Protestant support for Charles V, and the freedom given to Protestants within Austria by Maximilian. With reference to the second of these facts he remarks: 'Tout se faisait pour de l'argent dans l'Empire, qui dans ce temps-là n'en avait guère.'[2]

The *Annales*, then, show a marked development in Voltaire's conception of causation in history. Indeed, the work is more consistent in its attitude than the *Essai* itself. In the *Essai* he is dealing with a much vaster subject and is unable or unwilling to reduce it to any one central theme. All the ideas on causation which have already been examined reappear in the *Essai*, and in the final versions they are found side by side. Increasingly, too, Voltaire's interest in the struggle against *l'Infâme* is destroying his impartiality and turning the historian into a propagandist. But if this is visible in the *Philosophie de l'histoire*, in the body of the *Essai* it is still the historian who is in command.

These factors make the *Essai* a less unified work than the *Annales*. And other factors occasion further differences between the two works. Voltaire's philosophical views are becoming increasingly deterministic. And he comes into contact with a new form of historical determinism—that which he finds in the work of Montesquieu.

Voltaire and Montesquieu

Despite excellent studies such as that of Meinecke,[3] Montesquieu's own philosophy of history still awaits a really thorough treatment. Here we are concerned only with those aspects of his thought which appear to influence or, at any rate, to impress Voltaire.

Montesquieu may lay claim to the title of founder of modern sociology and is, at any rate, more of a sociologist than an historian. It is only in the *Considérations* that he adopts the form of narrative history. The analytical form of the *Esprit des Lois*, with its juxta-

---

[1] xiii. 303.   [2] xiii. 539.
[3] *Entstehung des Historismus*, i. 125 ff.

position of ancient and modern and of facts culled from every part of the world, is the antithesis of an historical presentation. Furthermore, he is notoriously lacking in any sense of historical criticism. Fueter observes that he treats his authorities like a jurist,[1] and Sorel comments on the unquestioning way in which he accepts Livy's account of early Roman history.[2] Yet his influence on historical thought is a vital one. 'Il a opéré une révolution entière dans l'esprit de la nation', asserts Grimm. And even his opponents would not disagree.

The problems which face Voltaire also face Montesquieu, and he can, at times, offer similar solutions. Thus he, too, can emphasize the disproportion between small causes and great events:

On verra dans *l'Histoire de la Jalousie* que ce n'est pas toujours la nature et la raison qui gouvernent les hommes, mais le pur hasard, et que certaines circonstances qui ne paraissaient pas d'abord considérables influent tellement sur eux et agissent avec tant de force et d'assiduité qu'elles peuvent donner un tour d'esprit à toute la nature humaine.[3]

Again, great men play a not unimportant part in his conception of historical causation. Thus with reference to the early successes of Rome, he remarks:

Une des causes de sa prospérité c'est que ses rois furent tous de grands personnages. On ne trouve point ailleurs une suite non interrompue de tels hommes d'état et de tels capitaines. Dans la naissance des sociétés, ce sont des chefs des républiques qui font l'institution; et c'est ensuite l'institution qui forme les chefs des républiques.[4]

Moreover, the influence of the individual is not restricted to the beginnings of society, as is shown by Montesquieu's comment on Caesar:

On parle beaucoup de la fortune de César; mais cet homme extraordinaire avait tant de grandes qualités, sans pas un défaut, quoiqu'il eût bien des vices, qu'il eût été bien difficile que, quelque armée qu'il eût commandée, il n'eût été vainqueur, et qu'en quelque république qu'il fût né, il ne l'eût gouvernée.[5]

However, if the dilemma which presents itself to Voltaire is also to be found in Montesquieu, it plays a less important role in his

---

[1] *Geschichte der neueren Historiographie*, p. 383.
[2] *Montesquieu*, p. 56.   [3] See Barrière, *Montesquieu*, p. 526.
[4] *Considérations (Œuvres*, 1866, i), p. 2.   [5] Ibid., p. 49.

work. For his purpose is to examine the relationships between laws and society and to find the fundamental causes of the nature and development of societies. In consequence, his search is directed to the social rather than to the individual, and to the type of cause which can be comprehended and analysed.

The *Considérations sur les Romains* already illustrates this. The whole work attempts to demonstrate a thesis expounded in the following well-known passage:

Voilà en un mot l'histoire des Romains; ils vainquirent tous les peuples par leurs maximes; mais lorsqu'ils y furent parvenus, leur république ne put subsister; il y fallut changer de gouvernement, et des maximes contraires aux premières, employées dans ce gouvernement nouveau, firent tomber leur grandeur.

Ce n'est pas la fortune qui domine le monde: on peut le demander aux Romains, qui eurent une suite continuelle de prospérités quand ils se gouvernèrent sur un certain plan, et une suite non interrompue de revers lorsqu'ils se conduisirent sur un autre. Il y a des causes générales, soit morales, soit physiques, qui agissent dans chaque monarchie, l'élèvent, la maintiennent ou la précipitent; tous les accidents sont soumis à ces causes; et si le hasard d'une bataille, c'est à dire une cause particulière, a ruiné l'État, il y avait une cause générale qui faisait que cet État devait périr par une seule bataille. En un mot l'allure principale entraîne avec elle tous les accidents particuliers.[1]

Montesquieu's views, as can be seen from the above statement, are rigidly deterministic. In practice, the determinism is not quite so rigid as in theory, for there are many determining factors, and Montesquieu is never quite consistent as to their relative importance. But he is consistent in his search for causes and in his rejection of picturesque details and of all facts which have no direct relevance to his theme.

Firstly, there are the material causes of the rise and fall of Rome. The economic structure, for example:

Ce fut le partage égal des terres qui rendit Rome capable de sortir d'abord de son abaissement, et cela se sentit bien quand elle fut corrompue.[2]

Or, again, technical superiority:

Le bouclier des Gaulois était petit, et leur épée mauvaise: aussi furent-ils traités à peu près comme, dans les derniers siècles, les Mexicains l'ont été par les Espagnols.[3]

[1] Ibid., p. 86.   [2] Ibid., p. 11.   [3] Ibid., p. 12.

Repeatedly Montesquieu emphasizes that it is the size of the empire which makes the laws of the earlier Republic impossible of application, and thus leads to decay.

Ainsi, comme la grandeur de la république fut fatale au gouvernement républicain, la grandeur de l'empire le fut à la vie des empereurs. S'ils n'avaient eu qu'un pays médiocre à défendre, ils n'auraient eu qu'une principale armée, qui, les ayant une fois élus, aurait respecté l'ouvrage de ses mains.[1]

Climatic determinism also plays its part in the *Considérations*, though it is not so important as it is to become in the *Esprit des Lois*, and Montesquieu cannot, as yet, explain its influence. Thus, with reference to the bravery of the Macedonians, he remarks:

Les peuples en étaient très-propres à la guerre, courageux, obéissants, industrieux, infatigables; et il fallait bien qu'ils tinssent ces qualités-là du climat, puisqu'encore aujourd'hui les hommes de ces contrées sont les meilleurs soldats de l'empire des Turcs.[2]

However, moral determining factors are equally important. They have their origin in the laws and customs of the Romans, which arise both from the natural qualities of the people and from the legislation, code of behaviour, and religious beliefs given to the state by its early kings and developed by its institutions. In Montesquieu's eyes they are primarily responsible for the rise of Rome and are revealed in the characteristic patriotism of the Roman people.

Social development is therefore determined by various factors. In the *Esprit des Lois* Montesquieu attempts to list them:

Plusieurs choses gouvernent les hommes: le climat, la religion, les lois, les maximes du gouvernement, les exemples des choses passées, les mœurs, les manières; d'où se forme un esprit général qui en résulte.[3]

And he proceeds to give examples of countries in which one or other of these factors is predominant.

But he is not usually so dogmatic as to assign particular causes to particular countries. Generally, he divides his causes into two groups—physical and moral, and spends much time trying to decide which is the more important. On the whole, he chooses the moral. 'Les causes morales forment plus le caractère général d'une

---

[1] *Considérations* (*Œuvres*, 1866, i), p. 68.   [2] Ibid., p. 21
[3] *Esprit des Lois*, Bk. XIX, ch. 4.

nation et décident plus de la qualité de son esprit que les causes physiques.'[1] Of the *Esprit des Lois* he claims that it forms 'un triomphe perpétuel de la morale sur le climat, ou plutôt, en général, sur les causes physiques'.[2]

Such may have been Montesquieu's aim. And the opening distinction between the three types of government—despotic, monarchical, and democratic—and the principles of fear, honour, and virtue on which each is based, gives a predominant place to moral values. But this is not the most influential part of the work. For Voltaire, and for others, too, it is the theory of material causes which appears most original; above all, the climatic determinism of Books XIV to XVIII of the *Esprit des Lois*.

Divorced from the rest of the work, these books suggest that society and its laws are largely determined by climatic conditions. Montesquieu opens with a 'scientific' analysis of the physical effects of temperature in determining human nature in different climates.[3] He proceeds to show how laws and customs correspond to climatic conditions. How, for example, Mahomet's prohibition of wine is related to the Arabian climate;[4] how the rigours of English weather are responsible for the high rate of suicide among the inhabitants;[5] and how the mildness of the Indian temper results from the beneficence of the climate.[6] Polygamy in hot climates is explained by the speed with which women lose their beauty there.[7] And in the XVIIth Book Montesquieu turns to a more important discussion of the relationship between climate and liberty, showing that different forms of government are appropriate to different regions, and that liberty is only attainable in temperate zones.[8]

Though for Montesquieu climate is only one of the factors determining what he terms the *esprit général* of a society,[9] the examples he gives suggest that in many things its influence is decisive. And in fact there is an unresolved conflict not only between the moral and physical determining forces, but between what Meinecke has called the 'rationalist' and 'naturalist' aspects of Montesquieu's

[1] See Dedieu, *Montesquieu*, p. 138, and also, on the nature of the *esprit général*, Shackleton, 'Montesquieu in 1948'.
[2] Dedieu, op. cit., p. 148.
[3] *Esprit des Lois*, Bk. XIV, ch. 2.
[4] Ibid., ch. 10.   [5] Ibid., ch. 12.   [6] Ibid., ch. 15.
[7] Ibid., Bk. XVI, ch. 2.   [8] Ibid., Bk. XVII, ch. 2.
[9] Ibid., Bk. XIX, ch. 4.

thought. His belief in Natural Law, like the principles behind his three different forms of government, is arrived at by *a priori* reasoning. In the name of Natural Law he condemns slavery. But he also shows that in hot climates slavery is based on 'raison naturelle'. The first of these conclusions is the result of his 'rationalist' approach; the second stems from his more empirical 'naturalism'.[1]

Of the two tendencies, it is the naturalist which has more influence on Voltaire. He has little respect for Montesquieu's *a priori* reasoning. He is often critical, too, of Montesquieu's natural determinism. Nevertheless, the latter has an important influence on his own explanations of causation in history.

The influence, however, is slow to develop. In the first place, the *Considérations sur les Romains* do not appear to make a very great impression. Voltaire mentions the work in a letter to Thiériot in the year of its publication, remarking that 'they call it the decadence of Montesquieu', and complaining that it treats a great matter far too lightly.[2] He speaks briefly in praise of it in his *Discours à l'Académie Française* of 1746,[3] and again in 1764 in his letter *Aux auteurs de la 'Gazette littéraire'*. But the latter praise is tempered with criticism: 'Il eût seul été digne de faire cette histoire, s'il eût pu résister surtout à l'esprit de système, et au plaisir de donner souvent des pensées ingénieuses pour des raisons.'[4] Yet if Voltaire criticizes Montesquieu's 'esprit de système', he never criticizes the system itself, and one may doubt whether he has ever really understood it. His early acquaintance with the work may well have been slight. The annotated copy in his library was that of the 1750 edition, which suggests that he only returned to the work after his interest in Montesquieu had been reawakened by the *Esprit des Lois*. And to judge from the notes themselves, Voltaire seems to have no interest in Montesquieu's theory of causation, and is chiefly interested in evidence to show that the Romans were really tolerant deists.[5]

It is only after the appearance of the *Esprit des Lois* that Voltaire becomes deeply interested in Montesquieu. In 1750 he discusses

[1] See Meinecke, *Die Entstehung des Historismus*, i. 141.
[2] xxxiii. 466.   [3] xxiii. 213.   [4] xxv. 183–5.
[5] See Price, 'The Opinions of Voltaire concerning Montesquieu's Theories of Roman Greatness'.

the work in a letter to the duc d'Uzès, approving Mme Du Deffand's description of it as 'de l'esprit sur les lois', criticizing its lack of method, but admiring its 'grandes maximes'.[1] And from this time onwards he constantly refers to it. Indeed, he probably comments on it more frequently than on any other work except the Bible.

In so far as Voltaire sees in Montesquieu a companion in the struggle for Enlightenment, he admires his work. In *l'A, B, C* he praises his sincerity,[2] and in a letter to Thiériot he remarks that 'ce livre n'a jamais été attaqué que par les idées qui font sa force; il prêche contre le despotisme, la superstition et les traitants'.[3] The same point is made in the *Dictionnaire Philosophique* article 'Lois'.[4] And in the article 'Esclaves' Voltaire praises Montesquieu's opposition to slavery, and defends him against the criticisms of Linguet who, in his *Théorie des lois civiles*, had suggested that the economic security of the slave was preferable to the physical freedom of the modern worker.[5]

However, this praise of Montesquieu's achievement is constantly vitiated by the many criticisms Voltaire makes of the *Esprit des Lois*. In the first place, he criticizes Montesquieu's erudition. He repeatedly asserts that the work is full of misquotations,[6] and devotes some fifteen pages of the article 'Lois (Esprit des)' to a section entitled 'Des citations fausses dans l'*Esprit des Lois*, des conséquences fausses que l'auteur en tire, et de plusieurs erreurs qu'il est important de découvrir'.[7] Here he exposes many misquotations, anachronisms, &c. He criticizes Montesquieu's method, asserting that 'ce livre m'a toujours paru un cabinet mal rangé',[8] and remarking of Montesquieu that 'c'est Michel Montaigne, législateur'. In particular he criticizes Montesquieu's tendency to treat the laws of Borneo or Formosa as if they were as certainly known as those of Greece or Rome.[9] He could have wished that Montesquieu 'n'eût point été chercher des incertitudes à six mille lieues'.[10]

Montesquieu's reasoning is also attacked. 'Je crois qu'il se trompe aussi quelquefois quand il raisonne', asserts Voltaire, and he gives enough examples to make the 'quelquefois' sound ironical.[11] He is unwilling to accept the initial distinction which Montesquieu

[1] xxxvii. 176.   [2] xxvii. 321–2.   [3] xxxviii. 351.
[4] xx. 14.   [5] xviii. 602.
[6] e.g. xxvii. 312, 316; xlvii. 578.   [7] xx. 1–15.
[8] xxxviii. 351.   [9] xxvii. 314–15.   [10] xxx. 431.
[11] xxvii. 312.

makes between the three principles of the three different forms of government. They are, as he says to Linguet, 'une antithèse qui se trouve fausse'.[1] In particular he ridicules the identification of virtue with the spirit of a republic, arguing that ambition, pride, and *esprit de propriété* all motivate the actions of the republican, and that there was far more honour in the offices of the Roman Republic than in the venal ones of the French monarchy.[2]

The theory of climatic determinism fares no better at Voltaire's hands. 'Sa prétendue influence des climats sur la religion est prise de Chardin', he asserts in *l'A, B, C*, 'et n'en est pas plus vraie', and he argues that both Mohammedanism and Christianity have spread to climates totally different from those of their origin.[3] In the *Commentaire sur l'Esprit des Lois* he is willing to accept the possibility of 'les rites' depending on climate, but asserts that 'la croyance' depends on education.[4]

It is, however, in the article 'Climat' in the *Dictionnaire Philosophique* that Voltaire deals most thoroughly with Montesquieu's views on this subject. He discusses the theory of climatic determinism, tracing it back to Bodin and Diodorus of Sicily. But he deals principally with the views of Montesquieu, for which he shows little sympathy. He quotes examples to show that the theory is at times completely wrong. The Emperor Julian admired the Parisians for 'la gravité de leurs caractères et la sévérité de leurs mœurs'; qualities which, according to Voltaire, are the antithesis of those possessed by the Parisians of his own time. 'Tout change dans les corps et dans les esprits avec le temps', he asserts, and he concludes that 'le climat a quelque puissance, le gouvernement cent fois plus; et la religion jointe au gouvernement encore davantage'.[5]

However, an examination of Voltaire's historical works reveals that, despite these criticisms, which may well owe more than a little to the personal antipathy between the two men, he has been much influenced by Montesquieu's theories.

The *Siècle de Louis XIV*, the *Annales de l'Empire*, and the 1753 *Histoire Universelle* show no trace of climatic determinism, although the first two are completed after Voltaire has read the *Esprit des Lois*. Only in the 1756 *Essay sur l'histoire générale* (the intermediate title of the work which subsequently became the

[1] xlv. 161.   [2] xxvii. 322–3.   [3] xxvii. 316.
[4] xxx. 444.   [5] xviii. 198–200.

Essai sur les mœurs) are the first signs of interest in Montesquieu visible. And here the additions which seem to be inspired by Montesquieu are mostly critical of the *Esprit des Lois*, as in the case of the discussion of the meaning of 'despot' or the assertion that Turkey is almost a democracy.[1] Yet there are two explanations added in this edition which, though not depending on climatic determinism, suggest a type of explanation akin to it, and may result from Montesquieu's influence. One is an explanation of the absence of progress in China:

Il me semble que la nature ait donné a cette espèce d'hommes si différente de la nôtre, des organes faits pour trouver tout d'un coup ce qui leur était nécessaire, et incapables d'aller au delà.[2]

The other accounts for the genius of the Etruscans:

C'est parce que, de tout temps, une des propriétés de cette terre a été de produire des hommes de génie, comme le territoire d'Athènes était plus propre aux arts que celui de Thèbes ou de Lacédémone.[3]

Whether or not these passages indicate the beginnings of Montesquieu's influence, by the time of the 1769 edition of the *Essai* (the first to include the *Philosophie de l'histoire*) that influence has become clearly visible.

It is most obvious in the sections which discuss India and Islam. The explanation of the 'mollesse' of the Indians is essentially the same as Montesquieu's;[4] that of many of the customs introduced or confirmed by Mahomet is, like Montesquieu's, based on climate.[5] Again, when discussing North America, Voltaire explains the absence of kings there on the basis of the difference between forms of government appropriate to different climatic zones.[6] And though he does not develop, as Montesquieu does, the concept of an 'esprit général' of a people, he makes use of analogous ideas of his own, sometimes using race and sometimes the qualities of the soil as the determining factor. These explanations, too, may well owe much to the stimulus afforded by Montesquieu.[7]

---

[1] See Caussy, *Supplément aux Œuvres de Voltaire*, i. 29, n. 3.

[2] *Essay sur l'histoire générale* (1758), i. 18.

[3] Ibid., p. 3. See xi. 160.

[4] Compare *Esprit des Lois*, Bk. XIV, ch. 3 with xi. 50.

[5] Compare idem., ch. 10 with xi. 220. These reflections are not found in the 1753 *Histoire Universelle*.

[6] xii. 410.

[7] e.g. xiii. 178 and xii. 25.

The *Dictionnaire Philosophique* also contains echoes of Montesquieu. The article 'Fanatisme' shows fanaticism resulting from the transplantation of laws and customs to climates other than that for which they were originally intended,[1] and in the article 'États' the following conversation takes place between a Brahman and a European:

Croyez-vous, dit l'homme d'Europe, que les lois et les religions soient faites pour les climats, de même qu'il faut des fourrures à Moscou et des étoffes de gaze à Delhi?

Oui, sans doute, dit le brame: toutes les lois qui concernent la physique sont calculées pour le méridien qu'on habite; il ne faut qu'une femme à un Allemand, et il en faut trois ou quatre à un Persan.[2]

The article 'Franc' observes that: 'Le climat et le sol impriment évidemment aux hommes, comme aux animaux et aux plantes, des marques qui ne changent point.'[3] In the *Histoire de Russie* the pessimistic religious beliefs of the Samoyeds are attributed to the rigours of the climate.[4] And in the *Précis du Siècle de Louis XV* Voltaire, looking for the causes of English naval superiority, suggests, 'Serait-ce enfin que le climat et le sol anglais produisent des hommes d'un corps plus vigoureux?'[5] Here, in view of the Norman conquest, he finds this unlikely. But a more striking assertion of the importance of physical causes is to be found in his account of the interrogation of Damiens:

Le physique a une si grande influence sur les idées des hommes qu'il protesta depuis, dans ses interrogatoires, que 's'il avait été saigné comme il le demandait, il n'aurait pas commis son crime'.[6]

Moreover, it is possible that this awareness of the way in which material factors influence human nature and action prompts Voltaire to greater relativism. This relativism, which contrasts with his more usual view that human nature is essentially unchanging, is found, for example, in the article 'Ézéchiel', where he remarks that 'il ne faut pas juger des usages anciens par les modernes',[7] and in the article 'Grégoire VII', where he goes so far as to assert that: 'Tout dépend, donc, du temps, du lieu où l'on est né, et des circonstances où l'on se trouve.'[8]

There are many other occasions on which he invokes Montes-

[1] xix. 73.   [2] xix. 33–34.   [3] xix. 179.
[4] xvi. 409.   [5] xv. 370.   [6] xv. 389.
[7] xix. 54.   [8] xix. 315.

quieu's theories. Often it is in order to reject them, or to suggest other explanations. But in the *Résumé* of the *Essai*, he concludes that climate is at least one of the vital factors governing human action: 'Trois choses influent sans cesse sur l'esprit des hommes; le climat, le gouvernement, et la religion: c'est la seule manière d'expliquer l'énigme de ce monde.'[1]

Determinism and progress

If Montesquieu's views offer Voltaire a theory of determinism, he is already conditioned to receive it. The young Voltaire, the Voltaire of the *Traité de métaphysique*, believed in Free Will, even though the amount of that Free Will was severely limited.[2] But in the late forties and the fifties, partly owing to the influence of Collins, partly through his correspondence with Frederick the Great, and partly owing to the series of misfortunes which preceded and followed his stay in Potsdam, he abandoned this belief for a rigid and pessimistic determinism. In 1752, for example, we find him writing to the duc de Richelieu:

> Nous sommes des ballons que la main du sort pousse aveuglément et d'une manière irrésistible. Nous faisons deux ou trois bonds, les uns sur du marbre, les autres sur du fumier, et puis nous sommes anéantis pour jamais.[3]

When he reaches the tranquillity of Ferney his pessimism becomes less extreme. His determinism, too, becomes less consistent, and when it suits his purpose he can, as in the *Histoire de Jenni*, preach once again the gospel of Free Will.[4] But the period during which most of his historical works appear is one in which the deterministic view is uppermost in his mind.

His determinism is at its most extreme in the article 'Philosophie' of the *Dictionnaire Philosophique*. Here he asserts that: 'Le hasard est un mot vide de sens; rien ne peut exister sans cause. Le monde est arrangé suivant des lois mathématiques: donc il est arrangé par une intelligence.'[5] The possible implications of this combination of deism and determinism are interesting. If human nature, too, is controlled by an intelligence, then history must have a plan and a purpose, and we are led back to a teleological view of

[1] xiii. 178. [2] xxii. 215–21. [3] xxxvii. 437.
[4] xxi. 564. [5] xx. 210.

history which differs from that of Bossuet only through the substitution of the deist Supreme Being for the Christian Jehovah.

On one occasion, Voltaire appears to be on the point of adopting this position. In the *Remarques sur l'Essai sur les mœurs* he opposes Boulainvilliers's suggestion that God created Islam in order to punish Eastern Christianity. However, he is willing to concede that the rise of Islam

est au moins un événement qu'on doit regarder comme une des roues de la machine de l'univers, et comme un effet nécessaire des lois éternelles et immuables: car peut-il arriver quelque chose qui n'ait été déterminé par le maître de toutes choses? Rien n'est que ce qui doit être.[1]

Such a view seems to follow naturally from Voltaire's premises. Yet it is clearly at variance with other strongly held beliefs. For the statement 'Rien n'est que ce qui doit être' is almost synonymous with the 'tout est bien' so fervently doubted in the *Poème sur le désastre de Lisbonne* and so mercilessly satirized in *Candide*. And if, in his last years, Voltaire almost becomes reconciled with the philosophy of Pangloss, such a reconciliation does not affect his historical writing. The statement from the *Remarques* quoted above is the only one in which he seriously suggests the divine control of historical events.

Instead, when he introduces determinism into his historical works, he introduces it as determinism by fate, by the inevitable concatenation of events. He writes, for example, that:

Dans la foule des révolutions que nous avons vue d'un bout de l'univers à l'autre, il paraît un enchaînement fatal des causes qui entraînent les hommes comme les vents poussent les sables et les flots.[2]

Events, moreover, are not merely inevitable; they are utterly unpredictable. The *Dialogue entre un Brachmane et un Jésuite* relates the story of how the Brahman one day stepped out with his right foot instead of his left, thereby starting a chain of events which led to the assassination of Henri IV. It is written to show that all events are determined and that great events may result from insignificant causes.[3]

This, of course, is not a new theme. But if Voltaire had originally stressed it because of his opposition to the deterministic views of

---

[1] xxvi. 555-6.   [2] xiii. 169.   [3] xxiv. 52-56.

Bossuet, his insistence on it, paradoxically enough, is now reinforced by the brand of determinism which he has adopted for himself. And in the *Essai* it appears frequently. In the *Annales* Voltaire considers the quarrel between orders of monks as the *étincelle* which sets off the Reformation. In the *Essai* it has become the cause again: 'Ce petit intérêt de moines dans un coin de la Saxe produisit plus de cent ans de discordes, de fureurs et d'infortunes chez trente nations.'[1] A similar emphasis on the disparity between cause and effect is seen in the attribution of the Crusades to the agitation of Peter the Hermit:

> Ce Picard, parti d'Amiens pour aller en pèlerinage vers l'Arabie, fut cause que l'Occident s'arma contre l'Orient, et que des millions d'Européens périrent en Asie. C'est ainsi que sont enchaînés les événements de l'univers.[2]

This is not the only result of Voltaire's increasing determinism. When he comes to believe in a fate which 'enchaîne tous les événements et se joue de la prévoyance des hommes',[3] he comes more and more to see history as a meaningless picture in which human cruelty and stupidity are the main *motifs*. History is 'un tableau des misères humaines' which must be depicted 'dans toute leur horreur'.[4] The *Essai* is an 'essai sur les sottises de ce globe'. To D'Argental he announces in 1754 that 'j'ai pris les deux hémisphères en ridicule'.[5]

This attitude leads to explosions of moral indignation and causes Voltaire to dismiss contemptuously many of those aspects and incidents of history of which he disapproves. It also leads him to delight in 'debunking' idealistic motives and replacing them by materialistic ones. Of the Peace of Prague, he asserts that: 'Peu de traités font mieux voir combien la religion sert de prétexte aux politiques, comme on s'en joue, et comme on la sacrifie dans le besoin.'[6] Of the Seven Years War he remarks: 'L'amour-propre de deux ou trois personnes suffit pour désoler toute l'Europe.'[7] And

---

[1] xii. 283.

[2] xi. 440. The remark is not found in the 1753 *Histoire Universelle*. Similar reflections occur in the discussion in the *Précis* of the plot against the Regent (xv. 156). Yet it is significant that Voltaire can, in the same place (xi. 440), give a far more shrewd and detailed analysis of the causes of the Crusades.

[3] xiii. 612.   [4] Letter to D'Argental, 1761 (xli. 225).

[5] xxxviii. 272. For similar statements, see xiii. 177; xxiv. 144; xv. 314; and xi. 293.

[6] xiii. 579.   [7] xv. 375.

the Fronde, the English Revolution, and the Rebellion of 1745 are all shown to result from economic causes.[1]

As well as resulting in an increased emphasis on economic factors, Voltaire's determinism also leads to a decrease in the importance attributed to great men. In the *Histoire du Parlement* he stresses the extent to which 'le hasard, l'intérêt présent, des volontés passagères' have been the real source of legislation.[2] And in a letter to the duc de Choiseul in 1761 he affirms that 'tous les hommes ont été, sont, et seront menés par les événements', and illustrates this from the career of his formerly all-powerful hero, Louis XIV himself.[3]

It would, however, be a mistake to believe, as has been suggested, that Voltaire's conversion to determinism brings about a complete change in his view of history.[4] Not only does it manifest itself in different ways, but it never entirely replaces older beliefs. The role of Peter in the *Histoire de Russie* is as important as that of Louis in the *Siècle*. Comparing the histories of Russia and Persia, Voltaire concludes that: 'Un seul homme, parce qu'il avait un génie actif et ferme, éleva sa patrie; et un seul homme, parce qu'il était faible et indolent, fit tomber la sienne.'[5] Of Peter, he asserts that 'jusqu'à la civilité de ses sujets, tout fut son ouvrage et celui du temps'.[6] Even in the *Essai* the role of great men remains an important one.

Voltaire's determinism, then, in so far as it is applied to history, is the antithesis of a unified theory. It can be a despairing fatalism, it can be based on universal moral laws, it can have many of the aspects of historical relativism, explaining the facts of history in terms of material conditions, forms of government, and religious beliefs. Yet it does not result merely in a series of dogmatic attitudes. For whilst Voltaire is becoming more deterministic, another concept is also becoming increasingly important in his historical writing: the concept of custom or opinion.

Under this heading he includes all the views, feelings, and beliefs of men which cannot be shown to be determined either by man's moral nature or by his physical situation. The importance he attaches to the concept may well owe something to his reading of

[1] xvi. 40 and xv. 284 and 305.
[2] xvi. 56.   [3] xli. 364.
[4] This is asserted by Bach, *Die Entwicklung der französischen Geschichtsauf-fassung im 18ten Jahrhundert*, p. 58.
[5] xvi. 620.   [6] xvi. 469.

Saint-Aubin's *Traité de l'opinion*,[1] but the concept is one which arises naturally as a reaction against the general deterministic tendency of Enlightenment historiography, and it is also to be found in Hume.[2] In the *Essai sur l'histoire générale* of 1756, Voltaire attaches considerable importance to 'l'Empire de la coutume',[3] and in the *Remarques sur l'Essai sur les mœurs* he devotes even more space to the power of 'opinion', asserting that it is often responsible not only for religious movements but also for the temporal power of potentates like the popes or the caliphs, and concluding that 'C'est donc l'histoire de l'opinion qu'il fallut écrire'.[4]

In the very existence of this concept there is implicit a criticism of Voltaire's own historical method, for one is led to ask whether, if these inexplicable facts are so important, analytical, 'philosophical' historical writing can have any real value. This point has been made by Cassirer,[5] who also notes that Voltaire himself makes no attempt to answer it. Yet it is not altogether true to say, as Cassirer does, that Voltaire chooses only those facts in history which can be analysed and explained. The very emphasis which he places on the concept of opinion shows that he (unlike many of his contemporaries) is, nevertheless, willing to admit the facts which he cannot explain. Understandably, he is not altogether pleased to do so, and 'opinion' tends to appear as the villain on the historical scene. But the fact that he stresses it at all is a testimony to the relative flexibility of his attitude.

A predominantly pessimistic determinism seems a far cry from a belief in progress, and to conclude this section with a discussion of Voltaire's concept of progress seems, perhaps, to be adding yet another to the many paradoxes already observed in his philosophy of history. Yet the concept does, in fact, occupy an important place in his work.

One can hardly speak of it as a theory. It is not until Condorcet unites Turgot's description of the development of society with the concept of perfectibility derived from Locke, that a theory of progress is born.

[1] Saint-Aubin's work of 1733 was among the books in Voltaire's library and may have influenced him not only in this connexion, but also in his suspicion of 'monuments'; see p. 132, n. 1.
[2] See Meinecke, *Die Entstehung des Historismus*, i. 116.
[3] See Pomeau, *La Religion de Voltaire*, p. 297.
[4] xxiv. 547–64.   [5] *Die Philosophie der Aufklärung*, p. 293.

Turgot's own views, expressed in the *Discours* which he delivered in the *Sorbonne* in 1750, are not based on any form of physical determinism; indeed, he goes out of his way to criticize Montesquieu.[1] Nor are they based on sensationalist philosophy, on a belief that human nature changes as its environment changes, and that progress, once begun, will thereafter continue indefinitely. His work is an affirmation that progress has happened, not that progress must happen. But he sees this progress as continuous, and is the first to conceive human history in this way as a unity.

> Les faits s'amassaient dans l'ombre des temps d'ignorance, et les sciences, dont le progrès, pour être caché, n'en était pas moins réel, devaient reparaître un jour accrues de ces nouvelles richesses; et tels que ces rivières qui, après s'être dérobées quelque temps à notre vue dans un canal souterrain, se montrent plus loin grossies de toutes les eaux filtrées à travers les terres.[2]

It is hardly to be expected that the old Voltaire could share the confident optimism of the youthful Turgot. Moreover, he probably had no knowledge of the *Discours*, which were not published till many years later. Nevertheless, the tone of optimistic confidence which animates Turgot's work is not infrequently to be found in that of Voltaire. This is particularly the case during the fateful period of Turgot's own ministry, for the spectacle of a *philosophe* in power raises the hopes of the patriarch of Ferney. But throughout the Ferney period, this almost apocalyptic note keeps sounding in his correspondence. 'Nous touchons au temps où les hommes vont commencer à devenir raisonnables', he announces to D'Alembert in 1763.[3] Two years later he writes to Helvétius: 'Je suis très persuadé que, si on veut s'entendre, et se donner un peu de peine, la tolérance sera regardée dans quelques années comme un baume essentiel au genre humain.'[4] And in 1771 he assures Allamand that: 'De la mer glaciale jusqu'à Venise, il n'y a pas un homme d'État aujourd'hui qui ne pense en philosophe.'[5]

In many works, among which perhaps the most noteworthy is the *Éloge historique de la raison*, the same attitude is visible.[6] And if it is never dominant in the historical works, it is nevertheless to be found there. Thus, in the *Défense de Louis XIV* one finds the

---

[1] Turgot, *Œuvres*, ii. 646–7.   [2] Ibid., p. 609.
[3] xliii. 49.   [4] xliv. 10.   [5] xlvii. 452.
[6] See also the frequently quoted line from *Les Lois de Minos*: 'Le monde avec lenteur marche vers la sagesse.'

statement that: 'Les bons écrits faits depuis quelques années ont percé dans toute l'Europe malgré les satellites du fanatisme qui gardaient tous les passages.'[1] The *Conclusion et examen de ce tableau historique* and the *Résumé* of the *Essai* both go out of their way to emphasize how much progress has been made by humanity during the period under review.[2]

Such statements, however, are rare in comparison with the many in which Voltaire denounces the barbarism and stupidity of human history as a whole. Yet despite this, it is a sense of progress and achievement rather than a feeling of futility which arises from a reading of the *Essai*. This results not from a stated belief in progress, but from the general attitude of the author. Despite its concentrated picture of human misfortune, *Candide* is not the book to drive anyone to suicide. The same is true of the *Essai*. Voltaire's constant denunciation of abuses, his condemnation of the past in the name of reason and tolerance, all imply the reality of progress. The author sits in judgement on the past, and the reader sits beside him. Together they represent the enlightened spirit of the modern world. Even if their humanitarian standards are not yet, and may never be, universally recognized, yet the very fact that they can occupy the seat of judgement shows that the human spirit has liberated itself from the shackles of the past. This feeling of triumph over the past, which the reader who enters into the spirit of the *Essai* must feel, is far more powerful than the many reminders that cruelty and intolerance are still with us, and will, perhaps, always be with us. For this reason, Voltaire's role in the creation of the *mystique* of progress is no small one.

If the phrase 'philosophy of history' implies a coherent view of the nature of historical development, then Voltaire has no philosophy of history. His mind is too agile, too intuitive, and too superficial to develop a consistent theory. But his failure also results from the duality which characterizes all his thought—the duality of what Meinecke has called 'mechanism' and 'moralism', the conflict between the rationalist and empirical approaches.[3] This duality, if it is visible from the beginning, becomes more and more pronounced in Voltaire's last years, especially in his excursions into ancient history.

---

[1] xxviii. 105.
[2] xiii. 183.
[3] *Die Entstehung des Historismus*, i. 86.

This lack of a philosophy of history lessens Voltaire's stature as a philosopher. But though the contradictions and superficiality of his explanations detract from the value of his historical writings, they do not do so nearly so much as would the imposition on the facts of any *one* of his many points of view. It is this open-mindedness, in a century given to various forms of rationalist dogmatizing, which constitutes much of the attraction of his work.

VI

HISTORICAL METHOD

Sources and critical method

IN the *Catalogue des écrivains* which accompanies the *Siècle de Louis XIV*, Voltaire remarks of the historian Dupleix:

> Il est le premier historien qui ait cité en marge ses autorités; précaution absolument nécessaire quand on n'écrit pas l'histoire de son temps, à moins qu'on ne s'en tienne aux faits connus.[1]

But this absolutely necessary precaution is one which Voltaire himself never takes. Sometimes he offers excuses, asserting, for example, that the events of the early years of the reign of Louis XIV are too well known to need the citation of authorities, and that he himself has 'witnessed' the closing years. At other times, as in the preface to the *Histoire de Russie*, he can affirm that 'on cite toujours ses garants',[2] though he actually does nothing of the sort. The *Essai*, too, is devoid of all but the vaguest citation of sources, though here more than anywhere, according to his own principles, they are necessary.

However, when such information as the historical works do give is added to that to be found in the correspondence, in the *Dictionnaire Philosophique*, in controversial writings like the *Supplément au Siècle de Louis XIV*, and in the statements of contemporaries, a fairly accurate picture of Voltaire's sources can be obtained. In the case of the *Siècle*, this task has been largely accomplished by Émile Bourgeois in his edition, though his conclusions may be supplemented by the far more detailed examination to which Lanson has subjected the final chapters of the work.[3] In the case of the *Essai* an introductory investigation on the same lines has been carried out by Hagmann.[4]

From this point of view Voltaire's works may be divided into

---

[1] xiv. 69.   [2] xvi. 381.

[3] Lanson, 'Notes pour servir à l'étude des chapitres 35–39 du *Siècle de Louis XIV* de Voltaire'. See also the recent study by Quignard, 'Un Établissement de texte: *Le Siècle de Louis XIV* de Voltaire'.

[4] Hagmann, *Über Voltaire's 'Essai sur les mœurs'*.

three classes. In one class may be placed those dealing with foreign countries of which he has no personal knowledge—works like the *Histoire de Charles XII* and the *Histoire de Russie*. The former has already been shown to be based on a combination of previous histories, memoirs, and the replies to personal inquiries directed to survivors of the events and others. The same is true of the *Histoire de Russie*. Here Voltaire uses the information sent by his Russian correspondent Schouvalow, supplemented by information he obtains from others such as Frederick the Great, and by a number of other memoirs and published works.[1] In both cases the results are similar. The historian has obtained as much material as he could, and has transformed it, through his graphic style and inquiring mind, into a valuable and eminently readable account. But his lack of direct knowledge of the countries he is dealing with, and their languages, necessarily prove to be grave limitations. The extent to which this is the case can be seen from an examination of the controversy relating to the *Histoire de Charles XII*.[2] Similar controversy follows the *Histoire de Russie*. If the comment which, according to Chamfort, Voltaire finally makes on this work, is unduly cynical, it is, perhaps, acceptable as a tacit recognition of the necessary limitations of this type of historical writing.[3]

In a second class may be placed works in which Voltaire deals with the more or less contemporary history of his own country. The *Précis du Siècle de Louis XV* and part of the *Histoire du Parlement* come within this category, but both are composed fairly rapidly, both have propagandist purposes, and in both his scope is to some extent restricted by the desire to avoid antagonizing, and sometimes by the desire to flatter authority. The work of this type on which, above all, Voltaire should be judged, is the *Siècle de Louis XIV*.

What are the sources of the *Siècle*? In the first place there are the printed works—histories, memoirs, letters. Voltaire claims to have read some 200 volumes of these.[4] The figure may be exaggerated, but Lanson's examination of the concluding chapters of the work illustrates the breadth of Voltaire's reading. D'Avrigny, Benoist, Bayle, Gourville, Brueys, Louvreleul, Dumas, Duval, Racine,

[1] The thoroughness of his documentation may be judged from the long list of MSS. on Russian history in F. Caussy's *Inventaire des MSS. de la bibliothèque de Voltaire conservée à la Bibliothèque impériale publique de Saint-Petersbourg*, Paris, 1913.

[2] See pp. 20 ff.   [3] See p. 74.   [4] xxxv. 29 ff.

Phélypeaux; these are only the more outstanding of the sources Lanson discovers. He concludes:

Il ne s'asservit jamais à un seul guide. Il complète et rectifie sa source principale par tout ce qu'il a pu trouver de sûr dans d'autres écrits, par des inédits authentiques, mémoires, pièces diplomatiques ou administratives, dont il a pu avoir communication, enfin par les témoignages oraux qu'il a pu recueillir.[1]

The role of unpublished sources in the *Siècle* is nothing like so great as that of the published ones, but it is considerable. He has consulted the memoirs of Torcy, Dangeau, and Villars before their publication, and also, probably, those of Saint-Simon. He takes great pains to acquire a *mémorial* written by Louis XIV, and when he finally obtains it in 1752 it is immediately included in the next edition of the *Siècle*. From the archives of the Louvre he obtains information regarding the secret treaty of 1668 and the correspondence of the duc d'Harcourt.[2] He has studied the reports of the *intendants*.[3]

It is impossible to assess his debt to those with whom he corresponds or converses. Bourgeois draws up a table of letters referring to the *Siècle* which contains about 200 items.[4] Even then it is not complete, for when he comes to revise the work in 1767 Voltaire writes to Damilaville, the duc de Bouillon, Chabanon, Morellet, and De Taubes with still further requests for information.[5] And he has also obtained much information orally. He has talked with people who knew the king, with those who guarded the Man in the Iron Mask, and with many other survivors of the age.[6] And he has many other sources, for details of which the reader is referred to the works of Bourgeois and Lanson. It is clear that in the breadth of its sources the *Siècle* reaches a very high standard.

Yet despite their variety, these sources, written or oral, published or unpublished, are nearly all personal memoirs or works composed from memoirs. And it is from the same type of source that Voltaire attempts to compose the historical works which fall into the third class—those dealing with the distant past. But here memoirs are

---

[1] Lanson, op. cit., p. 191.
[2] *Siècle de Louis XIV* (ed. Bourgeois), introduction, p. xlii.
[3] See xxxv. 29 ff.
[4] Bourgeois, introduction, pp. xlvi–l.
[5] xlv. 434, 436, 439, 450, and 453.
[6] See the letter to Dubos, xxxv. 29 ff.

few in number and hard to verify, and there are no surviving eye-witnesses. He is reduced to the published works of earlier historians. For he has neither the desire nor the technical skill to undertake a personal investigation into original documents.

Moreover, his attitude to all other forms of historical evidence is a highly sceptical one. In the article 'Histoire', he asserts that monuments are the only source of certainty in the field of ancient history. But except for early records of astronomical observations there is only one monument which he can produce in support of his contention: the Arundel marbles. The rest, like the Pyramids, can merely serve to indicate the great age of certain peoples. More-over, the majority have not even this simple use; Voltaire reverses the view of Hardouin, who regarded written documents with sus-picion and would only pin his faith on medals and inscriptions. He makes every effort to show the unreliability of such sources, giving examples of cases in which they have been shown to be pious frauds.[1]

This is a favourite theme. The *Résumé* of the *Essai* asserts that

La plupart des monuments, quand ils sont érigés longtemps après l'action, ne prouvent que des erreurs consacrées; il faut même quelque-fois se défier des médailles frappées dans le temps d'un événement.[2]

The *Précis du Siècle de Louis XV* offers the example of the medal struck to celebrate Admiral Vernon's capture of Cartagena—a 'capture' which never took place.[3] And the same point is made in the *Dictionnaire Philosophique* article 'Antiquité', and in a section of the *Fragment sur l'histoire générale*.[4]

In view of his opinions it is not surprising that Voltaire makes little or no use of such sources of historical information. He thereby shuts himself off from one of the more important achievements of the antiquarians. The use they had made of one form of 'monu-ment' may be judged from the article 'Médaille' in the *Encyclo-pédie*.

The vast increase in knowledge of the medieval world which took place in the late seventeenth and the eighteenth centuries was largely the result of the work of the scholars who discovered, pub-

---

[1] xix. 348 ff. A similar scepticism had already been shown by earlier writers in the Pyrrhonist tradition, such as Saint-Aubin; see Momigliano, 'Ancient History and the Antiquarian', p. 301.
[2] xiii. 175.   [3] xv. 206.
[4] xvii. 277 ff. and xxix. 224–7.

lished, and interpreted charters and other legal and ecclesiastical documents of the period. To this work Voltaire is in no position to contribute. Moreover, his attitude to it is full of contradictions.

As in the case of monuments, he shows considerable scepticism with regard to the value of charters. In *Le Pyrrhonisme de l'histoire* he remarks that

Pour pénétrer dans le labryinthe ténébreux du moyen âge, il faut le secours des archives, et on n'en a presque point. Quelques anciens couvents ont conservé des chartes, des diplômes, qui contiennent des donations dont l'autorité est très suspecte.[1]

In the *Dictionnaire Philosophique* this suspicion is uppermost in his mind. In the article 'Parlement de France' he demands:

Quelle foi peut-on avoir à ces anciens monuments après l'aventure des fausses décrétales qui ont été respectées pendant cinq cents ans?[2]

In the article 'Église' he remarks, speaking of Ruinarts's *Actes sincères*:

Ce n'est pas assez qu'un manuscrit soit tiré de l'abbaye de Saint-Benoît-sur-Loire, ou d'un couvent de célestins de Paris, conforme à un manuscrit des feuillants, pour que cet acte soit authentique.[3]

Yet his attitude towards the work of the *érudits* does not always show similar suspicion. He congratulates Rymer on the work he has done on English archives. He refers to or quotes from Tillemont, Du Cange, Muratori, and Giannone on more than one occasion.[4] During his stay at the Benedictine monastery of Senones he writes to D'Argental, 'Je m'occupe avec dom Mabillon, dom Martène, dom Thuillier, dom Ruinart',[5] and the work of Ruinart, together with that of Calmet the head of the congregation of Senones, is very well known to him, though he mentions both men more in order to mock their credulity than to praise their erudition.[6]

The *Catalogue des écrivains* of the *Siècle* contains references to many of the erudite historians. Achéri, Baluze, Chantereau, Cordemoi, Duchesne, Mabillon, Montfaucon, Tillemont, Pétau, and Simon all receive recognition and praise. The praise, however, does not always appear indicative of first-hand knowledge. Thus,

[1] xxvii. 255.   [2] xx. 172.   [3] xviii. 488.
[4] xvii. 306; xi. 501; and xxix. 361.   [5] xxxviii. 230.
[6] e.g. xxix. 455 and xviii. 488.

Mabillon's achievement is summed up in the one phrase, 'il a fait de profondes recherches'.[1] And Voltaire speaks of Dupleix, who is little more than a courtly popularizer, in the same sort of tone as that in which he speaks of Duchesne, one of the greatest of the seventeenth-century *érudits*.[2]

What emerges from these contradictions? As Voltaire has no first-hand knowledge of either the sources or the methods of medieval historians, he is able to offer criticism of the findings of the scholars only when their accounts seem contrary to *vraisemblance* or to the laws of the physical universe. For the rest, apart from occasional outbursts of scepticism, he accepts what they tell him. But his acquaintance with them, though fairly wide, is never profound. It is very rarely that he is able to weigh one against another. And in any case, he is usually exasperated by the type of detail they tend to debate. His attitude is summed up in the following passage from a letter to the Duchesse de Saxe-Gotha:

Je crois lui avoir déjà mandé que deux graves professeurs d'histoire examinaient scrupuleusement l'ouvrage pour voir si c'est le 25 ou le 26 d'un tel mois que telle sottise arriva il y a six siècles. Ces minutes seront pour les sots, dont ce monde est plein, et l'intérêt . . . les grands tableaux, la connaissance des hommes et des temps, l'histoire de l'esprit humain seront pour votre Altesse sérénissime.[3]

These are the limitations which characterize the *Essai sur les mœurs* and all the other works dealing with distant periods of history. The *Essai* is a compilation from earlier historians. Where the amount of material available is large, or where Voltaire is specially interested in a particular problem, the number of sources is often considerable. For his account of the Middle Ages, for example, he has used the Bollandist *Acta Sanctorum*, Ruinart's *Acta primorum Martyrum*, Achéri's *Spicilegium*; among contemporary historians, Gregory of Tours, Frédégaire, Eginhard, Joinville, and Froissart, and among more modern historians, Mézeray, Boulainvilliers, Daniel, Maimbourg, and Hénault.[4] For his discussion of the conquest of America he uses Herrera, Garcilaso de la Vega, de Solis, Zarata, and Las Casas.[5] He is thoroughly documented on Indian and Chinese history. On the other hand, his secretary Colini is horrified to find that Voltaire's account of the reign of Louis XIII

[1] xiv. 99.   [2] xiv. 67 and 69.   [3] xxxviii. 128.
[4] Hagmann, op. cit.
[5] See xii. 388, 395, 397, and 399.

is taken almost entirely from Le Vassor,[1] and Lanson has noted that what he has to say about Henri IV does not go very far beyond the account of Mézeray.[2] In his study of the *Essai* Hagmann has compiled a list of some eighty-nine works which Voltaire has used for his universal history. The list is far from complete. And some of the information he obtains, such as the translations of Persian poetry or the letters of Henri IV, are the result of personal efforts to trace original material.[3] Yet even if one were to double Hagmann's list, and allow for other examples of personal investigation, it is clear that the *Essai* cannot stand comparison with the *Siècle*. It is a reinterpretation of the accepted facts, not a piece of original research.

Even when the sources are numerous and varied, the way they are investigated leaves much to be desired. Voltaire is a rapid, but perhaps not always a careful reader. Many of the notes he makes for the *Siècle* and the *Essai* have been reproduced by Caussy. They are mostly jottings, and it is only occasionally that we find a detailed quotation, or a reference to the precise source from which the information comes. Again, Voltaire knew the *Mémoires* of Torcy before they were published. But after their publication he makes numerous changes in the *Siècle* on information drawn from them.[4] This suggests that the initial reading of them must have been a very cursory one. And the case of Saint-Simon illustrates the same point. There are verbal similarities between Voltaire and Saint-Simon which strongly suggest that the historian had read the work of the greatest of the memorialists.[5] But Voltaire never mentions Saint-Simon's work, and if he had read it, it seems to have made remarkably little impression on him. This again may result from a very cursory reading.

There is, however, another possible explanation. Voltaire may have obtained his information not from a first-hand reading of Saint-Simon, but from notes made by someone else. For among the sources of his historical works are many helpers and consultants.

[1] See Colini's letter to Dupont, xxxix. 8.

[2] Lanson, *Voltaire*, p. 123.

[3] He claims to have obtained the translations from a M. Dadiki, interpreter to George I (see Introduction to Geneva 1758 edition of the *Essai*); though he afterwards asserts that they are his own (xxxvii. 420). For Henri IV's letters, see xlii. 497.

[4] See Bourgeois, introduction, p. xlii and Quignard, op. cit., p. 312.

[5] Bourgeois, op. cit., p. 308, nn. 2 and 3.

And it is by no means easy to calculate how much he owes to them. His secretary Colini may have been the source of much information.[1] The early *Essai* and the *Annales* may owe a great deal to the two Colmar historians Lorenz and Dupont with whom he was in close touch when writing the latter work.[2] The *Siècle* may owe much to the long correspondence with Président Hénault.[3] The 1754 version of the *Essai* is published with the help of the Genevan historian Jacob Vernet, and as Vernet's letters show, he makes many corrections of fact and tones down the outspokenness of many of Voltaire's comments.[4]

Pour découvrir une vérité toujours incertaine et toujours prête à nous échapper, il faudra donc se jeter dans l'étude de nos diplômes, de nos formules anciennes, de nos capitulaires, et gémir sous ce fatras énorme de pièces propres à faire reculer d'effroi le savant le plus intrépide et le plus opiniâtre.[5]

These words are those of Mably, but the feeling of terror which informs them is common to the majority of the 'philosophic' historians. They are men of action, not contemplatives, and if they lack the faults of the Benedictines they also lack their virtues. And here Voltaire is no exception. For the most part he uses, as his raw material, the discoveries of others. It is in his interpretation of this material that he distinguishes himself from them.

'Dans tout ce que j'écrivais, je mettais toujours à la marge: *vide, quaere, dubita.*'[6] It is in this spirit that Voltaire reads the records of historians. And the outbursts of scepticism which characterize all his critical works from the 1748 preface to *Charles XII* to *Le Pyrrhonisme de l'histoire*, show that this is no passing crisis of doubt. In so far as this scepticism is based on philosophical principles, it has already been examined. What remains to be investigated is the way in which Voltaire criticizes those accounts in which there is no transgression of the laws of nature or of human nature. He has absorbed much of the sceptical spirit of Bayle and his

[1] See Caussy, *Supplément aux Œuvres de Voltaire*, p. 31.
[2] See Beuchot's *Avertissement* to the *Annales* (xiii. 187); Voltaire's letter to D'Argental (xxxviii. 185); and Colini, *Mon séjour auprès de Voltaire*, p. 112.
[3] For Hénault's views, see Lion, *Le Président Hénault*, pp. 67 ff.
[4] *Correspondance avec les Tronchin* (ed. Delattre), pp. 247–58.
[5] *De la manière d'écrire l'histoire*, p. 97.
[6] Preface to the 1754 edition of the *Essai* (xxiv. 42).

contemporaries. Of the Dark Ages he can remark that 'il fallut presser cent quintaux de mensonges pour extraire une once de vérité',[1] and even apropos of a period as recent as the seventeenth century, he can conclude that

Tous les grands événements de ce globe sont comme ce globe même, dont une moitié est exposée au grand jour, et l'autre plongée dans l'obscurité.[2]

And yet he differs profoundly from Bayle. For he wishes to write history which is moral, social, 'philosophical', and instructive. There results a fundamental dichotomy in his approach to history. On the one hand, his aim is positive and practical; on the other hand, his critical method is predominantly sceptical and negative. He wishes to create the new 'histoire de l'esprit humain'; but he has been taught to destroy rather than to create, to doubt rather than to affirm.

The conflict between these two tendencies is never completely resolved. If Voltaire had always doubted as consistently as he does in *Le Pyrrhonisme de l'histoire*, then works like the *Siècle* and the *Essai* would probably never have been written. But in practice he is able to suspend his disbelief. And in theory, he makes a distinction (already found in Bayle and Daniel) between ascertainable principal facts and doubtful details, and asserts that the latter are absent from his own works.[3]

The distinction is a convenient rule of thumb, but hardly very accurate. There may be occasions when some of the details are far more certainly established than the course of the main events of which they form part. Moreover, though Voltaire generally avoids details, he can, at times, attach considerable importance to them. The chapters of anecdotes in the *Siècle* occupy far more space than those dealing with the arts and sciences. And in the *Essai* some details are emphasized because the author considers that they serve to characterize their age. Edward III's challenge to Philippe de Valois throws light on medieval chivalry, and the fact that Galeazzo Sforza was assassinated in a cathedral illustrates the moral state of Italy at that time.[4]

Voltaire's views on critical method are never set forth in detail

---

[1] xxix. 236.   [2] xxvii. 296–7.
[3] e.g. xi. 34; xiii. 173; and xxvii. 285–6.
[4] xii. 150 and 167.

in any one place. But aspects of them are to be found throughout his historical works and his critical pamphlets. They are not always consistent but, taken as a whole, they present a reasonably clear picture.

In the first place, he insists that the facts must be established before they are explained. He has learnt the lesson of Fontenelle's parable of the golden tooth in the *Histoire des oracles*. More than once he uses words akin to those of Fontenelle himself. Thus in the *Dictionnaire Philosophique* article 'Chronologie' he remarks:

> Lenglet répète après quelques autres que ... Jupiter, âgé de soixante et deux ans commença de régner en Thessalie; que son règne fut de soixante ans, qu'il épousa sa sœur Junon. ... Mais y a-t-il eu un Jupiter? C'est par là qu'il fallait commencer.[1]

But how are the facts to be established? Voltaire answers this question more than once; but never very thoroughly or very consistently. In the *Siècle* he has this to say:

> Quand des contemporains comme le cardinal de Retz et le duc de La Rochefoucauld, ennemis l'un de l'autre, confirment le même fait dans leurs mémoires, ce fait est indubitable: quand ils se contredisent, il faut douter.[2]

In the *Résumé* of the *Essai* he is somewhat more exacting:

> Croyons les événements attestés par les registres publics, par le consentement des auteurs contemporains, vivant dans une capitale, éclairés les uns par les autres, et écrivant sous les yeux des principaux de la nation.[3]

The *Philosophie de l'histoire*, speaking of ancient Greece, lays down the general principle that:

> On peut croire un peuple sur ce qu'il dit de lui-même à son désavantage, quand ces récits sont accompagnés de vraisemblance et qu'ils ne contredisent en rien l'ordre ordinaire de la nature.[4]

These statements have at least one thing in common—a lack of detail and precision. The first and last both suggest critical criteria which are reasonable enough but obviously very incomplete. There may well be occasions when enemies agree, and yet are both wrong; and national legends can be satirical as well as heroic. The second

---

[1] xviii. 178. See also xxvii. 251.   [2] xiv. 421.
[3] xiii. 175.   [4] xi. 72.

statement, on the other hand, demands a degree of confirmation which the author of the *Siècle* rarely achieved. This he admits himself in the *Supplément* to the *Siècle* where, in reply to the criticisms of La Beaumelle, he offers far greater concessions to unproven testimony:

Le critique [i.e. La Beaumelle], sans rien approfondir, se contente de mettre en note 'ouï-dire'. Mais une grande partie de l'histoire n'est fondée que sur des ouï-dire rassemblés et comparés.[1]

La Beaumelle is also the occasion of another of Voltaire's statements on the criteria by which a document may be judged. In his examination of La Beaumelle's edition of the Letters of Mme de Maintenon, he remarks that many of the dates are clearly false, and concludes:

cette infidélité pourrait donner de violents soupçons sur l'authenticité de ces lettres, si d'ailleurs on n'y reconnaissait pas un caractère de naturel et de vérité qu'il est presqu'impossible de contrefaire.[2]

Here the criterion is a psychological one: the impression of truth and sincerity conveyed by the writer. It is unfortunate that Voltaire chooses, to illustrate these qualities, a work which has since been shown to be largely a forgery.

Voltaire, then, does not suggest many methods by which the authenticity of an historical testimony can be proved, and those he does suggest differ markedly from each other. But it is characteristic of his debt to historical Pyrrhonism that when it is a question of showing a testimony to be false, he has many methods at his disposal. To begin with, he is aware of the extent to which history can be falsified by prejudiced writers or invented by the creators of anecdotes. In *Le Pyrrhonisme de l'histoire* he remarks that the whole history of seventeenth-century France might be completely distorted in a hundred years' time if the works to survive were spurious *Testaments* like those of Colbert or Louvois, and works like the *Mémoires de Mme de Maintenon* by La Beaumelle.[3] Such reflections lead him to doubt all testimonies and to subject all accounts to careful scrutiny.

The *Défense de mon oncle* suggests a number of courses open to the critic:

Il peut, s'il veut, faire voir le peu de foi qu'on doit à cet auteur, par

[1] xv. 109. [2] xiv. 469. [3] xxvii. 295.

l'intérêt que cet auteur a eu de mentir, et par le goût de son pays pour les fables; il peut montrer que l'auteur même est supposé. Mais ce qui le détermine le plus, c'est quand le livre est plein d'extravagances. . . .[1]

Voltaire also uses many other critical methods. He points to anachronisms which reveal the unreliability of a testimony, to internal contradictions in an account, to the lack of corroborative evidence where such evidence could reasonably be expected, and to geographical errors.[2] The variety of methods at his disposal may be illustrated by the article 'Genèse' in the *Dictionnaire Philosophique*. Here he bases his criticisms on contradictions within the text (the double creation of Eve), the scientific impossibility of the account (the waters above the firmament), the fact that the account appears to borrow from previously existing legends (e.g. the serpent and Adam), and the anachronism of its origin (the impossibility of its having been written by Moses).[3]

The main criterion to which he appeals in his criticism of historical testimony is that to which he gives the name of *vraisemblance*. What is *invraisemblable* is either what is 'scientifically' impossible (in this sense the concept has already been examined), or what is unlikely in view of prevailing psychological or material conditions. In *Le Pyrrhonisme de l'histoire*, for example, he asserts that the cruelty of the punishment inflicted on Queen Brunehaut is unbelievable to a reader 'qui pèse les vraisemblances',[4] that it is not even *vraisemblable* that the Maréchal d'Ancre, as a Florentine, should have been in league with Spain, the hereditary enemy of his native land.[5] Similarly, he refuses to believe that Alexander VI plotted to poison all his cardinals: 'je n'en crois rien; et ma grande raison c'est qu'elle [the story] n'est point du tout vraisemblable.'[6] And the repetitions of history likewise arouse his suspicions. It seems unreasonable that Caligula should write down on his tablets the names of people he intended to have executed, and then allow these tablets to fall into their hands. When the same story is told of two other Roman emperors, 'la chose devient alors ridicule, et indigne de toute croyance'.[7] And when he finds exactly the same story told of Peter the Great, Voltaire dismisses it with contemptuous mockery.[8]

---

[1] xxvi. 400.
[2] e.g. xxiv. 487; xiv. 347; xxvii. 243; and xix. 176.
[3] xix. 226 ff.   [4] xxvii. 269.   [5] xxvii. 291.
[6] xxvii. 294.   [7] xxvii. 264.   [8] xvi. 591.

All these methods of procedure are examples of applied common sense. They are not in themselves new, nor do they reveal a method in the sense of a systematic approach to the verification of a testimony. Voltaire's criticism is not so much a method as a series of almost spontaneous and instinctive critical flashes. He is content to prick a story with the rapier of his wit, and rarely deems it necessary to crush it under the hammer of rigorous and detailed investigation. And despite the sharpness of his rapier, one is often aware (as in the case of some of the examples quoted above), that its thrusts are not always as lethal as Voltaire himself appears to think.

But if his criticism is often superficial, it has two qualities which go a long way to atone for this weakness. In the first place it is never silent. Throughout the whole course of history he is constantly on the look-out for the improbable story, the uncorroborated and probably prejudiced accusation, the base slanders, and the pious frauds. It would be futile even to begin to list them, and the reader has but to turn to *Le Pyrrhonisme de l'histoire* to find a whole volume of them. Voltaire, of course, is not always right; still less can he always prove himself to be right. But if he raises more problems than he answers, he performs a great service even in raising the problems. The majority of the *philosophes*—Montesquieu, Rousseau, Mably—tend to build their systems on historical facts without ever making sure that the facts themselves are true. Voltaire alone is constantly reminding them of Fontenelle's dictum: 'assurons-nous bien du fait avant de nous inquiéter de la cause.'

The second characteristic of Voltaire's criticism is its total lack of respect for established authority. This is, of course, most clearly seen in his attitude to the Bible. But here his own religious views are too deeply involved for his historical criticism to remain impartial. Almost equally striking, however, is his attitude to the historians of antiquity. To the humanists, Roman history was almost as much revealed truth as the Bible itself. Not so to Voltaire. He has no new information with which to attack the accounts of Livy and Tacitus. Indeed, he does not appear to be acquainted with the work of more erudite sceptics like Beaufort. His criticisms are all based on the inherent improbability of the accounts of the historians and on their psychology as it is revealed in their works and in their lives. But he finds sufficient evidence here to make him doubt much of Roman history. Livy contains fantastic *contes* which weaken his authority, although he remains Voltaire's favourite among the Romans.[1] But Tacitus and Suetonius are much more severely dealt with. A whole section of *Le Pyrrhonisme de l'histoire* is entitled *De quelques faits rapportés dans Tacite et dans Suétone*.[2] In it Voltaire examines the accounts of the atrocities imputed to Tiberius, Caligula, and Nero by these historians. He refuses, on the basis of their unsupported testimony, to believe in the debauches of the octogenarian Tiberius or the similar horrors of Caligula. He suggests that those who had a republican spirit hated the emperors and, in consequence, that

le malin Tacite et le faiseur d'anecdotes Suétone goûtaient une grande consolation en décriant leur maître dans un temps où personne ne s'amusait à discuter la vérité.

And his conclusion is in his typical sceptical vein:

Je voudrais au moins que nos compilateurs modernes . . . se bornassent à dire modestement, 'on rapporte, le bruit court, on prétendait à Rome, on soupçonnait'. Cette manière de s'énoncer me semble infiniment plus honnête et plus raisonnable.

Voltaire has not finished with Tacitus. He speaks of him again in *Le Pyrrhonisme de l'histoire*, this time with reference to Nero. The atrocity of Nero's killing of his mother is almost unbelievable. He examines Tacitus' text in order to try to find evidence of exaggeration. Again, Tacitus' visible prejudice against the state of affairs in his own country leads Voltaire to doubt the veracity of his account of the Germans which, he claims, is obviously written to satirize Rome. Tacitus 'aimait encore mieux la satire que la vérité'.[3]

Suetonius is also criticized elsewhere;[4] and Dion Cassius and Petronius fare little better.[5] The effect of all these doubts is cumulative. Voltaire is not the first to be sceptical about some of the Roman historians;[6] but he is the first to present a picture to the non-specialist reader, in which this scepticism is predominant.

To the eighteenth-century historian seeking to interpret early human history, three relatively new lines of approach were avail-

---

[1] xvi. 125 and xlvi. 88.   [2] xxvii. 256 ff.
[3] xxvii. 258. See also the *Traité sur la tolérance*, xxv. 72, n. 1.
[4] e.g. xlvi. 314 and xxv. 47 and 170.
[5] xviii. 299 and xxvii. 261.
[6] See Hazard, *La Crise de la conscience européenne*, pp. 37 ff.

able. The first was to attempt to discover the true 'meaning' of fables. The second was to compare customs and institutions in an attempt to observe similarities or, better still, sources. The third was to seek information about the relations between peoples by comparing their languages. All three methods were largely speculative, for neither linguistics nor social anthropology could, in the eighteenth century, be termed a science. Voltaire's attitude to all three is an ambivalent one.

The predominant method of interpreting primitive religions and fables was the euhemerist method: that of assuming that fables were really transpositions and magnifications of actual historical events. It is found in Lenglet du Fresnoy, in Pezron, or in the abbé Banier's *Explication historique des fables*.[1] It survives well into the eighteenth century with men like Calmet and Hardion.[2] It is applied to Germanic as well as classical legend, and we find Rapin de Thoyras constructing a genealogical tree of the Saxon kings of England, going back to Woden and Friga.[3]

Parallel to this approach is the attempt to interpret both the myths and customs of antiquity by comparing them and attempting to deduce a common meaning. The attempt is made particularly by theologians wishing to demonstrate the historical truth of the Bible. Thus, Huet emphasizes the similarities between the biblical story of Moses and the legends of Bacchus, Minos, &c.[4] Similarly, Lafiteau compares the customs of the American Indians with those of the Bible and the ancient world in order to show that customs, too, have a common origin.[5]

If the majority of the *philosophes* reject these views, they nevertheless work on similar lines. Thus Mairan and De Guignes who, believing in the primacy of Egyptian culture, try to demonstrate the influence of the Egyptians on China, both base themselves to some extent on the work of Huet who, from a somewhat different starting-point, had arrived at similar conclusions.[6] A Christian *philosophe* like Turgot combines something of the orthodox view with the 'philosophic' thesis when he suggests that the Chaldeans

[1] See p. 4, n. 3.   [2] See p. 86.
[3] *Histoire d'Angleterre*, Appendix to vol. i.
[4] His argument is based to no small extent on linguistic evidence; see Flottes, *Étude sur Daniel Huet*, p. 95.
[5] *Mœurs des sauvages amériquains comparées aux mœurs des premiers temps* (1724).
[6] See Engemann, *Voltaire und China*, p. 105.

are the people from which culture first spreads and gives as his reason the fact that they are 'plus voisins de la source des premières traditions'—a reference, presumably, either to the Garden of Eden or to Mount Ararat.[1]

However, the devotees of comparative method also search for affinities between languages and linguistic usages, as well as for those between customs. In the sixteenth century Bodin and others had sought to prove that Hebrew was the original human speech, and Bochart, in the following century, had pursued a similar aim. The *philosophes* adapt similar methods to their own purposes with no less fantastic results. Thus De Guignes, in his *Mémoire dans lequel on prouve que les Chinois sont une colonie égyptienne* of 1758, bases his argument in part on similarities to be found between certain Chinese and certain Egyptian customs, and also on the assumption that Sesostris, who was reputed to have conquered the Orient, must have left some traces behind him.[2] But his conclusive piece of evidence is purely linguistic. He shows that the symbols for the names of the first four Chinese emperors, if interpreted in a certain way, yield the names of the first four kings of Thebes. This is sufficient evidence for him to conclude that early Chinese history is really early Egyptian history in disguise; that it was brought to China by Egyptian conquerors, and that the Chinese are, therefore, a colony of the Egyptians.

Less abstruse linguistic arguments also come into De Guignes's thesis. The fact that the Hoang river and the Nile were both called black is adduced as evidence of the connexion of the two peoples.[3] It is largely because of the accounts of the conquests of Sesostris that De Guignes is convinced of the primacy of the Egyptians. But Gentil de Barbinais, ignoring Sesostris, used similar evidence to prove the Egyptians a colony of the Chinese.[4]

Voltaire's attitude to these speculative methods is characterized by the same duality which is seen in his approach to other new ideas—to those of Montesquieu, for example. On the one hand, his cautious scepticism is unable to accept them *in toto*, and he ridicules their more extreme results. On the other hand, he often

[1] Turgot, *Œuvres*, ii. 599.
[2] These arguments are also advanced by Mairan in his *Lettres . . . au R. P. Parrenin* (1759).
[3] De Guignes, op. cit., p. 77.
[4] See Engemann, *Voltaire und China*, p. 106.

borrows from them without acknowledgement, and uses them for his own purposes.

He does not show great interest in the attempt to interpret fables; the article 'Fables' in the *Dictionnaire Philosophique* hardly touches on the problem, and in the *Remarques de l'Essai*, he is content to suggest that fables are the result of idleness, superstition and self-interest.[1] The *Essai* itself, however, and some of the articles of the *Dictionnaire Philosophique* offer a euhemerist explanation, asserting confidently that Orpheus, Minos, or Hercules are deified men.[2] But if Voltaire commits himself in practice, he is unwilling to do so in theory. In the *Essai* he concludes:

> On pourrait faire des volumes sur ce sujet: mais tous ces volumes se réduisent à deux mots: c'est que le gros du genre humain a été et sera très-longtemps insensé et imbécile; et que peut-être les plus insensés de tous ont été ceux qui ont voulu trouver un sens à ces fables absurdes, et mettre de la raison dans la folie.[3]

However, his attitude to the conclusions of the *comparatistes* is clearer. On more than one occasion he attacks Huet's views. In the *Lettres chinoises* he remarks that Huet was the first to suggest that the Egyptians had populated India and China, but adds that 'comme il avait imaginé aussi que Moïse était Bacchus, Adonis et Priape, son système ne persuada personne'.[4] In *Dieu et les hommes* he tries to suggest that it is really Bacchus who is the original of Moses.[5] And that he is equally opposed to the more 'philosophic' *comparatistes* is illustrated by his determined opposition to the idea of the primacy of Egyptian culture.

Yet though Voltaire uses the comparative method in a different way, it is obvious that he does use it. The main thesis of the *Philosophie de l'histoire* is that all religions are fundamentally the same, in that all teach the same morality, and all recognize, however dimly, the existence of a Supreme Being. Voltaire proves this precisely as do the *comparatistes*. He searches for what is common to all religious thought by examining each religion in turn, and comparing the results. Where he differs from the others is that he tries to work back to abstract principles of reason and morality rather than to particular customs. It is only when he is dealing with the Jews that

[1] xxiv. 584–5.
[2] xi. 15 and 74. See also the article 'Idole' (xix. 406).
[3] xi. 15.
[4] xxix. 475.
[5] xxviii. 185. See also the *Examen important* (xxvi. 202–3).

he does the opposite, and his desire to show that the Jews are not the source of all truth and morality leads him to try to prove that the Jews owe everything to someone else.[1] If the results are almost as preposterous as those of De Guignes, the fault is in the initial prejudice rather than in the comparative method itself.

It is in the preface to the *Histoire de Russie* that Voltaire deals most thoroughly with the application of linguistics to history, and especially with the work of Mairan and De Guignes. This preface is one of the best examples of his witty invective. He satirizes the methods of the linguists by using similar arguments to prove that the French are a colony of the Trojans or, alternatively, of the Greeks. The legend of the Trojan origin of the monarchy, the existence of the French city of Troyes, and similar evidence prove the first of these origins, and there are innumerable similarities of language and customs to prove the second.[2] The preface does not name the people at whom its satire is directed. In 1760, however, Voltaire writes to his friend Mairan, asserting that De Guignes is the intended victim.[3] It is doubtful, however, whether Mairan was satisfied with this assurance, since Voltaire uses formulas which are direct parodies of Mairan's own.[4]

A study of this preface would suggest that Voltaire is contemptuous of all historical arguments based on linguistic evidence. But in practice this is far from being the case. The *Dictionnaire Philosophique* contains many linguistic discussions. Some of them, such as the survey of the words for *esprit* in different European languages illustrate the complexity of linguistic problems.[5] But others have a more direct historical purpose. The word *esclave*, for example, is discussed in the *Dictionnaire Philosophique*, in the *Histoire de Russie*, and in the *Annales* in an attempt to throw light on the Slav invasions of Europe.[6] In the *Histoire de Russie* the assertion that the word *czar* has nothing to do with the Latin *Caesar* is probably linked with Voltaire's neglect of Byzantine influences on Russia.[7] In the same work he insists that the Laplanders are a separate race, having nothing in common with their neighbours the Finns, and enforces his argument by asserting that common objects have totally differ-

---

[1] e.g. *Dieu et les hommes* (xxviii. 189 ff.); *Épître aux Romains* (xxvii. 89); and the article 'Fables' (xix. 59–60).

[2] xvi. 381–4.   [3] xl. 497.

[4] Compare the *Lettres de M. de Mairan au R. P. Parrenin*, p. 47 with xvi. 381.

[5] xix. 14 ff.

[6] xiii. 271; xvi. 403; and xviii. 599–600.   [7] xvi. 421 and 473.

ent names in the two languages. But he thinks two examples quite sufficient to prove this.[1]

In his general reaction to these methods, then, he exhibits the type of attitude already seen elsewhere. An outburst of scepticism at what appears exaggerated or over-systematic is followed by the silent adoption, when occasion demands it, of the method condemned. On the whole he adopts a 'common-sense' attitude to the more extreme views of his contemporaries. But common sense is not always a satisfactory substitute for a more systematic approach.

Richelieu's Testament Politique

Voltaire's method is perhaps most clearly visible in relation to particular problems. And no historical problem occupies his attention more frequently than that of the authenticity of the *Testament Politique* attributed to the Cardinal de Richelieu. For over forty years, until the eve of his death, he attacks the work and those who accept it as genuine.

His original suspicion is not surprising. The so-called *Testaments* of Colbert and Louvois had been shown to be the work of Courtilz de Sandras.[2] The Richelieu *Testament* had been published in Amsterdam in 1688 with no indication as to its origin, and its authenticity had immediately been questioned by Richelieu's biographer, Aubéry. Opinion, as Louis André has shown in his edition of the work, remained fairly evenly divided between those who accepted and those who rejected it. But none of these early critics subjected the work to close scrutiny, and the controversy tended to die out.[3]

Such was the position when Voltaire intervened in the dispute. His first attack on the authenticity of the *Testament* was contained in the *Conseils à un journaliste* which were printed in the *Mercure* in 1744. In the *Conseils* he gives twelve reasons for refusing to believe that Richelieu was the author.[4]

The first three all deal with the circumstances of publication. The work is printed thirty years after the Cardinal's death without previous announcement; the editor has not disclosed the source of

---

[1] xvi. 400.
[2] These had been published in 1693 and 1695.
[3] *Testament Politique* (ed. L. André), pp. 47–50.
[4] xxii. 258–60.

his manuscript nor is there any evidence that the manuscript was known to Richelieu's heirs.

Examination of the *Testament* itself increases Voltaire's doubts. He asserts (though without offering any evidence) that the style is different from that of the known works of Richelieu. The form of its signature is one never used by the cardinal. And it contains expressions and ideas 'peu convenables à un grand ministre qui parle à un grand roi'. Moreover, it contains contradictions both with itself and with the known facts. How could Richelieu have said that 'Dès qu'il fut appelé au conseil, il promit au roi d'abaisser ses ennemis, les huguenots et les grands du royaume', when it is known that Richelieu's original role in the *Conseil* was a very minor one? How could a man with the Cardinal's knowledge claim that, without extraordinary measures, the country spent annually during the war nearly double its peace-time income? And how could he mistake 'au denier cinq' (meaning 20 per cent.) for 5 per cent.? Could the real Cardinal have spoken of the *Parlements* as 'cours souveraines'? Could he have suggested suppressing the *gabelles*? And how could he, in the midst of war, entitle a chapter 'Succincte narration des actions du roi jusqu'à la paix'?

The argument of the *Conseils* is, however, only a preliminary skirmish. Voltaire continues to refer to the *Testament* in his correspondence, informing D'Olivet, for example, that he has good reason for attributing the work to Silhon, and that the abbé de Bourzeis has nothing whatever to do with it.[1] He then writes to Thiériot asking for copies of Silhon's other works. But three months later he has completely revised his opinion, and writes to d'Argenson affirming that: 'Je crois, en dépit de toute l'Académie française, que cet ouvrage fut fait par l'abbé de Bourzeis dont j'ai cru reconnaître le style.'[2]

Such a volte-face does not inspire confidence in his powers of stylistic analysis. But he is not yet having to defend his position, for the publication of the *Conseils* passes unnoticed. It is not till ten years later that he deals publicly with the *Testament* again. His new attack is prompted by the republicaion of the work, which appeared in 1749 in a *Recueil* of testaments, among which was that of Colbert. By this time, Voltaire's disbelief in the authenticity of the work has hardened.

His new criticisms appear first in *Des mensonges imprimés*, pub-

[1] xxxv. 207.   [2] xxxv. 290.

lished as a supplement to the edition of *Sémiramis* in 1749. In the following year, this time as a supplement to *Oreste*, there appeared an expanded version of the same work together with a more detailed attack on the *Testament* entitled *Raisons de croire que le livre intitulé 'Testament Politique du Cardinal de Richelieu' est un ouvrage supposé.*[1]

The *Raisons de croire* open with a declaration of the author's reasons for undertaking the work:

> Mon zèle pour la vérité, mon emploi d'historiographe de France qui m'oblige à des recherches historiques, mes sentiments de citoyen, mon respect pour le fondateur d'un corps dont je suis membre, mon attachement aux héritiers de son nom et de son mérite: voilà mes motifs pour chercher à détromper ceux qui attribuent au cardinal de Richelieu un livre qui m'a paru n'être ni pouvoir être de ce ministre.

Such a statement of motives hardly serves to create in the reader's mind a feeling of confidence in the impartiality of the author. Yet Voltaire appears to be completely unaware of this.

He begins, once again, with the external aspects of the work. The title itself is suspect, since 'Un homme qui parle à son maître n'intitule guère ses conseils respectueux du nom fastueux de *Testament politique*.' Moreover, after the cardinal's death, many works appeared, both in praise of and in condemnation of his administration. Voltaire claims to possess at least two of them with the title *Testamentum politicum*. These, he suggests, are the probable origin of later forgeries.

More important is the total absence of any reference to the work by the Cardinal himself, by the king, or by contemporaries. If Richelieu had really written such a work, 'il l'eût légué au roi comme un présent beaucoup plus précieux que le palais cardinal'. It will be seen that this objection, reasonable in itself, seems to contradict the first one. But Voltaire continues to amass further criticisms.

Turning to the work itself he begins by examining the question of its date. A statement that the war had lasted five years would suggest that the *Testament* was written in 1640. But it is almost unbelievable that the author, if he were writing at that date, should omit even to mention the birth of the dauphin two years earlier. The author, then, 'oubliant qu'il a feint d'écrire en 1639 et en 1640, s'avise ensuite d'écrire en 1635'. And the style of the work, too,

[1] xxiii. 443 ff.

could not conceivably be that of the cardinal. There are rhetorical flourishes 'dignes d'un professeur de rhétorique dans le seizième siècle ou d'un répétiteur irlandais qui dispute sur les bancs'; there is the recommendation to chastity which the licentious Richelieu would never have dared to make to the ascetic Louis XIII; there is the statement 'Vous êtes parvenu à la conclusion de la paix', although peace is not concluded till eight years later. And Voltaire notes that the author writes of a diminution in the number of Church benefices held by laymen, although this diminution did not take place until the reign of Louis XIV. He also writes against the 'droit de régale', though Richelieu himself appears to have upheld this right.

In the final series of the *Raisons de croire* Voltaire returns to the external history of the work. He rejects the affirmation of its authenticity furnished by Le Long. This is not accompanied by any proof and is contradicted by other authorities—Aubéri, Ancillon, Vigneul de Marville, and La Monnoie. Similarly, he is unimpressed by the story that, in 1664, the abbé des Roches, a former servant of Richelieu, gave his library to the Sorbonne and that in it was a manuscript conforming to the printed *Testament*:

C'est ce manuscrit même, remis à la Sorbonne, qui achève de prouver l'imposture. Il est remis vingt-deux ans après la mort du cardinal, sans aucun renseignement, sans la moindre indication de la part de l'abbé des Roches.

A more prudent critic might at least have thought of having the manuscript examined. But Voltaire is becoming more polemical. He is content to pour ridicule on a final piece of evidence:

On dit qu'on disait, il y a soixante et dix ans, que madame la duchesse d'Aiguillon avait dit, il y a quatre-vingts ans, qu'elle avait eu une copie manuscrite de cet ouvrage. On a trouvé une note marginale de M. Huet; et cette note dit qu'on avait vu le manuscrit chez madame d'Aiguillon, nièce du cardinal. Ne voilà-t-il pas de belles preuves?

However, the substitution of irony for reason at this juncture is probably very significant. In these last few points Voltaire is already replying to his critics.

The *Raisons de croire* of 1750 slightly expand the criticisms already made in the *Mensonges imprimés* of 1749. But between the two works there appeared Léon Ménard's *Réfutation du sentiment de M. de Voltaire*. Ménard, a member of the Académie des Inscriptions, criticizes particularly Voltaire's assertion that nothing is known about the history of the manuscript of the *Testament*. He refuses to believe that Richelieu's heirs were ignorant of its existence. He points to the existence of the Sorbonne copy which came from the abbé des Roches. He claims that the style of the *Testament* is the same as that of Richelieu's other works, though, like Voltaire, he offers no evidence.[1]

The *Mémoires de Trévoux* of February 1750 contain a review of Ménard's work. The anonymous reviewer writes approvingly and adds further evidence of his own to establish the authenticity of the *Testament*. Firstly, a second manuscript, once owned by the abbé de Rothelin, is in existence. The existence of two, or possibly three, manuscripts suggests it is unlikely that the publishers forged the document, especially as they appear to have used the least accurate manuscript. Further, the author draws attention to the existence of a note in Huet's copy of the *Testament* which says that the duc de Richelieu had informed him that he had often seen the manuscript.[2]

Voltaire does not refer to these criticisms directly, but it seems clear that he has read them both, and that the last of the *Raisons de croire* are written to refute them. They are possibly added to the work just before going to press, which may account for their lack of cogency.

But a more thorough refutation of Voltaire's criticisms appears in 1750 in the form of a *Lettre sur le Testament Politique du cardinal de Richelieu* by the erudite historian Foncemange, member of the Académie des Inscriptions, and friend of Gibbon. It is a letter which, as the *Journal des Savants* remarks, is written with 'cette politesse douce et honnête qui doit caractériser les gens de lettres'.[3] But it is none the less effective for this.

In his refutation, Foncemange follows, point by point, the argument put forward by Voltaire in the *Mensonges imprimés*. It is no proof of forgery, he asserts, that the work is only published long after it was written: the same is true of, for example, the *Mémoires* of Retz. Moreover, there is evidence concerning the history of the manuscript which Voltaire has overlooked. There is P. Le Long's statement that there were two copies of the *Testament*, one of which went to the king and the other, with the rest of Richelieu's papers,

[1] Menard, op. cit., pp. 5, 9, and 10.
[2] *Mémoires de Trévoux* (Feb. 1750), pp. 344 ff.
[3] *Journal des Savants* (June 1750), p. 441.

to the duchesse d'Aiguillon. And of this second manuscript further copies were taken. Foncemange asserts that two at least of these are in Paris, and that he also knows of the existence of others.

He then proceeds to answer Voltaire's criticisms of the text itself. Some are easily disposed of. The objection to the signature 'Armand du Plessis', for example, falls when the manuscripts are found to have no signature. The signature is clearly a copyist's or a printer's addition. The same is true of the date of the signing of peace, which has been left blank in the manuscripts. The style of the *Testament*, and particularly the disparagement of contemporaries, which Voltaire had considered unworthy of the cardinal, are shown to be typical of him. And, moreover, Voltaire has seen disparagement where none was intended. He has objected, for example, to the adjective 'pauvre' applied to the Duke of Mantua. Foncemange shows that the adjective is highly applicable to the situation of the duke, who was on the point of losing his capital, and that it should be interpreted in this sense. Voltaire has objected to the use of the term 'la Reine' for 'la Reine-mère' and to the familiarity of 'la Fargis' for the marquise du Fargis. Foncemange gives examples, including some from Richelieu's own *Journal*, to show that there is nothing unusual in these expressions.

His quotations show, in general, a scholarly approach which is in marked contrast to that of Voltaire, who never gives precise references. It is not without a certain malice that Foncemange observes: 'Comme M. de Voltaire ne cite point, je suis réduit à deviner sur quoi tombent ses objections. Vous verrez la même chose dans toute cette lettre.'

Careful study of the text is often enough to enable Foncemange to refute Voltaire's objections. This is the case, for example, with the apparent contradiction between revenue and expenditure in the first years of war. It is the case with Richelieu's recommendation of chastity, which Foncemange shows to be quite general in intention and to have no specific message for Louis XIII himself. And if 'au denier cinq' for 5 per cent. is a real slip, it is a slip which could easily be made by anyone, as 'au denier dix' is 10 per cent.

Foncemange, too, has a greater historical erudition which enables him to refute other points of Voltaire's. Thus Voltaire stigmatizes the whole ninth chapter of the *Testament* as the work of an ignorant 'faiseur de projets'. Foncemange shows that in fact most of the chapter is borrowed from Sully. Equally, he proves that the 'affaire des comptants', which, according to Voltaire, only became prominent at the time of Fouquet's disgrace, was in fact already important before the time of Richelieu.[1]

The controversy arouses considerable interest. Raynal notes in the *Nouvelles littéraires*: 'Notre nation qui se passionne souvent pour des objets frivoles, vient de se partager avec beaucoup de vivacité sur une question assez peu importante.'[2] And he follows this with an account of the controversy. He himself leans strongly towards Voltaire's point of view, and dismisses the existence of the Sorbonne manuscript as a 'préjugé'! And Voltaire, for the time being at any rate, has the last word, for Foncemange does not reply to the *Raisons de croire*, judging, as he later says, that he has already answered all that was important in Voltaire's argument.

In 1764, however, Foncemange persuaded Mme d'Egmont, who had inherited the Richelieu papers, to have a new edition of the *Testament* printed.[3] This edition was accompanied by an appendix consisting of a greatly enlarged version of Foncemange's letter of 1750. Moreover, the editor, Marin, adds his own refutation of Voltaire's point of view. Though noting that Voltaire's doubts have had the salutary effect of stimulating the defenders of the *Testament* to produce a more accurate text, he rejects Voltaire's arguments, asserting that there was a constant tradition in the Richelieu family to the effect that the cardinal was the author of the work, and stating that four manuscripts of the *Testament* have now been discovered, as well as a continuation of the first chapter ('Succincte Narration') which contains notes in the handwriting of the cardinal himself.[4]

Foncemange's letter, in its expanded form, is an even more thorough refutation of Voltaire's argument.[5] And Foncemange begins by carrying the war into the enemy camp. To illustrate his contention that minor factual errors in the *Testament* are no proof that the work is a forgery, he quotes examples from the *Essai sur les mœurs* of similar mistakes, and concludes, with a touch of irony:

Au reste, comme M. de Voltaire ne cite jamais ses garants, on ignore

[1] *Lettre sur le 'Testament Politique' du cardinal de Richelieu.*
[2] *Correspondance littéraire*, i. 393.
[3] André, op. cit., p. 52.
[4] *Maximes d'État ou 'Testament Politique' du cardinal de Richelieu* (1674), preface.
[5] *Lettre sur le 'Testament Politique'* (1764), pp. 71 ff.

si c'est à lui ou aux écrivains qu'il a consultés qu'on doit imputer les fautes qui ont pu lui échapper.

As before, Foncemange makes good use of his erudition. He shows that the abuse of laymen possessing ecclesiastical benefices had already decreased in Richelieu's time, and that Voltaire is therefore wrong in asserting that because the author refers to this as something in the past, he is therefore writing at a much later date. And one argument which Voltaire introduced with the words 'en voici une qui est sans réplique' is shown to depend on his having mistaken a nephew for his uncle. Similarly, Richelieu's promise to the king to 'relever son nom' on his entry into the *Conseil* is understandable because of Richelieu's rapid rise to power, his pride, and his desire to pass over the period before he had attained power.

Foncemange then proceeds to the more positive side of his argument. He sets out to show that the *Testament* is both a convincing autobiographical document and a fine political treatise. However, he makes one concession, on which Voltaire is to seize. He concedes that certain parts of the work, to judge by the display of erudition which is contained in them, are not by Richelieu himself, but by secretaries.

To these new criticisms Voltaire replies with considerable alacrity. Three works, the *Doutes nouveaux sur le Testament attribué au cardinal de Richelieu*, the *Nouveaux Doutes*, which supplement them, and a *Lettre écrite depuis l'impression des Doutes*, which is, in fact, published with them, appear together in the last months of 1764.

With the discovery of the manuscripts, and especially of one annotated in Richelieu's own hand, the basis of the debate has clearly altered. If the authenticity of one of them can be established, then minor errors or infidelities in the printed text cease to be of crucial importance. But Voltaire does not seem altogether aware of the new situation. After insinuating that Foncemange himself is really in doubt as to the authenticity of the *Testament*, and quoting as evidence his admission that part of the work may have been written by someone other than the cardinal, he goes on to repeat the list of all those who, even before his own intervention, have doubted the authenticity of the work. Aubéry's testimony, in particular, he sees as irrefutable, for Aubéry was working under the direction of the duchesse d'Aiguillon, and it seems inconceivable that, if she were aware of the existence of the *Testament*, she would not have informed him of the fact when he denied the authenticity of the 1688 edition. Voltaire proceeds to quote some of Aubéry's objections, which he has already used elsewhere.

Yet his tone has become more conciliatory. 'Je fais lire la lettre de M. de Foncemange, je dicte mes doutes, et je lui demande des éclaircissements', he asserts, and, in particular, he begs Foncemange to make quite sure that it is in fact Richelieu's handwriting which has been discovered on one of the manuscripts. Not that he is willing to accept this as proof of authorship. His own *Histoire de la guerre de 1741* has marginal notes by the comte d'Argenson; but this hardly proves that D'Argenson wrote the work. He is, however, now forced to abandon some of his earlier arguments. But his method of doing so is not very honest. Foncemange has refuted two of his points, regarding the 'million d'or' and the 'affaire des comptants'. These points were made in the *Mensonges imprimés*, the text which Foncemange was using for his earlier criticisms. The passage in the *Mensonges imprimés* dealing with the *Testament* was, however, cut out of the 1751 edition of Voltaire's works, probably because most of its points already appeared in the *Conseils à un journaliste*. In the *Doutes nouveaux*, however, Voltaire, no longer capable of defending these arguments, adopts the alternative course of implying that he has never made them. He refers Foncemange to the 1757 edition of his works (where, of course, these arguments no longer appear):

Il aurait vu que, dans cette édition, il n'est point question des millions d'or dont il parle. Ne mêlons point des bagatelles à l'essentiel de la cause: des discussions inutiles détournent des grands objets: allons toujours au fait principal dans toute affaire.

In the rest of his reply he often avoids the criticisms of Foncemange himself, and instead reiterates his previous objections, repeats his assertion that the *Testament* was the work of the abbé de Bourzeis, and lists once again all the small errors of fact which would never have been made by the cardinal, asserting that they add up to a practical certainty.[1]

The *Lettre écrite depuis l'impression des Doutes* is, in general, even more conciliatory in tone, and also somewhat vaguer. The whole dispute, Voltaire suggests, is futile: 'Il n'importe guère de qui soit un livre pourvu qu'il soit bon.' He has been led to his suspicions by

[1] xxv. 277–306.

other forgeries—including testaments of Louvois, Colbert, and the duc de Lorraine. 'Les testaments politiques sont devenus si fort à la mode qu'on a fait enfin celui de Mandrin.' And he adds his own reasons for rejecting these other testaments, concluding, with Montaigne, that the only reasonable course in the face of all these errors is to doubt.[1]

But he is not willing for this to be his final answer. Almost immediately after the *Lettre* he writes the *Arbitrage entre M. de Voltaire et M. de Foncemange*,[2] which is published anonymously at the end of 1764 or early the following year. Here, in effect, he is trying to accept defeat and yet retain most of his positions. He begins by attempting, as he has already done in the *Lettre*, to widen, and thereby to confuse, the subject under debate:

> Le sujet qui les divise paraît très important: il s'agit de savoir non-seulement si le plus grand ministre qu'ait eu la France est l'auteur du *Testament Politique*, mais encore s'il est digne de lui. . . .

He then makes a significant concession to Foncemange. He admits that the 'Succincte Narration' (the first chapter of the *Testament*) is probably by Richelieu or approved by Richelieu, as is suggested by the presence of the cardinal's notes on the manuscript; though the fact that Richelieu never signed the manuscript suggests that it contained many things of which he did not approve. But as for the rest of the work (the *Testament* proper) it has no necessary connexion with the 'Succincte Narration' and is probably the work of the abbé de Bourzeis, who has later joined the two together.

With this partial, but only partial, admission of error, Voltaire ends his last work on the *Testament*. But it is far from being his last reference to the *Testament*, for in many later writings, and in his correspondence, he often goes out of his way to denounce the work as a forgery with all the vehemence of his earliest pronouncements on the subject.[3]

What conclusions can be drawn from this long controversy?

In the first place it is now generally accepted that Voltaire was wrong, and that the *Testament* was genuine, though genuine in the sense that it was edited rather than written by the cardinal himself. But the evidence for this conclusion, which may be found in the

[1] xxv. 306–8.   [2] xxv. 321–34.
[3] e.g. xiii. 31; xv. 561; xvi. 17; xix. 30; and xlv. 550.

introduction to Hanotaux's edition of the *Maximes d'état et fragments politiques du cardinal de Richelieu*, was for the most part not available either to Voltaire or to his opponents.

Yet there is one source of evidence probably available to Voltaire which he appears to ignore deliberately. He insists that Richelieu's heirs were unaware of the existence of a testament. Yet others who interrogate the Richelieu family receive a different reply. Huet and Ménard are both assured of the authenticity of the work, and Mme de Genlis later tells of a conversation between herself and Mme d'Egmont, daughter of the maréchal de Richelieu:

> Elle m'a confirmé dans l'opinion que j'avais sur le *Testament* du cardinal de Richelieu. Elle nous a dit que le maréchal de Richelieu avait écrit et répété à Voltaire qu'il était inconcevable qu'il s'obstinât à revoquer en doute *l'acte le plus authentique dont l'original existait*, etc. Mais qu'à tout cela, Voltaire avait répondu qu'à cette occasion, la vérité était si peu vraisemblable, qu'il ne se rétracterait point.[1]

The anecdote may be apocryphal. But its concluding aphorism does seem to correspond fairly accurately with Voltaire's final position on the issue. And as he is unwilling to submit to the arguments of Foncemange, it may be that he has already refused to accept the assurances of the duc de Richelieu. But how is this attitude to be explained?

Three questions appear to be involved. Firstly, how reasonable are his original objections to the *Testament*? Secondly, how far is he guilty of unreasonable stubbornness in refusing to admit his error? And thirdly, can this refusal be attributed to external causes —to his dislike of the cardinal himself, or of his policies, or to his desire to further a 'liberal' cause?

Voltaire's original suspicions are reasonable enough. The *Testament* is published with no indications as to its origin at a time when forgeries are frequent, and its authenticity is denied by Richelieu's official biographer, Aubéry, who could reasonably have been expected to be aware of the existence of a testament if such a work were among the treasured possessions of the Richelieu family. Aubéry's own objections are the starting-point of those of Voltaire. But Voltaire soon finds new objections of his own, and his ever-present critical sense is quick to spot errors, anachronisms, and other *invraisemblances* in the text.

[1] André, op. cit., p. 459.

And yet a comparison of his work with that of Foncemange soon lays bare the incompleteness of his method. So many of his arguments reveal that he does not know the history of the first half of the seventeenth century, that he is scarcely acquainted with the writings of Richelieu's contemporaries, and that he is constantly assuming that the standards of politeness and accuracy of his own age applied equally rigorously a century before. And when, faced with Foncemange's arguments, his attitude hardens, he becomes more obviously prejudiced, refusing to admit that Richelieu's own heirs have proclaimed the *Testament* authentic, and resorting to various tricks in order to repel the assaults of his adversary.

The latter stages of the argument are marked by two opposing tendencies on Voltaire's part. The one is to accept the evidence put before him (particularly that drawn from the discovery of the various manuscripts), and admit that he was wrong. He does this to the extent of agreeing in the *Arbitrage* (though, be it noted, not under his own name) that the 'Succincte Narration', at least, may be attributed to the cardinal. But in contrast to this reasonableness, his determination not to give way completely appears to stiffen, and he continues to denounce the *Testament* as a whole. And a third tendency, already visible in his early writings on the subject, becomes more pronounced in the later ones : the tendency to refuse to separate the question of the authenticity of the *Testament* from the question of its value as a political treatise.

Is this the real reason for Voltaire's consistent opposition? This has more than once been suggested. Grimm, for example, writing in the *Correspondance littéraire* at the time of the controversy, suggests that Voltaire refuses to believe the work authentic because he finds it stupid, whilst he thinks Richelieu himself wise. Grimm believes in the authenticity of the *Testament*, but not in its value.[1] Similarly, Louis André, in his edition of the *Testament*, finds a political reason behind Voltaire's intransigence: that of his fundamental opposition to absolutism and to those who founded it in France.[2]

Both these points of view probably represent an aspect of the truth. Yet neither carries complete conviction. In the first place, although as an Academician, and as a protégé of the maréchal de Richelieu, Voltaire frequently praises the cardinal, his real attitude,

---

[1] *Correspondance littéraire*, vi. 148–54.
[2] André, op. cit., p. 52.

as many of his writings testify, is one of profound hostility.[1] He can even say, with reference to the *Testament* controversy: 'Au reste je hais tant la tyrannie du cardinal de Richelieu, que je souhaiterais que le *Testament* fût de lui, afin de le rendre ridicule à la dernière postérité.'[2] It cannot, then, be admiration for Richelieu which makes Voltaire reject the *Testament*. Nor can it be deference to Richelieu's heirs, since they insist that the work is genuine.

Can it be, as André suggests, that Voltaire attacks the *Testament* because he wishes to discredit its absolutist doctrines? This hardly seems likely, since he could attack the doctrines of a genuine *Testament* just as effectively as those of a forgery. Moreover, Voltaire's opposition to absolutism is itself by no means absolute. And an investigation of exactly what he is criticizing in the *Testament* does not reveal a fundamental opposition between an autocratic Richelieu and a liberal Voltaire. Indeed, the correspondence between Voltaire and Gamonet, which André publishes, reveals a Voltaire defending feudal privileges against the egalitarian suggestions of the *Testament* itself.[3] It is not that Voltaire is opposed to Richelieu's principles and wishes to attack them. It is rather that he does not even understand them and regards them as nonsensical. In his references to Richelieu's remarks about the 'reign of God' or the future of the Sainte-Chapelle, he reveals not a reasoned hostility but a complete failure to understand how any sensible man can waste time discussing such things when he ought to be talking politics.[4]

That Voltaire's attitude is not purely that of the 'philosophical' propagandist is shown also by the way in which he rejects the anti-clerical grist which the *Testament* brings to his mill. The cardinal, for example, warns the king against the increased power of the Jesuits. Far from being delighted with this warning, Voltaire refuses to accept its authenticity, asserting that Richelieu could never have made such a statement when the Huguenots constituted a far more serious threat.[5]

On the whole it does not seem true to say that Voltaire's attitude

[1] In his Notebooks, Voltaire speaks of Richelieu as 'vindicatif, impérieux, sanguinaire' and criticizes him strongly. See *Voltaire's Notebooks* (ed. Besterman), pp. 111 and 318–19.
[2] xlv. 550.
[3] André, op. cit., pp. 488–506.
[4] xxv. 292 and 298–9.   [5] xxiii. 450–1.

to the *Testament* results from any definite political or 'philosophic' considerations. Rather is it due to a lack of any sense of historical relativity. Constantly, but unconsciously, Voltaire judges the seventeenth century by eighteenth-century standards. Hence a conclusion like 'Le *Testament* du cardinal de Richelieu n'est pas d'un homme poli', because he writes of a lady of the court as 'la Fargis'; hence his amazement at high-flown phrases like 'le roi d'Espagne, en secourant les Huguenots, avait rendu les Indes tributaires de l'Enfer' or 'les éléments n'ont de pesanteur que lorsqu'ils sont en leur lieu'.[1] Voltaire fails to make any allowance for changes in speech, customs, and mental attitudes which have taken place in the century or more between the writing of the *Testament* and his own criticisms.

The controversy over the *Testament*, then, reveals both sides of Voltaire's historical criticism. It reveals his deep scepticism and his acute and incisive logical approach. But it reveals, too, his superficiality, his lack of really profound historical erudition, and, above all, a lack of a full sense of historical relativism, a complete failure to conceive of, or believe in, ways of thought different from those of his own age. And this same duality is visible throughout his historical work.

Form and style

On exige des historiens modernes plus de détails, des faits plus constatés, des dates précises, des autorités, plus d'attention aux usages, aux lois, aux mœurs, au commerce, à la finance, à l'agriculture, à la population: il en est de l'histoire comme des mathématiques et de la physique; la carrière s'est prodigieusement accrue.[2]

Voltaire is perhaps not fully aware of the extent to which these new demands necessarily imply a change in the form of historical writing. For he can still envisage history, as did the humanists, as being first and foremost a work of art. More than once, for example, he insists that history should be presented as drama. To D'Argenson he writes in 1740:

Il faut, dans une histoire, comme dans une pièce de théâtre, exposition, nœud, et dénouement.[3]

[1] xvii. 210–11 and xxiii. 448.   [2] xix. 365.
[3] xxxv. 374.

And to Schouvalow, explaining the plan of the *Histoire de Russie*, he asserts:

> J'ai toujours pensé que l'histoire demande le même art que la tragédie, une exposition, un nœud, un dénouement, et qu'il est nécessaire de présenter tellement toutes les figures du tableau, qu'elles fassent voir le principal personnage, sans affecter jamais l'envie de le faire valoir.[1]

As late as 1773 he writes to Marin in similar terms.[2] And one of his last words on history, appearing in a letter to Frederick the Great in 1778, is the apparently disillusioned conclusion that

> Pour l'histoire, ce n'est, après tout, qu'une gazette; la plus vraie est remplie de faussetés et elle ne peut avoir de mérite que celui du style.[3]

It is hardly surprising, in view of the frequency with which this view is expressed, that some critics have tended to see in it the theory behind Voltaire's practice of history.[4] But to do so is to disregard entirely the whole tendency of development of his work. The early *Histoire de Charles XII* has some affinity with tragedy. Lanson has suggested that the narrative part of the *Siècle* has a similar form.[5] But even if this is true, Voltaire has destroyed the dramatic effect of the work as a whole by making the last part of it a series of purely descriptive chapters on arts, sciences, and religious affairs. And in the *Essai sur les mœurs*, the *Histoire du Parlement*, the *Annales de l'Empire*, and the *Précis du Siècle de Louis XV* there is no hint of such dramatic construction. Even in the *Histoire de Russie* the narrative of the life of the emperor is subordinated to the description of society.

Moreover, it is not only in his overall plan that Voltaire breaks with the humanists. He does so equally in matters of detail. In the first place, he makes repeated attacks on three features typical of the humanist historians—harangues, portraits, and anecdotes.

Harangues were regarded by the later humanists themselves with some disfavour,[6] and even the *Histoire de Charles XII* is free from all but the shortest reported speeches. Voltaire's opposition,

---

[1] xxxix. 470.   [2] xlviii. 398.   [3] l. 338.

[4] e.g. Bellessort, *Essai sur Voltaire*, p. 207, and Thompson, *A History of Historical Writing*, ii. 66.

[5] Lanson, *Voltaire*, pp. 118–19.

[6] Fénelon (*Lettre à l'Académie*, p. 128) is sceptical, whilst Daniel (see p. 27) is openly hostile. But Rapin de Thoyras can still quote the harangue of a Breton ambassador to the invading Saxons, and excuse himself by saying that it does not appear to 'pécher contre la vraisemblance' (*Histoire d'Angleterre*, i. 92).

however, becomes more pronounced. In the *Supplément* to the *Siècle*, he insists that harangues should be totally omitted, asserting that there are only two examples of direct speech in the *Siècle* itself, and that both these speeches were actually made.[1] Further criticism appears in the *Dictionnaire Philosophique* article 'Histoire', in the *Annales*, and elsewhere.[2] In all these works Voltaire rejects the fabrication of harangues as being contrary to the spirit of truth which should be that of history.

Portraits are similarly rejected. The article 'Histoire' is willing to allow portraits of contemporaries, but it is ridiculous for the historian to produce those of people he has never seen.[3] This is emphasized in the preface to the *Histoire de Russie*, where Voltaire pours scorn on Sarrasin's portrait of Wallenstein. In the *Supplément* to the *Siècle* he indignantly takes La Beaumelle to task for having dared to suggest that the *Siècle* itself should have contained more portraits. And further criticism is to be found in the preface to the 1754 edition of the *Essai*.[4]

On the whole anecdotes are equally strongly condemned. We have seen that they played a considerable part in the *Histoire de Charles XII*. They are still prominent in the *Siècle*, but Voltaire feels it necessary to excuse their presence there with a special plea: 'Louis XIV mit dans sa cour, comme dans son règne, tant d'éclat et de magnificence, que les moindres détails de sa vie semblent intéresser la postérité.'[5] And usually he has no time for such trivial details, as can be seen from his ironical comments on the *Mémoires* of Dangeau which are full of them.[6] Moreover, he is equally convinced that the majority of anecdotes are false. This is emphasized in the article 'Anecdotes' in the *Dictionnaire Philosophique*, in the letter *À M.* * * * *sur les anecdotes*, and in many other places.[7]

It is not surprising that the imaginative reconstructions of the historical novelist infuriate him even more. He finds them in the work of La Beaumelle, and in the *Lettre à l'auteur des Honnêtetés littéraires* he protests indignantly:

> On voit à chaque page un homme qui parle au hasard d'un pays qu'il n'a jamais connu, et qui ne songe qu'à faire un roman.

[1] xv. 124.   [2] xix. 361–2; xiii. 503; and xxv. 185.
[3] xix. 362.   [4] xvi. 388; xv. 122; and xxiv. 47.
[5] xiv. 422.   [6] xxviii. 251 ff.
[7] xviii. 193 ff. and xxix. 407. See also xvi. 385 and xxxix. 70.

'Mademoiselle de La Vallière, dans un déshabille léger, s'était jetée dans un fauteuil: là elle pensait à loisir à son amant; souvent le jour la retrouvait assise sur une chaise, accoudée sur une table, l'œil fixe dans l'extase de l'amour.'

Hé, mon ami, l'as-tu vue dans ce déshabille léger? l'as-tu vue accoudée sur cette table? est-il permis d'écrire ainsi l'histoire?[1]

All these criticisms are aimed at the various kinds of untruthfulness which characterize humanist historiography. But if Voltaire succeeds in defending and preserving factual truth, nevertheless, in rejecting the descriptive and anecdotal he is largely destroying the life and colour of history. The *Histoire de Charles XII* has been shown to be the least typical of his histories. The whole trend of his later development is away from the sort of approach it typifies. Yet the fact that some critics can think of it as his best work suggests that this later development was perhaps misdirected.

For it is not just the anecdote which is absent from Voltaire's later historical work: it is man himself, the living individual, facing the problems of his age and deciding his course of action. In the preface to the *Histoire de Russie* Voltaire asserts that it is no part of his task to pry into the inner secrets or motives of Peter the Great.[2] In this particular instance, this is a prudent way of avoiding saying anything which might embarrass his Russian patrons. But it is not only in the *Histoire de Russie* that he fails to bring his characters to life. Indeed, he hardly ever succeeds. The accumulation of anecdotes about Louis XIV helps to give some picture of the king, but this is because of their own intrinsic value, and is not the result of illuminating comment from Voltaire himself. Even Charles XII and Peter the Great remain figures seen from outside; characters in a swift-moving adventure story rather than beings whose real personality is revealed. And other individuals in whom Voltaire is deeply interested, Cromwell, Richelieu, or Mahomet, for example, are never comprehended except in the most mechanistic terms.

This is not the fault of Voltaire's theory. It results from his general lack of psychological insight, visible in his *contes* and dramas, and in his tendency to assume that everyone who does not think as he does is either a fool or a hypocrite. But the weakness is a serious one in an historian. If Collingwood is right, and the historian's task is to rethink the thoughts of the past, then Voltaire

[1] xxvi. 162.   [2] xvi. 385.

is hardly an historian at all. And not only does he fail to penetrate the mind of the individual; he is no more successful in dealing with that of the group. S. G. Tallentyre's assertion, with reference to the *Essai sur les mœurs*, that 'It was the first history which dealt not with kings, the units, but with the great, panting, seething masses they ruled'[1] is a masterpiece of misstatement. No one, least of all the masses, is allowed to pant or seethe in the *Essai*. The dress, habits, and customs of the people are portrayed, but they are portrayed from the outside, dispassionately, never, as with the romantic historians, with the aim of resurrecting a dead world. And when Voltaire does attempt something more vivid, he rarely succeeds. One cannot but applaud his decision to reject the majority of accounts of battles, when one reads a description such as this:

> Après la première charge, on vit encore un effet de ce que peut la fortune dans les combats. L'armée ennemie et la française, saisies d'une terreur panique, prirent la fuite toutes deux en même temps, et le maréchal de Villars se vit presque seul quelques minutes sur le champ de bataille: il rallia les troupes, les ramena au combat, et remporta la victoire.[2]

This impersonal, analytical style, which characterizes all Voltaire's historical works, but above all, the *Essai*, has an emotional aridity which is never really compensated for by the human feeling which obviously exists behind his outbursts of moral indignation at the events related, and the rarer expressions of approval when some brighter gleam is descried in the dark picture of human miseries. It is because of this that Voltaire, great as is his contribution to the science of history, cannot rank among the great historical artists. And yet this emotionally arid but intellectually sparkling style is obviously the one which most perfectly suits his peculiar gifts. It is an inimitable style, too, equally remote from the ornateness of the humanists, the lyricism of a Rousseau, and the picturesqueness of the romantics. It gives his work an unmistakable stamp of individuality.

---

[1] Tallentyre, *The Life of Voltaire*, i. 365.   [2] xiv. 359.

CONCLUSION

IT is in the work of Voltaire that the outline of universal history, as we know it today, is first clearly discernible. Earlier European historians describe a world some 6,000 years old, and their account of ancient history is dominated by a literal interpretation of the Bible and confined almost exclusively to the Middle East and Europe. Voltaire describes a world of great antiquity, in which societies have gradually come into being and decayed, and he emphasizes the importance of non-European civilizations such as those of India and China. It is he who, more than any other individual, brings about the Copernican revolution in historiography, displacing the Christian European from his comfortable seat at the centre of the universe.

In so doing, however, he creates as many problems as he solves. He postulates the existence of thousands of years during which man is engaged in learning the rudiments of civilized life. But he has no knowledge of pre-history, no evidence of what actually happened during this long period. His attempts to fill the gap are almost pure speculation, and this speculation, inspired by the deist propagandist rather than by the historian, is as unsatisfactory in the way it deals with man's spiritual progress as it is in its failure to deal, except in the barest outline, with his material advancement.

These are important limitations; but they are largely imposed by the absence of knowledge of anthropology and pre-history which characterizes the eighteenth century. If it is legitimate to show the extent to which Voltaire clings to patterns of thought which have their origin in doctrines he sought to oppose, it is more important to stress the change which he does bring about and the extent to which his work stimulates his successors to further discoveries.

This is perhaps Voltaire's greatest achievement. Yet he has an important part to play in another transformation which may well be considered even more significant. In the nineteenth century history comes to be regarded as the equal of the natural sciences: the historian claims to show, in Ranke's words, 'wie es eigentlich gewesen', and does not merely point a moral or adorn a tale.

Modern historiography is not just concerned with the doings of the great or the adventures of the individual, but seeks to describe the totality of past human experience, the history of societies and civilizations in all their different aspects.

This transformation is not the work of any individual, but Voltaire's part in it is an important one. Not only is he one of the most outstanding advocates of 'l'histoire de l'esprit humain', but in his own historical works he gives to social, economic, and cultural developments a far more important place than that allotted by most of his predecessors.

Once again, of course, there are obvious limits to his achievement. He is a popularizer rather than a scholar, and has to make what use he can of such information about social and economic history as others have provided for him. He is often narrow-minded and dogmatic—particularly in his views on art. Above all, though he is not a moralist in the seventeenth-century sense, he is a propagandist interested in changing society as much as in describing it. He shares the humanitarian ideals which characterize the Enlightenment, and if there is much in these ideals which is timeless, there is also much which is peculiar to the eighteenth-century *bourgeoisie* or to the struggle against Catholic authoritarianism.

Yet it is only rarely that these propagandist aims result in serious distortion. In the major works, like the *Siècle* and the *Essai*, they are balanced by a sincere desire for impartiality. If they flavour all Voltaire's work, they do not destroy its value as social history.

Voltaire attempts to recount the history of society. He also attempts to explain it; and here he must be considered less successful. If the puppets on the historical stage are not moved by the finger of God, there must be some other mechanism which is responsible for their antics. Yet Voltaire's thought lacks the profundity (or should one say, the rigidity?) to discover such a mechanism. Instead, he seizes upon the various explanations offered by others, and interprets history sometimes as the work of great men, sometimes as the result of the machinations of a capricious and ineluctable fatality, and sometimes as the product of the deep-seated determining influence of climate, religion, and government. Anxious as he is to explain, he will rarely ponder over his explanation, and the result is often a disappointing superficiality.

It is to Montesquieu, Condorcet, or Lessing that one must turn

if one wishes to discover an Enlightenment philosophy of history or
a coherent explanation of causality, and not to Voltaire. Yet if his
views are inconsistent, this does not mean that, individually, they
are not important. In the emphasis he places, particularly in his later
years, on economic causes, he appears to serve as a link between
Machiavellian realism and nineteenth-century theories of economic
determinism. His admiration for his heroes perhaps looks forward
to Carlyle. And his ever-present scepticism tends to restrain the
readers of Montesquieu, Turgot, or Mably from an uncritical
acceptance of theories not always rooted in fact.

This same scepticism is most clearly visible in his critical
method. It is he who, more than anyone else, inherits and, at the
same time, fructifies the tradition of historical Pyrrhonism.
Montesquieu does not appear to be affected by it, and the younger
men, Rousseau, Mably, or Raynal, represent an age which is trying
to construct a new faith rather than question an old one.

Voltaire's most positive achievement in this field is his application to history of principles drawn from the natural sciences in the
belief that nature and human nature are unchanging. But these
principles prove to be a mixed blessing. If they allow him to ex-
punge the miraculous from the pages of history, they also tempt
him to delete everything else which is not in accordance with his
own nature or with the standards and values of eighteenth-century
French society. As a result, and particularly because of his own lack
of psychological profundity, his scepticism is often carried too far,
and he is often led to denounce as fraudulent statements which
can be shown to be in no way contrary to the 'trempe du cœur
humain'.

His scepticism is equally visible in what may be termed the field
of lower criticism. Here it is particularly striking because the
majority of the *philosophes* tend to be more credulous. It is because
his historical method has been compared to theirs that its virtues
have tended to be magnified. But when it is compared to that of
the erudite historians, it is its inadequacy which is chiefly revealed.
Voltaire's sources, except when he is dealing with the history of his
own times, are almost exclusively second-hand. Moreover, he is
entirely lacking in the technical skills necessary for a first-hand
investigation of the distant past. In his treatment of evidence he
shows an awareness of the importance of eyewitness accounts
and the need for corroboration of testimonies, and he is adept at

spotting anachronisms, contradictions, and improbabilities. Yet the rules he applies are those contained in every primer. If he applies them more boldly than many, his boldness is at times rashness. The extent to which he tends to leap to conclusions on the basis of insufficient evidence is exemplified by his criticisms of the *Testament Politique* of Richelieu. His controversy with Foncemange on this subject reveals the inferiority of his method to that of the more scholarly, if less imaginative, of his contemporaries.

Finally, the poet who hoped to create the French epic and to be the worthy successor of Racine reveals himself as an indifferent devotee of Clio the muse. His style has all the logical clarity and wit which everywhere characterize his prose. Yet though he has an intellectual understanding of things and ideas, he has no sympathetic understanding of men: and it is men, after all, who make history. Voltaire makes little attempt to explore the psychology of his characters; he lacks the deep interest in the past for its own sake which alone can lead to that 'résurrection intégrale' of men and events of which Michelet spoke. In this context, at any rate, those who have accused him, and the Enlightenment in general, of being 'anti-historical' have some justification. His effort to understand the past is an effort to review it in the light of the present, not to recreate it. He despises tradition, and is never willing to accept history as an authority; to argue from an historical fact to a right. Instead he uses history as a warning; as a constant reminder that men have long been stupid, cruel, and intolerant, and that the price of civilization is eternal vigilance. A society which cannot look back on the course of history with a certain contempt would, he seems to say, be a society in decay. If such an attitude can be the strength of a social reformer, it can be the weakness of an historian.

Can Voltaire, as some have suggested, be claimed as the father of modern historiography? It would clearly be absurd to answer such a question categorically. It is more valuable to observe how French Enlightenment historiography, as typified by its greatest and most universal figure, stands midway between that of the seventeenth century and that of modern times. The distance between Bossuet and Voltaire is great, but so, too, is the distance between Voltaire and Michelet or Taine. The gradual accumulation of knowledge and the impact of the Revolution and of romanticism brought about vast changes. So, too, did the development of the seed of a more imaginative understanding of the past which had lain dormant in the *Scienza Nuova* throughout the greater part of the eighteenth century. Yet Vico's seed would not have prospered had not the ground been prepared for it. Among those who accomplished this task, Voltaire's role is one of the greatest.

BIBLIOGRAPHY

Principal sources

1. ANON., *A History of the Wars of Charles XII*. London, 1715.
2. —— *An Universal History from the Earliest Account of Time to the Present*. 22 vols. London, 1737–44.
3. BANIER, A., *Explication historique des fables*. 3 vols. Paris, 1715.
4. BAYLE, P., *Œuvres diverses*. 4 vols. The Hague, 1725–7.
5. —— *Dictionnaire historique et critique*. 16 vols. Paris, 1820–4.
6. BOLINGBROKE, H. ST. J., *Works*. 4 vols. Philadelphia, 1841.
7. BOSSUET, J.-B., *Discours sur l'histoire universelle*. Paris, 1681.
8. BOULAINVILLIERS, H. DE, *Histoire de l'ancien gouvernement de la France*. 3 vols. The Hague, 1727.
9. —— *La Vie de Mohamed*. 2 vols. Amsterdam, 1730.
10. CALMET, A., *Histoire universelle, sacrée et prophane*. 8 vols. Strasbourg, 1735–47.
11. CORDEMOY, G. DE, *Divers traitez de métaphysique, d'histoire et de politique*. Paris, 1691.
12. D'ALEMBERT, J. LE R., *Discours sur la meilleure méthode d'écrire l'histoire*. Paris, 1761.
13. —— *Discours préliminaire de l'Encyclopédie*, ed. F. Picavet. Paris, 1929.
14. DANIEL, G., *Histoire de France*. 10 vols. Paris, 1729 (1st edn. 1713).
15. DUBOS, J.-B., *Histoire critique de l'établissement de la monarchie françoise dans les Gaules*. 3 vols. Paris, 1734.
16. FÉNELON, F. DE LA M., *Lettre à l'Académie*, ed. A. Cahen. Paris, n.d. (1st edn. 1716).
17. FLEURY, C., *Discours sur l'histoire ecclésiastique*. Paris, 1771 (1st edn. 1708).
18. FONCEMANGE, E. L. DE, *Lettre sur le Testament Politique du cardinal de Richelieu*. Paris, 1750.
19. FONTENELLE, B. LE B. DE, *Œuvres complètes*. 3 vols. Paris, 1818.
20. —— *De l'origine des fables*, ed. J.-R. Carré. Paris, 1932.
21. —— *Histoire des oracles*, ed. L. Maigron. Paris, 1908.
22. FORBONNAIS, F. V. DE, *Recherches et considérations sur les finances de France*. 2 vols. Basle, 1758.
23. GIANNONE, P., *Istoria civile del regno di Napoli*. 4 vols. Naples, 1723.
24. GRIFFET, H., *Traité des différentes sortes de preuves qui servent à établir la vérité de l'histoire*. Liège, 1769.
25. GRIMM, F. M., *Correspondance littéraire*, ed. M. Tourneux. 16 vols. Paris, 1877–82.
26. GUIGNES, J. DE, *Mémoire dans lequel on prouve que les Chinois sont une colonie égyptienne*. Paris, 1759.
27. HARDION, J., *Histoire universelle, sacrée et prophane*. 18 vols. Paris, 1754–65.

28. HÉNAULT, C. F. F., *Nouvel abrégé chronologique de l'histoire de France*. 2 vols. Paris, 1761 (1st edn. 1741).
29. JUVENEL, F. DE, *Principes de l'histoire*. Paris, 1733.
30. LAFITEAU, J.-F., *Mœurs des sauvages amériquains comparées aux mœurs des premiers temps*. Paris, 1724.
31. LA MOTHE LA HODE, *Histoire de Louis XIV*. 5 vols. The Hague, 1737.
32. —— *Vie de Philippe d'Orléans*. 2 vols. London, 1736.
33. LA MOTTRAYE, A. DE, *Historical and Critical Remarks on the History of Charles XII, King of Sweden, by Mr. de Voltaire*. London, 1732.
34. LARREY, I. DE, *Histoire de France sous le règne de Louis XIV*. 4 vols. Rotterdam, 1718.
35. LENGLET DU FRESNOY, N., *Méthode pour étudier l'histoire*. Paris, 1713 (2 vols.) and 1729 (4 vols.); and *Supplément*, 1739.
36. LIMIERS, H. P. DE, *Histoire du règne de Louis XIV*. 7 vols. Amsterdam, 1717.
37. —— *Histoire de Suède sous le règne de Charles XII*. 12 vols. Amsterdam, 1721.
38. MABLY, G. B. DE, *Œuvres*. 12 vols. London, 1789.
39. —— *De l'étude de l'histoire*. Printed in Condillac, *Œuvres*. Paris, 1798, vol. xxi.
40. MAIRAN, D. DE, *Lettres de M. de Mairan au R. P. Parrenin*. Paris, 1759.
41. MELON, J. F., *Essai politique sur le commerce*. Amsterdam, 1735.
42. MÉNARD, L., *Réfutation du sentiment de M. de Voltaire qui traite d'ouvrage supposé le 'Testament Politique' du cardinal de Richelieu*. Paris, 1750.
43. MONTESQUIEU, C.-L. DE S. DE, *Œuvres*. 3 vols. Paris, 1866.
44. NORDBERG, J. A., *Histoire de Charles XII*. 4 vols. The Hague, 1748.
45. PONIATOWSKI, S., *Remarques d'un seigneur polonais sur l'Histoire de Charles XII, roi de Suède, par M. de Voltaire*. The Hague, 1741.
46. RAPIN DE THOYRAS, P., *Histoire d'Angleterre*. 10 vols. The Hague, 1724–7.
47. RICHELIEU, A. DU PLESSIS, CARDINAL DE, *Testament Politique*. Amsterdam, 1688.
48. —— *Testament Politique*, ed. L. André. Paris, 1947.
49. SAINT AUBIN, G.-C. LE GENDRE DE, *Traité de l'opinion pour servir à l'histoire de l'esprit humain*. 6 vols. Paris, 1733.
50. SAINT-RÉAL, V. DE, *Œuvres*. 4 vols. The Hague, 1722.
51. TURGOT, A. R. J., *Œuvres*. 2 vols. Paris, 1844.
52. VERNET, J., *Abrégé d'histoire universelle*. Geneva, 1753.
53. VOLTAIRE, *Œuvres complètes*, ed. L. Moland. 52 vols. Paris, 1777–85. (References to editions published in Voltaire's lifetime, where these differ from Moland, are given in the footnotes.)
54. —— *Correspondance de Voltaire (1726–29)*, ed. L. Foulet. Paris, 1913.
55. —— *Correspondance avec les Tronchin*, ed. A. Delattre. Paris, 1950.
56. —— *Correspondence*, ed. Th. Besterman. Geneva, 1953–.
57. —— *Voltaire's Notebooks*, ed. Th. Besterman. 2 vols. Geneva, 1952.

58. VOLTAIRE, *Supplément aux œuvres de Voltaire: Œuvres inédites: Tome I, Mélanges historiques*, ed. F. Caussy. Paris, 1914.
59. —— *Histoire de Charles XII*, ed. M. A. Geffroy. Paris, 1847.
60. —— *Le Siècle de Louis XIV*, ed. E. Bourgeois. Paris, 1906.

Secondary authorities

61. ASCOLI, G., 'Voltaire historien', *Revue des cours et conférences*, 28 Feb. 1925.
62. BACH, R. L., *Die Entwicklung der französischen Geschichtsauffassung im 18ten Jahrhundert*. Freiburg i. B., 1932.
63. BARBER, W. H., *Leibniz in France*. Oxford, 1955.
64. BARRIÈRE, P., *Un Grand Provincial: Charles-Louis de Secondat, baron de La Brède et de Montesquieu*. Bordeaux, 1946.
65. BELLESSORT, A., *Essai sur Voltaire*. Paris, 1925.
66. BLACK, J. B., *The Art of History: A Study of Four Great Historians of the 18th Century*. London, 1926.
67. BRAILSFORD, H. N., *Voltaire*. Oxford, 1935.
68. CARRÉ, J.-R., *Consistance de Voltaire le philosophe*. Paris, 1938.
69. CASSIRER, E., *Die Philosophie der Aufklärung*. Tübingen, 1932.
70. CAZES, A., *Pierre Bayle*. Paris, 1905.
71. CHASE, C. B., *The Young Voltaire*. London, 1926.
72. COLLINGWOOD, R. G., *The Idea of History*. Oxford, 1946.
73. DESNOIRESTERRES, G., *Voltaire et la société au XVIIIᵉ siècle*. 8 vols. Paris, 1869–76.
74. DILTHEY, W., 'Das 18te Jahrhundert und die geschichtliche Welt', *Deutsche Rundschau*, July–Sept. 1901.
75. DULONG, G., *L'Abbé de Saint-Réal*. Paris, 1921.
76. EDSALL, H. L., 'The Idea of History and Progress in Fontenelle and Voltaire', *Yale Romanic Studies*, vol. xviii. New Haven, 1941.
77. ENGEMANN, W., *Voltaire und China*. Leipzig, 1933.
78. EVANS, W. H., *L'Historien Mézeray et la conception de l'histoire en France au XVIIᵉ siècle*. Paris, 1930.
79. FLINT, R., *Historical Philosophy in France*. Edinburgh, 1893.
80. FUETER, E., *Geschichte der neueren Historiographie*. Munich and Berlin, 1936.
81. GANDAR, E., 'Voltaire historien', *Lettres et souvenirs d'enseignement*, vol. ii. Paris, 1869.
82. GIARRIZZO, G., *Edward Gibbon e la cultura europea del settecento*. Naples, 1954.
83. GOOCH, G. P., 'Voltaire as historian', *Catherine the Great and Other Studies*. London, 1954.
84. HAGMANN, J. G., *Über Voltaires Essai sur les mœurs*. Rapperswil, 1883.
85. HAXO, H. E., 'Pierre Bayle et Voltaire avant les Lettres Philosophiques', *P.M.L.A.*, vol. xlvi (1931).
86. HAZARD, P., *La Crise de la conscience européenne*. 2 vols. Paris, 1942.
87. HUBERT, R., *Les Sciences sociales dans l'Encyclopédie*. Paris, 1923.
88. HURN, A. S., *Voltaire and Bolingbroke*. Paris, 1915.

89. LANSON, G., *Voltaire*. Paris, 1910.
90. —— 'Notes pour servir à l'étude des chapitres 35–39 du *Siècle de Louis XIV* de Voltaire', *Mélanges offerts à M. Charles Andler*. Strasbourg, 1924.
91. LION, H., *Un Magistrat homme de lettres au 18e siècle: le président Hénault*. Paris, 1903.
92. LUPORINI, C. *Voltaire e le 'Lettres Philosophiques'. Il concetto della storia e l'illuminismo*. Florence, 1955.
93. MAYR, R., *Voltaire-Studien*. Vienna, 1879.
94. MEINECKE, F., *Die Entstehung des historismus*. Munich and Berlin, 1936.
95. MOMIGLIANO, A., 'Ancient History and the Antiquarian', *Journal of the Warburg and Courtauld Institutes*, vol. xiii (1950).
96. PINOT, V., *La Chine et la formation de l'esprit philosophique en France (1640–1740)*. Paris, 1932.
97. POMEAU, R., *La Religion de Voltaire*. Paris, 1956.
98. PRICE, E. H., 'The Opinions of Voltaire concerning Montesquieu's Theories of Roman Greatness', *Philological Quarterly*, vol. xvi (1937).
99. QUIGNARD, J., 'Un Établissement de texte: Le "Siècle de Louis XIV" de Voltaire', *Les Lettres romanes*, vol. v (1951).
100. ROWBOTHAM, A. H., 'Voltaire, sinophile', *P.M.L.A.*, vol. xlvii (1932).
101. SAKMANN, P., 'Die Probleme der historischen Methodik und der Geschichtsphilosophie bei Voltaire', *Historische Zeitschrift*, vol. xcvii (1906).
102. —— 'Universalgeschichte in Voltaires Beleuchtung', *Zeitschrift für französische Sprache und Literatur*, vol. xxx (1906).
103. SCHARGO, N. N., *History in the Encyclopédie*. New York, 1947.
104. SÉE, H., 'Les Idées politiques de Voltaire', *Revue historique*, vol. xcviii (1908).
105. SEZNEC, J., 'Falconet, Voltaire and Diderot', *Studies on Voltaire and the 18th century*, vol. ii (1956).
106. SHACKLETON, R., 'Montesquieu in 1948', *French Studies*, vol. iii (1949).
107. SICHEL, W., *Bolingbroke and his Times*. London, 1901.
108. SIMON, R., *Henry de Boulainviller, historien, politique, philosophe, astrologue*. Paris, 1942.
109. SONET, E., *Voltaire et l'influence anglaise*. Rennes, 1926.
110. THIERRY, A., *Œuvres*. 4 vols. Paris, 1859.
111. THOMPSON, J. W., *A History of Historical Writing*. 2 vols. New York, 1942.
112. TORREY, N. L., 'Bolingbroke and Voltaire: a fictitious influence', *P.M.L.A.*, vol. xlii (1927).
113. —— *Voltaire and the English Deists*. New Haven, 1930.
114. WADE, I. O., *Voltaire and Mme du Châtelet*. Princeton, 1941.
115. WEULERSSE, G., *Le Mouvement physiocratique en France*. Paris, 1910.
116. ZERFFI, G. G., 'Voltaire in his relation to the Study of General History from a Philosophical Point of View', *Transactions of the Royal Historical Society*, vol. x (1882).

GENERAL INDEX

Bold figures refer to more important references.

INDEX OF REFERENCES TO
VOLTAIRE'S WORKS